Applied Econometrics with SAS®

Modeling Demand, Supply, and Risk

Barry K. Goodwin
A. Ford Ramsey
Jan Chvosta

§.sas®

sas.com/books

The correct bibliographic citation for this manual is as follows: Goodwin, Barry K., A. Ford Ramsey, and Jan Chvosta. 2018. *Applied Econometrics with SAS®: Modeling Demand, Supply, and Risk*. Cary, NC: SAS Institute Inc.

Applied Econometrics with SAS®: Modeling Demand, Supply, and Risk

Copyright © 2018, SAS Institute Inc., Cary, NC, USA

ISBN 978-1-62960-407-7 (Hard copy)
ISBN 978-1-63526-050-2 (EPUB)
ISBN 978-1-63526-051-9 (MOBI)
ISBN 978-1-63526-052-6 (PDF)

Contents

Chapter 1.   Introduction 1
   1.1   Overview 1
   1.2   Applications of Economic Analysis 2
   1.3   Intended Audience 3
   1.4   Examples for Hands-On Practice 4
Chapter 2.   Theory of Demand 5
   2.1   Overview 5
   2.2   Preference Axioms and the Utility Function 6
   2.3   Utility and Marshallian Demands 8
      2.3.1   A Graphical Look at Utility and Demand 9
   2.4   Indirect Utility 14
   2.5   Hicksian Demands and Expenditures 15
      2.5.1   The Slutsky Equation 17
   2.6   Elasticities 18
   2.7   Separability and Aggregation 20
Chapter 3.   Empirical Approaches to Demand Analysis 23
   3.1   Overview 23
   3.2   Double Logarithmic Demand Functions 24
      3.2.1   The Double Log Form 25
      3.2.2   Empirical Analysis 25
   3.3   Rotterdam Model 29
      3.3.1   Absolute Price and Relative Price Rotterdam Formulations . . 30
      3.3.2   Empirical Analysis 33
   3.4   Almost Ideal Demand System 44
      3.4.1   Full and Linear Approximate AIDS Models 44
      3.4.2   Empirical Analysis 46
   3.5   Demand for Differentiated Products 54
      3.5.1   Discrete Choice 55
      3.5.2   Logit Models 57
      3.5.3   Empirical Analysis 60
   3.6   Conclusion 74
Chapter 4.   Theory of Supply 75
   4.1   Overview 75
   4.2   The Production Function 76
   4.3   The Cost Function and Derived Factor Demands 77
   4.4   The Profit Function 79
      4.4.1   Profit Derived Factor Demands 80
      4.4.2   Elasticities 80
   4.5   Concepts of Time in Production 81
   4.6   Separability and Aggregation 81
Chapter 5.   Empirical Approaches to Supply Analysis 83
   5.1   Overview 83
   5.2   Cobb–Douglas Production 84
      5.2.1   Econometric Analysis 85
   5.3   Translog Functional Form 91
      5.3.1   Empirical Analysis 93
   5.4   Frontier Production Functions 104

5.4.1 Empirical Analysis 107

Chapter 6. Empirical Approaches to Risk 113

6.1 Overview 113

6.2 Frequency and Severity Modeling 114

6.2.1 Compound Distribution Model 115

6.2.2 Empirical Analysis 116

6.3 Agricultural Insurance 124

6.3.1 Yield Insurance 125

6.3.2 Empirical Analysis 125

6.3.3 Revenue Insurance 142

6.3.4 Dependence and Copulas 143

6.3.5 Empirical Analysis 146

References 159

About the Authors

 **Barry K. Goodwin, PhD**, is the William Neal Reynolds Distinguished Professor in the Department of Agricultural and Resource Economics, as well as a Graduate Alumni Distinguished Professor in the Department of Economics, at North Carolina State University, where he teaches and conducts research on policy, risk, trade, and applied econometrics. He is a fellow and past president of the Agricultural and Applied Economics Association. He has coauthored three books and more than 150 peer-reviewed journal articles, receiving numerous research awards, including best article awards from the *American Journal of Agricultural Economics*, the *Journal of Agricultural and Resource Economics*, and the *Canadian Journal of Agricultural Economics*. Professor Goodwin completed his PhD in economics at North Carolina State University in 1988.

 **A. Ford Ramsey, PhD**, is an assistant professor in the Department of Agricultural and Applied Economics at Virginia Polytechnic Institute and State University. His research interests are risk and insurance, agricultural economics, and applied econometrics. He has been a SAS user since 2012 and was a consultant for SAS from 2014 to 2017. He was honored with an Australian Agricultural and Resource Economics Society / Agricultural and Applied Economics Association *Heading South Award* and the National Science Foundation *East Asia and Pacific Summer Institutes Fellowship*. Professor Ramsey completed his PhD in economics at North Carolina State University in 2017.

 **Jan Chvosta, PhD**, is Senior Manager of Economics Technology Solutions, Advanced Analytics, in Research and Development at SAS. His research interests are econometric modeling, cross-sectional and panel data analysis, spatial econometrics, and high-performance computing. Dr. Chvosta was born in the Czech Republic. Shortly after receiving an MS in Informatics from the Czech University of Life Sciences in 1994, he relocated to the United States to pursue a career in economics and econometrics. He received an MS in applied economics from Montana State University in 1996. In 2004, he graduated from North Carolina State University with an MS in applied statistics and a PhD in economics.

Learn more about these authors by visiting their author pages, where you can download free book excerpts, access example code and data, read the latest reviews, get updates, and more:
http://support.sas.com/goodwin
http://support.sas.com/ramsey
http://support.sas.com/chvosta

Acknowledgments

We thank Jeffrey Dorfman, Thomas Marsh, George Davis, Wen Bardsley, and Donna Woodward for taking time to review the book and for providing us with many helpful comments, which greatly improved the final draft. We also thank our editors Jenny Jennings Foerst and Julie McAlpine Palmieri for guiding us through the writing process. Their numerous edits, comments, and coordination of the review process are truly appreciated. In addition, we thank Mark Little for making this project possible, and we acknowledge the many other colleagues at SAS Institute who in various ways contributed.

Chapter 1
Introduction

Contents

1.1	Overview	**1**
1.2	Applications of Economic Analysis	**2**
1.3	Intended Audience	**3**
1.4	Examples for Hands-On Practice	**4**

1.1 Overview

As computing speed has increased, applied econometric analysis has significantly expanded its scope and scale. Analysis that only 20 years ago was infeasible can now be completed in the blink of an eye. These developments have helped to shape economics as an empirical science. Modern analysts have a multitude of tools at their disposal, and SAS remains the first choice for many in research, academia, and the business analytics sector. SAS has a number of important advantages. First and foremost, it is thoroughly tested and validated for critical applications. It is fast, with many procedures being optimized for multi-threaded applications. SAS offers extraordinary technical support. Finally, SAS is robust, is flexible, and can be easily adapted to *any* application.

The examples contained in this volume represent a wide variety of applications that we have covered in over 25 years of teaching. We've used SAS in graduate teaching at four universities (North Carolina State, Ohio State, Kansas State, and Virginia Tech) and have had the pleasure of training hundreds of graduate students in its use and application. The examples included in this volume were collected from doctoral classes in demand analysis, production analysis, risk modeling, and microeconometrics. The examples are intended to illustrate an approach to applied analysis that can easily be modified to fit general problems of interest encountered by applied practitioners. They may be easily altered for application in any software environment or through the SAS OnDemand for Academics.

Before considering specific examples, a few points merit emphasis. Applications that lack careful attention to the theory, policies, institutions, and idiosyncrasies of any specific problem are less than worthless. They may lead to inaccurate or inadequate conclusions regarding the economic phenomena of interest. Many empirical results can have multiple, contrasting implications. For example, a finding of perfect spatial market integration may reflect the efficiently competitive behavior of traders or perfect collusion among monopolists. One must look closely at the institutional setting and the economic facts before attempting an interpretation of empirical results. Applied analysis must be guided by economic theory.

A common example lies in the behavior of consumer demand functions. Our theory tells us that such demand functions should be homogeneous of degree zero, must satisfy concavity requirements of the utility function, and must satisfy adding-up conditions across equations. Further, we often expect to see symmetry reflected in preferences, an implication of Young's Theorem as applied to continuously differentiable utility functions. One may choose to impose these restrictions when estimating a demand system or may choose to test the restrictions. In practice, one often finds that the available data lead to a statistical rejection of a hypothesis implied by economic theory. This does not imply that such theory should be ignored. Any analysis carries with it many unexpressed and maintained hypotheses.

Recent developments in open source software have led to widespread adoption of packages and programs that lack the error validation that is inherent in SAS. The R software package is of course the most prominent example. R is indeed a very useful tool and offers a wide range of user-based packages that have been submitted to its package repository. These packages, though useful and certainly attractively priced, have not undergone the extensive vetting that commercial software such as SAS has had. As users of R, our experience has been that many of the packages are fragile and can fail when one departs from the included examples. User support is voluntary and legions of R devotees are often gracious in offering their support to those that ask. However, R remains a user-supported, open-source software platform and thus may not be suitable for many critical applications. It is also the case that R and SAS can peacefully coexist on a computer. R readily reads SAS data sets and SAS has excellent provisions in the IML procedure for passing values to and from an R session. We frequently use R within SAS/IML software and have found the flow of programming to be seamless.

Through the use of PROC IML, *any* empirical problem can be addressed on the SAS platform. SAS/IML software has a number of valuable optimization routines that offer considerable flexibility in estimation. Likewise, the ETS procedures are comprehensive and address the vast majority of empirical techniques that applied economists are likely to face. The developers at SAS are continually updating existing packages and are providing new packages that mirror developments in the academic and research arenas. In teaching, we often ask our students to hard code problems for which existing software routines are readily available. There certainly is educational value in such an exercise. However, the potential for error is high when one is hard coding a problem, and thus we typically recommend that students and other practitioners use comprehensive procedures such as those contained in SAS when possible.

The examples that follow are not intended to be comprehensive or representative of what is typical in any graduate economics class. Rather, they are examples drawn from our own research and teaching. As such, they reflect our particular interests and research areas. Any empirical problem is amenable to estimation and evaluation in SAS. These examples provide only a brief hint at the types of applied problems that a SAS user can tackle.

1.2 Applications of Economic Analysis

This text covers three major areas of economic analysis: demand, supply, and risk. Examples in each area are drawn from real research and coursework problems. In applied economics specifically, these three areas can reasonably be said to have constituted the bulk of empirical analyses. As an empirical discipline, economics is situated at the nexus of economic theory, econometrics, and statistics. For this reason, we feel justified in structuring this book such that our empirical applications are preceded by chapters that delineate and explain relevant theoretical considerations. Armed with knowledge of theory and computational tools, you will be well equipped to address problems in all three of the topic areas.

The earliest demand studies focused on agricultural products. One reason for this focus is the notion that demands for agricultural commodities are relatively stable. Likewise, in the absence of storage and with cyclical production, the demand curve can be precisely traced from movements of the supply curve. Some of the earliest classical studies on the topic are Lehfeldt (1914), a paper on the elasticity of demand for wheat, and comments–nearly a decade later–by Schultz (1925). The modern work of the past half century or so can be roughly divided into demand for commodity aggregates and demand for individual products and brands. As an example of the first case, we could be interested in demand for various types or cuts of meat. If the user has data on the aggregate consumption and prices of meat across a country or region (which this text provides), the models analyzed in the third chapter demonstrate how to conduct an economic analysis of the demand for homogenous goods.

Because problems of demand and supply involve functions with shape restrictions, there has been a large body of econometric work aimed at discovering flexible parametric functions that can meet such restrictions. These flexible functional forms have been applied in both demand and supply contexts. The most popular forms are derived in the text and applied to empirical problems in chapters 3 and 5. The most basic functional forms, the transcendental logarithmic and generalized Leontief, were developed in the early 1970s by Christensen, Jorgenson, and Lau (1975) and Diewert (1971) respectively. A watershed moment in demand analysis was the development of the almost ideal demand system (AIDS) of Deaton and Muellbauer (1980a). The AIDS model is now viewed by many economists as the dominant approach in the analysis of demand for homogenous goods.

Demand studies for individual products or brands matured more slowly in the 1970s and 1980s, but have since experienced an explosion in growth. The increasing availability of scanner data collected from registers at supermarkets and retail stores has enabled exciting new research in discrete choice modeling. Likewise, online sales have led economists to confront problems involving big or massive data. Perhaps the most popular method for estimating demand functions for heterogeneous goods was developed by Berry, Levinsohn, and Pakes (1995). This approach and its generalizations have since been applied to numerous types of goods in order to understand the structure of underlying markets. Some applications include Nevo (2001), who used BLP methods to measure market power in cereals, and Villas-Boas (2009), who investigated the effects of a policy banning price discrimination.

Concurrent with the development of methods for the analysis of demand, advances have also been made in problems on the supply side. Many of the derived demand problems in production are similar to problems of consumer demand, and thus lend themselves to estimation by similar techniques. Building on early research in flexible functional forms, extensions to these models were developed by authors like Morrison (1988), who applied them in production contexts. Estimation of production functions, whether at the firm level or at larger levels of aggregation, has been a popular topic. Results of such studies have been used to explain technological change and its impact on economic development and growth (Hayami and Ruttan 1970; Mundlak, Butzer, and Larson 2012).

The use of stochastic frontier production functions has become popular for the measurement of technical efficiency at the firm level. In contrast to the assumptions of classical production analysis, in which producers are treated as successful optimizers, empirical results indicate that many firms do not produce at the production frontier. The distance of these firms from the frontier is a measure of inefficiency. In stochastic frontier analysis, the factors causing firm inefficiency (or efficiency) are of primary interest. Kumbhakar and Lovell (2000) present a detailed history of the development of the frontier paradigm and theoretical results. Chapter 5 of this text contains an application of stochastic frontier analysis and demonstrates the simplicity with which these techniques can be enabled in SAS.

The last third of this book focuses on problems of risk, with applications to the measurement of risk in various contexts. In agricultural economics particularly, risk measurement has taken on increased significance with the prominence of the federal crop insurance program. This program, with over $100 billion in total liability in any given year, is the cornerstone of contemporary agricultural policy. Much attention has been paid to the design and pricing of the policies offered through the program. The accurate pricing of such policies involves problems that are of interest both statistically and economically. For instance, revenue insurance policies require accurate modeling of dependence between agricultural yields and prices of the commodity. Economic theory tells us that the relationship between the two is negative, with high prices accompanying low yields, and vice versa.

1.3   Intended Audience

The content and tools presented in this book have been designed for a general audience of applied economists. This includes graduate students who are just beginning their studies, practitioners in policy organizations, government analysts, and those in private industry. We cannot claim to provide exhaustive coverage of economic theory, statistics, or econometrics. There are many books better suited to these objectives. What we do provide are empirical examples with SAS code and freely available data. These are the elements so sorely lacking in many other texts.

You should be able to run all of the examples in their own SAS environment. The idea is that you will be able to use the code contained here as a building block for more advanced analyses. You might be embarking on a graduate thesis, or working in a government organization to better understand the impacts of different policies. We suggest that you use the models in the book as needed, and then continue to develop and refine the models as your problem requires. Because you will develop knowledge of both economic theory and SAS software, this refinement process should be relatively pain free.

1.4   Examples for Hands-On Practice

This book includes tutorials for you to follow to gain hands-on experience with SAS. The majority of examples in this book were created using SAS/ETS 14.2 software. Other packages used include SAS/BASE, SAS/IML, and SAS/STAT.

Applied econometrics–as a discipline–is so broad that there are countless methods and techniques available to the researcher. However, the majority of the models covered in this text can be handled with a handful of SAS procedures. In the sense that the content of the book is oriented toward major topics in economic analysis, knowledge of these same procedures is sure to serve any empirical researcher well:

1. **PROC COUNTREG**: As its name implies, PROC COUNTREG is a procedure for performing regression when the dependent variable is a non-negative count. It supports several different models for count data including Poisson regression, negative binomial regression, and zero-inflated models.

2. **PROC COPULA**: To generate probabilities and magnitudes of loss, practitioners in finance and insurance often require a joint probability distribution over several variables. PROC COPULA allows the user to fit a number of copula functions that capture dependence relationships between variables. The copula functions are then used to construct joint distributions. The COPULA procedure provides a number of options to assist the user in determining model fit and simulating from the estimated copulas.

3. **PROC IML**: A complete interactive matrix language (IML) can be accessed with a call to PROC IML. While SAS provides ready-made procedures for the vast majority of econometric problems you are likely to encounter, PROC IML provides an environment for hard-coding any routines that may not be available in SAS. It can also be used for data manipulation involving matrix calculations.

4. **PROC MODEL**: It's not a stretch to claim that linear simultaneous equation models are the applied economist's bread and butter. PROC MODEL is designed to analyze both linear and nonlinear systems of equations. The equations are parsimoniously specified using SAS programming statements, and many of the most popular methods for parameter estimation (OLS, 2SLS, ITSUR, GMM, etc.) are available.

5. **PROC QLIM**: The QLIM procedure analyzes univariate and multivariate limited dependent variable models in which dependent variables take discrete values or in which dependent variables are observed only in a limited range of values. It can also be used to fit stochastic frontier production and cost functions.

6. **PROC REG**: The REG procedure is the most general regression procedure in SAS. While PROC MODEL can also handle many of the same regressions, PROC REG provides a number of standard tables and graphics to assist the user in assessing model fit.

7. **PROC SEVERITY**: The fitting of parametric distributions to random variables is common in econometrics and statistics. In many actuarial applications, the variables of interest are losses which must be non-negative. PROC SEVERITY allows the user to fit a variety of non-standard distributions for continuous non-negative random variables. Fit criteria are provided so that the user can efficiently choose between competing models.

You can access the example code and data for this book by linking to its author page at https://support.sas.com/authors. This book is compatible with SAS OnDemand for Academics. If you are using SAS OnDemand for Academics, then begin here: https://support.sas.com/.

Chapter 2
Theory of Demand

Contents

2.1	Overview	5
2.2	Preference Axioms and the Utility Function	6
2.3	Utility and Marshallian Demands	8
	2.3.1 A Graphical Look at Utility and Demand	9
2.4	Indirect Utility	14
2.5	Hicksian Demands and Expenditures	15
	2.5.1 The Slutsky Equation	17
2.6	Elasticities	18
2.7	Separability and Aggregation	20

2.1 Overview

Consumer theory, or the demand side of economics, is concerned with the constrained choices that consumers face. The consumer's problem can be stated in several ways, but we will see that nearly all of these approaches boil down to problems of optimization. As you consume in the course of your daily life, you make the best use of your available resources and income. In order to characterize consumption choices mathematically, some definition must be given to the consumer's idea of what goods are "best". This is achieved by specifying an objective function that the consumer purposefully aims to maximize. Likewise, if a problem of choice is to be economically interesting, resources must be treated as scarce. Without scarcity, the consumer would have no reason to choose between different wants. The notion of scarcity can be mathematically implemented by placing constraints on the maximization of the objective function; the problem is then one of constrained optimization.

The framework that we will operate in for the majority of this book is one of rationality. We assume that there is a logic to the choices of the consumer – and the producer as well, although this content is relegated to later chapters. If the consumer's choices are rational, then we can say that they are consistent with a given objective function. Even though the task of describing consumption behavior with a single objective function seems quixotic, there have been major developments in the last century that allow economists to do just that. By the end of this chapter, you will be prepared to describe consumer choice and to formulate the behavioral equations that represent the decision–making process.

The economic theory in this chapter sets the stage for empirical and econometric analyses that come later in the book. This theoretical treatment is by no means comprehensive, and the bibliography at the end of the text lists a number of references. Two of the most complete sources for demand theory are Deaton and Muellbauer (1980a) and Cornes (1992). Instead of trying to cover all aspects of the theory, we aim to provide foundational material that clarifies the link between economic theory and applied analysis. By providing code to estimate these models in SAS, we hope that you will be able to immediately take the theory to the data.

Economists have spent a significant amount of effort to construct economic models that adhere to the results of economic theory. They have also developed a number of econometric techniques that allow for the validity of these models to be tested. While our treatment of demand begins with theory, and then moves to application, such one–sided presentation is not borne out in the overall history of economics. As we show, it has often been the case that careful empirical analysis has motivated advances in purely theoretical areas. Given this interplay, we believe that it is worthwhile for the applied economist to devote time to the consideration of both theory and application. This necessarily includes the use of statistical software to obtain practical results from real data.

2.2   Preference Axioms and the Utility Function

Our study of the theory of demand begins with recognition of the main economic decision of the consumer: to choose between the consumption of different goods. Goods do not need to be physical commodities; it is quite common to include leisure time as a good, for example. Nomenclature is important, as we have explicitly defined the consumer's choice over goods, not bads. This implies that consumers have some preference toward consumption. We can always define a bad as the negative of a good. In this sense, a new good can be created by defining the good to the the negative of the bad. Let the quantity of any good be represented by the scalar x_i where $i = 1, \ldots, n$ indexes the goods available for consumption. Instead of listing each good separately, a collection of goods can be thought of as a consumption bundle and represented by a vector $\mathbf{x} = [x_1, \ldots, x_n]$. We occasionally use i, j, and k to represent different consumption bundles. Rational consumers will choose amongst the many bundles available to them in a consistent fashion.

We have noted that the choices of a rational consumer must be consistent, but we have not given an explicit account of what is meant by this term. There are several axioms of choice that give structure to an individual's preferences and will allow us to construct utility functions that describe individual behavior. In the rest of this chapter, consumers that adhere to these axioms, and behave in a way that is compatible with their associated utility functions, will be considered rational. Some of the choice axioms are economically important while others serve a more mathematical purpose. But because the utility function is a mathematical object, axioms with less economic content are necessary to maintain congruence between preferences and utility. With a utility function, the advantages of calculus become available. This is the main benefit of using a utility function to represent preferences.

The preference axioms are most easily stated in terms of set notation with the bundles thought of as collections or sets of goods. The symbol $\succeq$ will mean weakly preferred or "as good or better than" while $\succ$ will mean strictly preferred or "better than." Consider two different bundles $\mathbf{x}_j$ and $\mathbf{x}_k$. If the consumer always prefers to consume bundle $\mathbf{x}_j$ over bundle $\mathbf{x}_k$, we can write $\mathbf{x}_j \succ \mathbf{x}_k$. If the consumer may prefer $\mathbf{x}_j$, but we cannot exclude the possibility that the consumer is indifferent between the bundles, we write $\mathbf{x}_j \succeq \mathbf{x}_k$. In the special case that both $\mathbf{x}_j \succeq \mathbf{x}_k$ and $\mathbf{x}_j \preceq \mathbf{x}_k$, the consumer is indifferent between the two bundles and we write $\mathbf{x}_j \sim \mathbf{x}_k$

There are six basic axioms that must be imposed on a consumer's preferences to generate the classical theory of demand. The breakdown or omission of these axioms implies some irrationality on the part of the consumer. Though not impossible, it is considerably more difficult to analyze economic agents who partake in irrational behavior. Completely irrational actors simply do not have enough structure in their behavior to allow for a full and thorough analysis. The rational consumer that we consider in this chapter must adhere to the following axioms.

1. **Reflexivity**: For any $\mathbf{x}_j, \mathbf{x}_j \preceq \mathbf{x}_j$.

   Every bundle of goods is as good or better than itself. Perhaps an uninteresting statement, but one that is necessary if consistency of choice is to be maintained.

2. **Completeness**: For any $\mathbf{x}_j$ and $\mathbf{x}_k, \mathbf{x}_j \preceq \mathbf{x}_k$ or $\mathbf{x}_j \succeq \mathbf{x}_k$.

   The consumer can compare and order any bundle in the choice set. When comparison is made between two bundles, one bundle must be considered better than the other, or the consumer must be indifferent between the two bundles.

3. **Transitivity**: For any x_j, x_k, and x_l, if $x_j \preceq x_k$ and $x_k \preceq x_l$, then $x_j \preceq x_l$.

   The completeness axiom implies that the consumer can compare and rank any two bundles. The transitivity axiom extends this notion to a preference ordering over the entire set of possible bundles. Taken together with the axioms of reflexivity and completeness, the consumer is able to create an ordering of all of the bundles available for consumption.

4. **Continuity**: For any bundle x_j, the "no worse than" and "no better than" sets are closed.

   Consider the possible collections of goods at the consumer's disposal. Define the "no worse than" set as $A(x_i) = \{x|x \succeq x_i\}$ and the "no better than" set as $B(x_i) = \{x|x \preceq x_i\}$. With respect to x_i, the consumer prefers or is indifferent to any bundle in $A(\cdot)$. On the other hand, he weakly prefers x_i to any bundle in $B(\cdot)$. If the sets $A(\cdot)$ and $B(\cdot)$ are closed, they contain their boundaries. When considering any particular bundle of goods, all other bundles must fall into either $A(\cdot)$ or $B(\cdot)$. If we think about moving through the space of possible bundles, when the border between $A(\cdot)$ and $B(\cdot)$ is reached, we can transition smoothly between these sets as a consequence of the continuity axiom.

5. **Nonsatiation**: If $x_j \geq x_k$ and $x_j \neq x_k$, then $x_j \succ x_k$.

   If two bundles have equal amounts of all goods except one, the bundle with the greater quantity of the differential good will be strictly preferred. Because choice is defined over goods, the consumer will always prefer to have more rather than less. The nonsatiation axiom is often questioned because of the cases in everyday life where people appear to be satiated. Such incidents do not present a problem for theory and accompanying applied analysis as long as the economic problem is properly posed. The illusion of satiation is often a result of failure to consider decision making over a long period of time. In other words, a consumer may be satiated over a short period of time, but they are not satiated over longer intervals. In the majority of situations, it seems unlikely that the point of satiation will be reached.

6. **Convexity:** If $x_i \preceq x_j$, then $\lambda x_j + (1 - \lambda)x_i \succeq x_i$ for $0 \leq \lambda \leq 1$.

   The consumer has a preference toward consumption of some amount of every good in the bundle, rather than consumption of a single good. This has implications for the shape of indifference curves, which we discuss in the next section and illustrate graphically. The practical consequence of this axiom is that, for any given set of prices and income, the consumer's optimization problem will be solved by a single, unique bundle of goods.

If the first four preference axioms are satisfied, the consumer's preferences can be represented by a utility function. The last two axioms are "axioms of convenience" in the sense that they are not necessary for the derivation of a utility function. Nonetheless, they turn out to be quite useful in achieving certain theoretical results. The scalar–valued utility function

$$u = u(x) \tag{2.1}$$

is related to the consumer's preference ordering; if $x_i \succeq x_j$ then $u(x_i) \geq u(x_j)$. The utility function is a tool that allows for the preference ordering to be represented in a mathematically convenient way. It is also the objective function that was mentioned in the introduction to this chapter. The values obtained from the utility function are called utils, and we can now say that if a bundle is at least as good as another, then it must generate at least as many utils.

We must be careful not to take the concept of utility too far. The utility function is an ordinal representation of preferences, not a cardinal one. Cardinal numbers denote quantity and the size of the number is meaningful, while ordinal numbers order or define an object's position in a series of numbers. The amount of utils obtained from any given bundle is only useful as far as it allows us to order or rank bundles. If $u(x_i) = 2$ and $u(x_j) = 4$, we can say that x_j is preferred to x_i, but we cannot say that it is "two times as good." Regardless of the ordinality of the utility concept, the utility function will prove to be extremely useful in deriving the demand functions that we will use in empirical analysis.

2.3   Utility and Marshallian Demands

The primal problem for the consumer is to maximize his utility function subject to limitations on his budget. He has the freedom to choose goods for consumption, but inherent restrictions on this choice arise as a consequence of the prices óf the goods and his income. The budget constraint is binding because money is scarce and income is finite. An implicit assumption is that the consumer can buy all he wants at given prices, without affect the prices. Even the wealthiest individuals must make decisions subject to a budget constraint. More precisely, the consumer's problem is to $\max_{\mathbf{x}} u(\mathbf{x})$ subject to $\mathbf{px} = m$ where $\mathbf{p} = [p_1, \ldots, p_n]$ is a vector of prices for the goods in $\mathbf{x}$ and m is the consumer's scalar income.

This problem may be formulated in terms of a Lagrangean and solved through differential calculus. The Lagrangean is

$$L = u(\mathbf{x}) + \lambda(m - \mathbf{px}) \tag{2.2}$$

where λ is the Lagrange multiplier. The first order conditions are

$$\frac{\partial u(\mathbf{x})}{\partial x_i} = \lambda p_i \quad i = 1, \ldots, n \tag{2.3}$$

$$m = \mathbf{px} \tag{2.4}$$

which is a system of $n + 1$ equations in $n + 1$ unknowns. Substituting, and solving the system for all x_i, we can obtain demand functions for each of the goods under consideration. It is a common assumption that the consumer will demand a strictly positive quantity of each good, thereby ruling out the possibility of corner solutions. A corner solution occurs when the consumer does not purchase one of the goods. In fact, the convexity axiom ensures that a corner solution will not be optimal under a linear budget constraint. Solving the system of equations in 2.3 for the optimal bundle of goods yields

$$x_i = x_i(\mathbf{p}, m) \quad i = 1, \ldots, n \tag{2.5}$$

These demand functions give the utility maximizing quantity of each good that is demanded by the consumer under a given income and set of prices. The functions in equation 2.5 are known as uncompensated, or Marshallian, demand functions. This name comes from the work of Alfred Marshall, a founder of neoclassical economics. The n Marshallian demand functions form a system of equations. Because the demands were derived from an optimization problem with a satisfactory utility function, we should expect to find the system as a whole to be consistent with rational choice.

Uncompensated demand functions will satisfy several properties when derived under the conditions described above. Indeed, a number of these properties can be obtained without considering the consumer's preferences at all. One must only assume the existence of a Marshallian demand function and a linear budget constraint. We have not pursued such an approach in this chapter, but both Deaton and Muellbauer (1980a) and Cornes (1992) derive some properties of demands without appealing to preferences and utility. The properties of the Marshallian demand functions are:

1. **Positivity**: Given that prices and income are non–negative, the consumer will never demand a negative amount of any good. Because corner solutions are assumed away, it is also the case that the consumer will always demand a small amount of every good. Thus, every Marshallian demand function in the system of demands is strictly positive and $x_i > 0$ for all i.

2. **Adding–Up**: Because the budget constraint is an exact equality, $\mathbf{px}(\mathbf{p}, m) = m$. The consumer will not hold any unspent income, so the total value of the demanded bundle must be equal to income. This property is not

as strict as it might seem; there are various ways of dealing with saving, investment, or other inter-temporal problems that might arise. These boil down to one general approach: creatively defining the goods in the budget constraint.For instance, savings can be thought of as a good.

3. **Homogeneity**: The demand functions are homogenous of degree zero in prices and income so that $x_i(\mathbf{p}, m) = x_i(\theta \mathbf{p}, \theta m)$ for any scalar $\theta > 0$ and $i = 1, \ldots, n$. If we scale both prices and income by the same amount, then the optimal quantity demanded of each good must be the same. This property is a statement of an absence of "money illusion." The actual level of prices and income are inconsequential. As long as relative prices and income are maintained, the outcomes of a consumer choice problem will be identical.

4. **Symmetry**: Define the matrix of substitution effects as

$$S = \begin{vmatrix} \frac{\partial x_1}{\partial m} x_1 + \frac{\partial x_1}{\partial p_1} & \cdots & \frac{\partial x_1}{\partial m} x_n + \frac{\partial x_1}{\partial p_n} \\ \vdots & \ddots & \vdots \\ \frac{\partial x_n}{\partial m} x_1 + \frac{\partial x_n}{\partial p_1} & \cdots & \frac{\partial x_n}{\partial m} x_n + \frac{\partial x_n}{\partial p_n} \end{vmatrix}$$

This matrix will be symmetric negative semi-definite, with the consequence that properties of symmetry and negativity must hold. Even though both of these properties are related to the matrix of substitution effects, they have somewhat distinct economic implications. Symmetry implies that for $i \neq j$, $\frac{\partial x_i}{\partial m} x_j + \frac{\partial x_i}{\partial p_j} = \frac{\partial x_j}{\partial m} x_i + \frac{\partial x_j}{\partial p_i}$. The off–diagonal elements of the matrix must be symmetric.

5. **Negativity**: The elements on the diagonal of the substitution matrix must be non–positive. Thus $\frac{\partial x_i}{\partial m} x_i + \frac{\partial x_i}{\partial p_i} \leq 0$ for all $i = 1, \ldots, n$.. This implies that the substitution effect of every good with respect to its own price cannot be positive. Note, however, that this property does not rule out the possibility of an increase in quantity demanded with an increase in price. The change in the quantity of good x_i with respect to its own price p_i, which is given by the term $\frac{\partial x_i}{\partial p_i}$, could be positive. Negativity would still hold as long as $\frac{\partial x_i}{\partial m} x_i$ is strongly negative.

The properties that characterize Marshallian demand functions can be taken as restrictions in the statistical estimation of demand systems. In the next chapter, we will give some form to the demand functions and then estimate their parameters using a variety of statistical methods. Because of the shape and curvature properties of the theoretical demands, we will want to use functional forms that allow us to test whether the estimated demand system adheres to these properties. We may also want to be able to impose restrictions from theory a priori.

If all of the theoretical properties are satisfied for an entire system of demands, then the demand system is integrable. This means that a utility function exists, consistent with the axioms of preference from the previous section, that will generate the system of demands. A geometric treatment of integrability can be found in Samuelson (1950) with a more concise statement of the Integrability Theorem available in Hurwicz and Uzawa (1971). For our purposes, it is enough to recognize that if a system of demands is integrable, it is consistent with utility theory and the idea of the rational consumer.

2.3.1 A Graphical Look at Utility and Demand

It can be instructive to view utility functions graphically, although this practice is not common as the functional form of the utility function is usually unknown and the number of dimensions of the function is typically greater than three. This section provides a graphical look at one of the most common utility functions – the Cobb–Douglas utility function – and allows us to demonstrate some of the plotting functions available in SAS. Consider an individual who can choose between goods x_1 and x_2. The bundle that the consumer chooses is represented arbitrarily by the two–dimensional vector $\mathbf{x}$. The Cobb–Douglas utility function takes a bundle from the choice space and returns the amount of utils that the given bundle generates. The form of the Cobb–Douglas utility function is

$$u(\mathbf{x}) = x_1^\alpha x_2^\beta \tag{2.6}$$

where it is usually assumed that $\alpha + \beta = 1$. For simplicity of exposition, we will take both α and β to equal $\frac{1}{2}$. What does the utility function look like? We can answer this question by creating a 3D plot of the function in SAS.

First, we need to generate a set of grid points where the utility function will be evaluated. The values on the X and Y axes of the plot will represent quantities of the two goods so it makes sense to start the grid of points at the origin. The grid will go out to 100 in both dimensions with a step size of one, so that the utility function will be evaluated at a total of 10,000 grid points. The following SAS code creates a data set of grid values using do loops. The evaluation of the Cobb–Douglas utility function occurs inside the loops.

```
data cobb_douglas;
    do x1 = 0 to 100 by 1;
        do x2 = 0 to 100 by 1;
            u = sqrt(x1 * x2);
            output;
        end;
    end;
run;
```

The TEMPLATE procedure is used to define statistical graphics in SAS. The following code defines the graphic "cobbdouglas_3d_graph" which is a 3D overlay defined by three parameters. We can also instruct SAS to fill or color in the surface of the function by modifying the SURFACETYPE option. Once the template has been defined, the graph is rendered by calling PROC SGRENDER. One advantage of using PROC TEMPLATE is that it is easy to make graphics that can be applied to different data sets.

```
proc template;
    define statgraph cobbdouglas_3d_graph;
        begingraph;
            entrytitle "Cobb-Douglas Utility Function";
            layout overlay3d;
                surfaceplotparm x = x1 y = x2 z = u /
                    surfacetype = fill;
            endlayout;
        endgraph;
    end;
run;


proc sgrender data = cobb_douglas template = cobbdouglas_3d_graph;
run;
```

Figure 2.1 3D Plot of Cobb–Douglas Utility

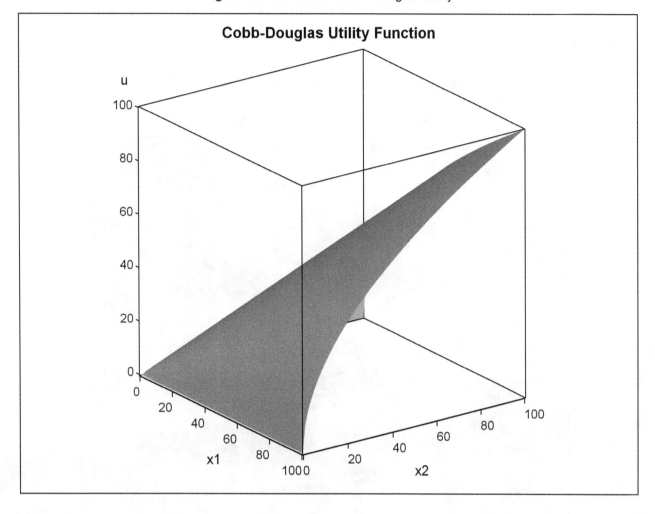

Another type of graphic that is commonly used to visualize utility functions is a contour plot. Contour plots show a cross section of a 3D plot, like the one we generated above, but with contour lines indicating the points where the function has a constant value. In the economic lexicon, these contour lines are referred to as indifference curves. Because the level of utility is constant for any bundle of goods along the curve, the consumer is indifferent between any of the bundles. Remember that the convexity axiom ensures that indifference curves have certain properties.

As with the 3D plot, we must first define a statistical graphic template for the contour plot. We have several different options for the overlay. The NHINT option requests that the z value (utility) be split into roughly 10 different ranges or bins. The contour plot is then displayed using PROC SGRENDER.

```
proc template;
    define statgraph cobbdouglas_contour;
        begingraph;
            entrytitle "Cobb-Douglas Utility Function";
            layout overlay;
                contourplotparm x = x1 y = x2 z = u /
                    contourtype = fill nhint = 10 colormodel = twocolorramp name = "Contour";
                continuouslegend "Contour" / title = "Utility";
            endlayout;
        endgraph;
    end;
```

```
run;
```

```
proc sgrender data = cobb_douglas template = cobbdouglas_contour;
run;
```

Figure 2.2 Contour Plot of Cobb–Douglas Utility

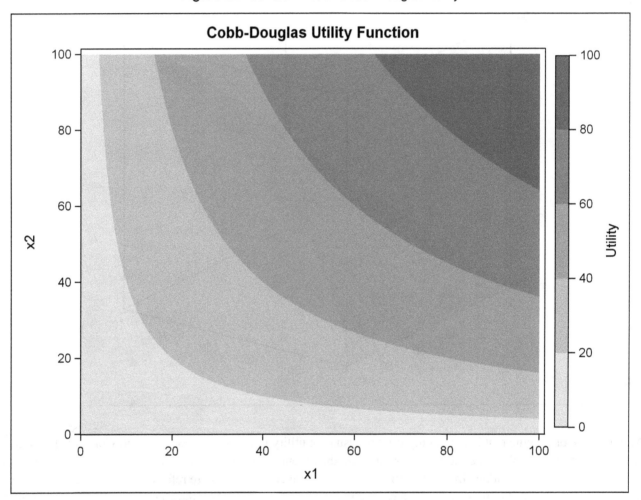

We can see from Figure 2.1 and Figure 2.2 that the Cobb–Douglas utility function is continuous. It is also convex and all of the level sets of the utility function are convex sets. The property of convexity is reflected in the smoothness of the indifference curves. Notice that these curves do not contain any kinks or straight segments. If we were to draw a linear budget constraint on these plots, it would be tangent to the utility surface at precisely one point. This point, which would maximize utility for the given budget constraint, would lie somewhere in the interior of the plot and not on one of the axes.

If you go through the steps of setting up and then solving the consumer's primal problem assuming a Cobb–Douglas utility function, the resulting Marshallian demands will be

$$x_1(\mathbf{p}, m) = \alpha \frac{m}{p_1} \tag{2.7}$$

$$x_2(\mathbf{p}, m) = \beta \frac{m}{p_2} \tag{2.8}$$

The demand functions can be visualized in much the same way that we considered 3D and contour plots of the utility function. We will visualize the demand function for the first good to see how the optimal quantity of x_1 responds to changes in its own price. Assuming that nominal income is held constant at 100, and that $\alpha = \frac{1}{2}$, the following code generates a grid of prices. Quantity demanded is evaluated at each price.

```
data cobb_douglas_demand;
    do p = 1 to 100 by 1;
            x = (1/2) * 100 / p;
            output;
    end;
run;


proc sgplot data = cobb_douglas_demand;
    series x = p y = x;
    title 'Cobb-Douglas Demand Function';
run;
```

When plotting the demand curve, the dependent variable is on the x axis, as is the common practice in economics. The demand curve slopes downward which is consistent with the Law of Demand. Notice that the quantity demanded goes to infinity as the price approaches zero. In other words, the consumer cannot be satiated. Similarly, as the price goes to infinity, the quantity demanded approaches zero. As a result of strictly convex preferences, the consumer always demands a positive amount of the good.

Figure 2.3 Plot of Cobb–Douglas Demand Function

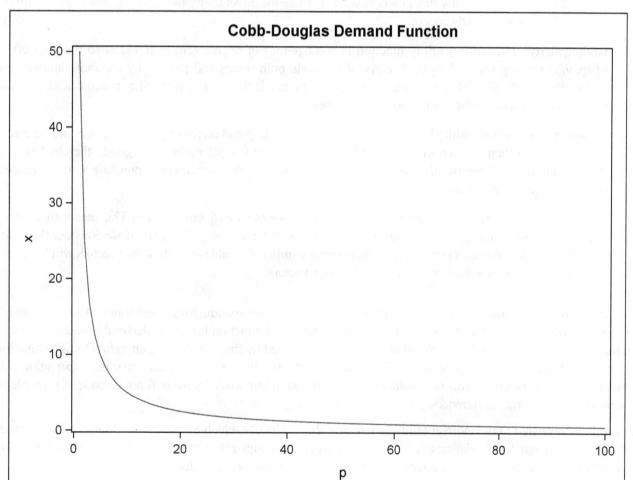

2.4   Indirect Utility

In the previous section, demand functions were derived by maximization of the consumer's utility function subject to a linear budget constraint. The Marshallian demand functions allow us to determine an optimal consumption bundle from a given set of prices and income. The optimal bundle, in turn, will yield a maximal amount of utility when taken as an input to the utility function. Because of this connection between prices, income, and utility, we might also consider a utility function based on prices and income alone. Substituting the demand functions of equation 2.5 back into the utility (objective) function results in what is known as the indirect utility function,

$$v = v(\mathbf{p}, m) \tag{2.9}$$

Remember that the rational consumer's wellbeing is affected by consumption of goods. For better or worse, this is all that he cares about, as embodied in the axioms of preference. Prices and income do not affect the consumer directly, but indirectly, as they act as constraints on the quantities of the goods that can be consumed. The indirect representation of utility has some intuitive appeal because prices, rather than quantities, are the exogenous variables in the consumer's problem. The consumer chooses quantities with prices taken as given; the usual assumption forcing this exogeneity is that of perfectly competitive markets.

The indirect utility function has the properties of:

1. **Positivity**: The indirect utility function is positive, but like the direct utility function, we should be careful not to treat utility as a cardinal concept.

2. **Homogeneity**: The indirect utility function is homogenous of degree zero in $\mathbf{p}$ and m so that $v(\mathbf{p}, m) = v(\theta\mathbf{p}, \theta m)$ for any scalar $\theta > 0$. Clearly, if we scale both prices and income by the same amount, the optimizing bundle of goods is the same. Because the bundle is the same, direct utility is equivalent, and thus we should not expect indirect utility to change either.

3. **Monotonicity**: Indirect utility is monotonically decreasing in $\mathbf{p}$ and increasing in m. If prices increase with income held constant, the consumer will be forced to purchase a smaller amount of goods, thereby lowering the level of utility. If income increases with prices held constant, the consumer can purchase a greater amount of goods, thereby raising utility.

4. **Strict Quasi–Convexity**: The indirect utility function is strictly quasi–convex in $\mathbf{p}$. This means that $v((1 - \lambda)\mathbf{p}_i + \lambda\mathbf{p}_j, m) < \max(v(\mathbf{p}_i, m), v(\mathbf{p}_j, m))$ with $0 < \lambda < 1$ and $i \neq j$. Roughly, if we consider the utility available from two different price vectors, the maximum utility attainable from these two vectors will be greater than the utility obtained from an average of the price vectors.

The indirect utility function and the (direct) utility function are corresponding representations of the consumer's preferences. Because of this equivalence, it does not matter which function is used to derive demands. Several of the functional forms used in the empirical examples are motivated by first considering an indirect utility function. One important point is that the direct and indirect utility functions will generally contain the same information only if preferences are convex. As this is a maintained assumption in our analysis, we will not consider the problems generated by non–convex preferences.

A useful result related to the indirect utility function is Roy's identity which allows for the Marshallian demands to be derived through differentiation (Roy 1947). This process is simpler than the optimization problem that would confront us were we to begin with a direct utility function. Roy's identity formally says that

$$x_i(\mathbf{p}, m) = -\frac{\partial v(\mathbf{p}, m)/\partial p_i}{\partial v(\mathbf{p}, m)/\partial m} \tag{2.10}$$

If we know the indirect utility function, then it is possible to obtain the uncompensated demands by differentiating with respect to prices and income to form the ratio in equation 2.10. For an application of Roy's identity to the derivation of a system of empirically applied demands, see Fleissig and Swofford (1996).

2.5   Hicksian Demands and Expenditures

The primal problem is to maximize utility subject to the budget constraint. From this process we obtain utility maximizing quantities. An alternative representation of the same problem – or dual representation – to consider the consumer who minimizes expenditures, again by choosing a bundle of goods, subject to a given level of utility. More formally the consumer will $\min (\mathbf{px})_\mathbf{x}$ subject to $u(\mathbf{x}) = u$. The dual problem is also solved by application of calculus with the Langrangean taking the form

$$L = \mathbf{px} + \lambda(u - u(\mathbf{x}))$$ (2.11)

As in the primal problem, there are $n + 1$ first order conditions which are

$$p_i = \lambda \frac{\partial u(\mathbf{x})}{\partial x_i} \quad i = 1, \ldots, n$$ (2.12)

$$u = u(\mathbf{x})$$ (2.13)

Solving the system for each x_i yields expenditure minimizing demands known as compensated, or Hicksian, demand functions. Hicksian demands are named after the twentieth century British economist John Hicks. Recall that solving for quantities in the primal problem produces Marshallian demand functions in income and prices. In the dual problem, the demands are functions of prices and utility and written as

$$h_i = h_i(\mathbf{p}, u)$$ (2.14)

The Hicksian demands give the quantities necessary to minimize expenditures for a target level of utility at a given set of prices. It is possible to arrive at the same demanded quantities by either taking income as in the primal problem or taking the corresponding utility in the dual problem. The Hicksian demands are called compensated demands because the level of utility is held constant.

The relationship between the Hicksian and Marshallian demands is, at the optimum,

$$x_i(\mathbf{p}, m) = h_i(\mathbf{p}, u)$$ (2.15)

Hicksian demands satisfy the following properties:

1. **Positivity**: Given that prices and income are non–negative, the consumer will never demand a negative amount of any good. As the Marshallian and Hicksian demands are equivalent at the optimum, the Hicksian demands must also be positive with $h_i > 0$ for all i.

2. **Adding–Up**: Just as the Marshallian demands must satisfy the adding-up property, so must the Hicksian demands. The quantities demanded are the same, so it follows that the Hicksian demands must also satisfy the budget constraint equality. Thus, $\mathbf{ph}(\mathbf{p}, u) = m$.

3. **Homogeneity**: Hicksian demands are homogenous of degree zero in prices so that $h_i(\mathbf{p}, u) = h_i(\theta \mathbf{p}, u)$ for any scalar $\theta > 0$. These demands are compensated because unlike the Marshallian demands, where real income may vary with a change in price, real income implicitly adjusts to compensate for any price change. Thus, if all prices are scaled, income compensates for this scaling and we are left purchasing the same bundle of goods.

4. **Symmetry**: We must first define the Slutsky matrix of compensated price responses. This matrix

$$S = \begin{vmatrix} \frac{\partial h_1(p,u)}{\partial p_1} & \cdots & \frac{\partial h_1(p,u)}{\partial p_n} \\ \vdots & \ddots & \vdots \\ \frac{\partial h_n(p,u)}{\partial p_1} & \cdots & \frac{\partial h_n(p,u)}{\partial p_n} \end{vmatrix}$$

must be symmetric negative semi-definite. Unlike the substitution matrix associated with the Marshallian demands, we have explicitly defined the Slutsky matrix as a matrix of first order derivatives. In fact, these two matrices are equivalent, which is why we have used S to represent both. As the off–diagonal elements of S must be symmetric, $\frac{\partial h_i(p,u)}{\partial p_j} = \frac{\partial h_j(p,u)}{\partial p_i}$ for all $i \neq j$. If we know the compensated demand response of good i to a change in the price of good j, then we also know the compensated demand response of good j to a change in the price of good i.

5. **Negativity**: The diagonal of the Slutsky matrix must be non–positive. This has some important implications, mainly the connection of this property to the ubiquitous Law of Demand. As the diagonal of the Slutsky matrix is composed of own–price compensated demand responses, we can say that compensated demand curves will never slope upward.

If we substitute the Hicksian demands into the general formula for expenditures, we obtain the expenditure function

$$e(\mathbf{p}, u) = \mathbf{p}h(\mathbf{p}, u) \tag{2.16}$$

The expenditure function returns the minimum amount of income necessary to obtain a level of utility at a given set of prices. The expenditure function, also referred to as the cost function, has the following properties:

1. **Continuous**: The expenditure function is continuous in both $\mathbf{p}$ and u.

2. **Homogeneity**: The expenditure function is homogenous of degree one in prices so that $\theta e(\mathbf{p}, u) = e(\theta \mathbf{p}, u)$. If all prices are scaled, and we wish to remain at the same level of utility, then expenditures will also need to be scaled by the same amount. This is a result of the linearity of the budget constraint.

3. **Monotonicity**: The expenditure function is monotonically increasing in $\mathbf{p}$ and u. If prices increase, but utility is constant, then expenditures must increase to allow the consumer to remain at the same level of utility. If the target level of utility increases, but prices are held constant, then expenditures must increase in order for the consumer to purchase more goods to reach the higher target utility.

4. **Concavity**: Concavity must hold for prices. Thus $e((1 - \alpha)\mathbf{p}_i + \alpha \mathbf{p}_j, u) \geq (1 - \alpha)e(\mathbf{p}_i, u) + \alpha e(\mathbf{p}_j, u)$ for any price vectors i and j and any $0 \leq \alpha \leq 1$.

From the representation of the expenditure function given in equation 2.16, it is clear that if one differentiates this function with respect to a given price, we arrive back at the Hicksian demands (Shephard 1953). This result is known as Shephard's lemma which formally says that

$$h_i(\mathbf{p}, u) = \frac{\partial e(u, \mathbf{p})}{\partial p_i} \tag{2.17}$$

Just as with Roy's identity, Shephard's lemma provides us with an easy approach for the derivation of demand functions; our analysis of the theory of demand has come full circle. We first began with a direct utility function and showed that we could obtain Marshallian demands. If we instead begin with expenditures, we can also obtain demand functions, although they are the Hicksian demands. The suitability of the primal and dual approaches to any particular analysis will depend on the question at hand. It will be useful to have both concepts in the theoretical toolbox.

2.5.1 The Slutsky Equation

A key result, that will be used to derive some of the demand functions in the next chapter, is known as the Slutsky equation. The Slutsky equation links what we have termed the matrix of substitution effects and the Slutsky matrix. It also provides the link between Marshallian and Hicksian demands. Because it is so deeply embedded in the primal and dual approaches to demand analysis, understanding the Slutsky equation is crucially important. We earlier arrived at the conclusion that, at the optimum,

$$x_i = x_i(m, \mathbf{p}) = x_i(e(u, \mathbf{p}), \mathbf{p}) = h_i(u, \mathbf{p}) \tag{2.18}$$

At the optimal point, the Marshallian and Hicksian demands must coincide. Taking this equality and differentiating with respect to a single price results in

$$\frac{\partial h_i}{\partial p_j} = \frac{\partial x_i}{\partial m} x_j + \frac{\partial x_i}{\partial p_j} \tag{2.19}$$

which is usually written in the form

$$\frac{\partial x_i}{\partial p_j} = \frac{\partial h_i}{\partial p_j} - \frac{\partial x_i}{\partial m} x_j \tag{2.20}$$

The term on the left is the Marshallian demand response to a change in price. This response can be decomposed into two sources. The first term on the right hand side of the equation is the pure substitution effect of the price change. The second term is the income effect, which results from the notion that a change in any of the prices in the consumer's bundle implicitly adjusts the consumer's real income. To think about this concept, consider a consumer who faces a constant nominal income and rising nominal prices for all of the goods available for his consumption. Clearly the consumer's real income must fall; it would not be possible to maintain a given level of utility.

Nowhere in this chapter have we implied that the response of uncompensated demands to a change in own–price must be negative. The Slutsky equation shows why such an implication would not hold. We have already hinted at this result in our discussion of properties of the Marshallian demands. The pure substitution effect must be negative – this results from the negativity property of the Hicksian demands – but the income effect could be large and negative, thereby causing the uncompensated price response to be positive. Goods with positive own–price Marshallian demand responses are called Giffen goods, and while theoretically possible, they are very rarely observed.

There should be no confusion at this point that the matrices defined as the matrix of substitution effects in the section on Marshallian demands, and the Slutzsky substitution matrix in the section on Hicksian demands, are in fact the same matrix. This matrix is particularly important in demand theory. The integrability condition relies on the Slutsky substitution matrix being symmetric and negative semi-definite. These properties have been restated due to their importance. You may sometimes see these two properties referred to in other texts as Slutsky symmetry.

We now have enough theory to allow us to start with either the primal problem or the dual problem and arrive at a system of demands. These demands may be either Marshallian or Hicksian demands. Some discussion was also made of the indirect utility function and expenditure function. What we view as primarily important for applied work are the restrictions that the theory implies for the demand functions. For instance, the Marshallian demands should satisfy the conditions of adding–up, homogeneity, symmetry, and negativity. The rest of this chapter does not deal with demand theory directly, but expands on the ideas developed so far. In particular, we discuss elasticities and problems of separability and aggregation, two topics that are never far from applied work.

2.6   Elasticities

The quantities that are usually of the most economic interest in the study of demand systems are elasticities. Elasticities are defined as the ratio of a percentage change in one variable to the percentage change in another variable. These quantities are popular because they are scale free measures. We will primarily be involved in computing own–price, cross–price, substitution, and income elasticities. However, there are several different elasticity measures – with varying interpretations – of which the applied economist must be aware. Elasticities naturally extend to producer theory and our presentation of several major elasticity concepts in this chapter allows us to economize on text in subsequent chapters. Throughout the book we will use ϵ_{ij} to denote the price elasticity of demand for good i with respect to good j. Income elasticities will be denoted by η_i in the case of good i and substitution elasticities denoted by ω_{ij} for good i with respect to good j. Superscripts are used to denote different types of elasticities; these distinctions are made clear in the text.

The most common elasticities, at least in the sense that they are the first elasticities to which most students of economics are exposed, are the uncompensated or Marshallian price elasticities of demand. These are closely related to income elasticities of demand as both are obtained by taking logarithmic derivatives of the Marshallian demand functions. The uncompensated price elasticity of demand is recovered by taking this derivative with respect to price. The elasticity is then given by

$$\epsilon_{ij} = \frac{\partial \log (x_i(\mathbf{p}, m))}{\partial \log (p_j)} = \frac{\partial x_i(\mathbf{p}, m)}{\partial p_j} \frac{p_j}{x_i(\mathbf{p}, m)} \tag{2.21}$$

The income elasticity of demand results from the logarithmic derivative of the Marshallian demand with respect to income or expenditure. More formally

$$\eta_i = \frac{\partial \log (x_i(\mathbf{p}, m))}{\partial \log (m)} = \frac{\partial x_i(\mathbf{p}, m)}{\partial m} \frac{m}{x_i(\mathbf{p}, m)} \tag{2.22}$$

It is apparent from equation 2.21 and equation 2.22 that elasticities are unitless measures of the response of one variable to changes in another. The level changes in the formulas are scaled by price-quantity or income-quantity ratios. More precisely, the elasticity provides a comparison of the percentage change of one quantity to a percentage change in another quantity. This unitless feature of the elasticities facilitates comparison between different goods and prices which will naturally vary in their scale.

Goods can be classified according to the magnitude and sign of their elasticities. In particular, goods with $\epsilon_{ij} > 0$ are classified as gross substitutes while those with $\epsilon_{ij} < 0$ are gross complements. We can also classify goods by considering their income elasticities. If $\eta_i > 0$ then good i is considered a normal good, whereas it is considered inferior if $\eta_i < 0$. Among the normal goods, if $\eta_i > 1$ then the good is a luxury. These may be contrasted with necessities where $0 < \eta_i < 1$.

As the uncompensated elasticities are derived from the Marshallian demands, so are the compensated elasticities derived from the Hicksian demands. Thus the compensated price elasticities of demand are given by

$$\epsilon_{ij}^h = \frac{\partial \log (h_i(\mathbf{p}, u))}{\partial \log (p_j)} = \frac{\partial h_i(\mathbf{p}, u)}{\partial p_j} \frac{p_j}{h_i(\mathbf{p}, u)} \tag{2.23}$$

Goods can be said to be Hicksian substitutes if $\epsilon_{ij}^h > 0$ and complements if $\epsilon_{ij}^h < 0$. There is, of course, no compensated income elasticity of demand as income is precisely what is being compensated!

The uncompensated and compensated elasticities can be related by the Slutsky equation. Beginning with the Slutsky equation in 2.20, multiply both sides of the equation by $\frac{p_j}{x_i}$. Multiplying the last term on the right by $\frac{m}{m}$ and reducing to elasticities gives the elasticity form of the Slutsky equation which is

$$\epsilon_{ij} = \epsilon_{ij}^h - \eta_i s_j \tag{2.24}$$

Here, s_j denotes good j's budget share. The uncompensated price elasticity of good i with respect to the price of good j is the difference between the compensated price elasticity and the income elasticity of good i when scaled by good j's budget share. Alternatively, we could think of the compensated price elasticity as the sum of the uncompensated price elasticity and an elasticized income effect. The Slutsky equation is particularly useful in this context because, provided that estimates for two of the three elasticities are available, the third elasticity can be calculated directly. We will make use of this identity in the next chapter where many of the empirical demand systems have parameters that may be interpreted as income and uncompensated price elasticities, but the derivation of compensated price elasticities is somewhat more difficult.

The elasticity form of the Slutsky equation clearly shows the conditions that must hold for a Giffen good. Remember that a Giffen good has a positive own–price Marshallian demand response so that $\epsilon_{ii} > 0$. We know that ϵ_{ii}^h will always be negative, so the only way a Giffen good can exist is if the term $-\eta_i s_i$ is positive and larger than ϵ_{ii}^h. The budget share will always be nonnegative, so a necessary condition is that $\eta_i < 0$. The good must also have a very small compensated own–price elasticity or it must be a relatively large portion of the overall budget.

The language of elasticities can be useful for stating, in more succinct fashion, the properties or restrictions that characterize consumer demand functions. The elasticity formulas are particularly useful in the derivation of the Rotterdam and AIDS models in the next chapter. There are four principle restrictions and the elasticized form of each restriction is given below.

1. **Adding-Up**: The adding-up condition implies two restrictions on the elasticities, which have come to be known as Engel aggregation and Cournot aggregation. The Engel aggregation condition is $1 = \sum_i s_i \eta_i$. The Cournot aggregation condition is $0 = \sum_i s_i \epsilon_{ij} + s_j$ for all j.

2. **Homogeneity**: The homogeneity condition is also known as Euler aggregation with the elasticity form $\sum_j \epsilon_{ij} + \eta_i = 0$ for all i. Using the Slutsky equation this can be restated as $\sum_j \epsilon_{ij}^h = 0$ for all i.

3. **Symmetry**: The symmetry condition does not imply symmetry in the cross-price elasticities of demand. This is a common mistake. Rather, it implies symmetry in the compensated elasticities multiplied by their budget shares. The mathematical form is $s_i \epsilon_{ij}^h = s_j \epsilon_{ji}^h$. Again using the Slutsky equation, this further implies that $\epsilon_{ij} = \frac{s_j}{s_i} \epsilon_{ji} + s_j(\eta_j - \eta_i)$.

4. **Negativity**: With negativity, $\epsilon_{ii}^h < 0$ for all i.

Several other elasticities have been developed with the goal of accurately measuring substitution and complementarity relationships between goods. Allen (1938) and Uzawa (1962) developed arguably the most common elasticity used to measure substitution relationships. The Allen–Uzawa Elasticity is given by

$$\omega_{ij}^a = \frac{\partial h_i(\mathbf{p}, u)}{\partial p_j} \frac{p_j}{h_i(\mathbf{p}, u)} \frac{m}{p_i x_i} = \frac{\epsilon_{ij}^h}{s_i} \tag{2.25}$$

which is the Hicksian elasticity divided by its budget share. Two goods will always have the same classification as complements or substitutes whether the compensated price elasticity or Allen–Uzawa elasticities are used. One interesting feature of the Allen–Uzawa elasticity is that $\omega_{ij}^a = \omega_{ji}^a$ for all i and j. When $\omega_{ij}^a > 0$ the goods can be classified as substitutes and when $\omega_{ij}^a < 0$ the goods may be classified as complements.

Morishima (1967) proposed another elasticity to measure substitution, although his contribution was not fully recognized in the United States until Blackorby and Russell (1989). The Morishima Elasticity is

$$\omega_{ij}^m = \frac{-\partial \log(h_i(\mathbf{p}, u) / h_j(\mathbf{p}, u))}{\partial \log(p_j / p_i)} = s_j(\omega_{ij}^a - \omega_{jj}^a) \tag{2.26}$$

Some care must be taken when using elasticities of substitution to characterize substitution and complementarity relationships. Hicks original concept of the elasticity of substitution applied to the case of production with two inputs. In cases where there are more than two inputs, the Hicks concept can still be applied, but output and all other inputs beside the pair under investigation must be held constant. The Allen–Uzawa elasticity presented here (referred to occasionally as the Allen or Hicks–Allen elasticity) attempts to rectify the inadequacies of the Hicks concept when applied to more than two inputs or goods. As Blackorby and Russell (1989) show, the Hicks-Allen elasticity is a poor measure on this account. What little information the Hicks-Allen elasticity does contain can be found in parameter estimates alone. In the case of many factors of production, the best measure of substitution between inputs is the Morishima elasticity. Developed by the economist of the same name, this elasticity is both an exact measure of the ease of substitution and provides complete comparative statics information about relative factor shares in production. It comes much closer to realizing the goals of Hicks' original elasticity in the case of many inputs or goods.

The elasticity proposed by Mundlak (1968) is similar to the Morishima elasticity, but the application is to the Marshallian demands, not the Hicksian. The Mundlak elasticity is

$$\omega_{ij}^u = \frac{-\partial \log \left(x_i(\mathbf{p}, m)/x_j(\mathbf{p}, m) \right)}{\partial \log \left(p_j/p_i \right)} = \omega_{ij}^m + s_i(\eta_i + \eta_j) \tag{2.27}$$

All of the elasticities of substitution that have been mentioned can be used to classify goods as substitutes or complements. TheAllen-Uzawa elasticity is a one-good, one-price elasticity, while the Morishima and Mundlak elasticities are two-good, one-price elasticities. The Allen-Uzawa elasticity measures the percent change in the demand for the level of the good from a percent change in price. The Morishima and Mundlak elasticities measure the percent change in the ratio of goods from a percent change in price. This point is developed by Davis and Gauger (1996) in a comparison of different elasticity measures. One complication is that some goods could be classified as complements under one elasticity measure and substitutes under another. For this reason it is important to recognize the differences between the various elasticities of substitution. In the empirical sections that follow, we are explicit in reporting the elasticity that is being estimated. There is a substantial literature devoted to the topic of substitution elasticities, and the interested reader can find an overview in Stern (2010).

2.7   Separability and Aggregation

In many cases, economists do not have price and quantity information on narrowly defined goods. It is far more common to be confronted with a data set that includes information on commodity aggregates, price indices for commodity aggregates, and perhaps a measure of income or consumption expenditures. As an example, consider the case of the demand for milk. If we were not willing to accept some commodity aggregation, we would need to specify demand functions for whole milk, skim milk, buttermilk, and many specific brands and subcategories of milk products. It is time consuming and expensive to collect such detailed data on consumer expenditures, and it is for this reason that many budget studies restrict themselves to commodity aggregates. However, with the advent of online shopping and scanner data, it is the case that more thorough data sets are now increasingly available.

Even if we were able to specify demand equations for all the different goods available to the consumer, the demand system would be intractably large. Any sort of time series analysis would become quite difficult as the number of variables would quickly exceed the number of observations in the data. Because of these practical concerns, economists have spent a great deal of time on issues of separability and aggregation. The basic idea is to constrain the group of commodities under consideration to a reasonable size. Naturally, we will want our analyses under aggregation to be theoretically consistent as well as tractable.

There are three major separability classifications. Consider dividing the n commodities of the consumer's problem into S different aggregates or subgroups which we denote with different capital letters A, B, C and so on. The vector of commodities in each group can be given by $\mathbf{x}_G = [x_1, \ldots, x_{n_G}]$ where n_G is the number of commodities in group G. There are three forms of separability with which we should be concerned.

1. **Weak Separability**: Weak separability holds if and only if the utility function can be written in the form

$$u(\mathbf{x}) = f[u_A(\mathbf{x}_A), \ldots, u_S(\mathbf{x}_S)] \tag{2.28}$$

    As a consequence of weak separability

$$\frac{\partial[(\partial u/\partial x_i)/(\partial u/\partial x_k)]}{\partial x_j} = 0 \tag{2.29}$$

    for $i, k \in G$, $j \in H$, and $G \neq H$.

2. **Strong Separability**: Strong separability, also known as additive separability, holds if the utility function takes the form

$$u(\mathbf{x}) = f[u_A(\mathbf{x}_A) + \cdots + u_S(\mathbf{x}_S)] \tag{2.30}$$

    Another implication is that

$$\frac{\partial[(\partial u/\partial x_i)/(\partial u/\partial x_k)]}{\partial x_j} = 0 \tag{2.31}$$

    for $i, k \in G$, $j \in H$, and $G \neq H$.

3. **Implicit or Homogenous Separability**: The utility function is implicitly separable if the expenditure function can be written in the form

$$e(u, \mathbf{p}) = e[u, e_A(u, \mathbf{p}_A), \ldots, e_S(u, \mathbf{p}_S)] \tag{2.32}$$

    where $\mathbf{p}_G = [p_1, \ldots, p_{n_G}]$ is a price vector associated with the commodities of subgroup G.

The weak separability assumption allows you to write demand functions in terms of expenditure and prices of the goods in the group in question. Weak separability is an imposed assumption. However, it is an assumption that can be tested as shown in Moschini, Moro, and Green (1994). Consider the following short proof of the implications of weak separability for demand systems. Let all quantities except those in group G be predetermined. Then the primal problem gives the following first order conditions.

$$\frac{\partial u(\mathbf{x})/\partial x_i}{\partial u(\mathbf{x})/\partial x_k} = \frac{p_i}{p_k} \tag{2.33}$$

$$\sum_{i \in G} p_i x_i + \sum_{j \in H} p_j x_j = m \tag{2.34}$$

Group H is a catch-all group that includes all of the predetermined goods not found in group G. As the $n_G - 1$ equations are independent of x_j, provided that j is in H and $H \neq G$, the conditional demand functions can be written as

$$x_i = x_i(m - \sum_{j \in H} p_j x_j, \mathbf{p}_G) \tag{2.35}$$

Now suppose that the predetermined quantities are equal to their Marshallian optimal quantities. Then

$$x_i = x_i(m - \sum_{j \in H} p_j x_j(m, \mathbf{p}), \mathbf{p}_G) = x_i^G(m_G, \mathbf{p}_G) \tag{2.36}$$

where m_G is the expenditure allocation to goods in group G. We have thus demonstrated that under the assumption of weak separability, if we know the expenditures and prices for group G, the conditional demand functions for the group can be treated the same as any other demand system. For this reason, the assumption of weak separability is one of the most ubiquitous assumptions in demand analysis.

Assumptions of weak separability can be motivated by considering the consumer's budgeting process. If this process proceeds in stages, it may be consistent with the consumer's single stage maximization problem. Consider a consumer that budgets by first allocating income to several groups, such as food, housing, transport, etc. In the second stage the consumer allocates the within-group expenditures among different goods. This process could include more stages as consumers decide between different brands or individual items.

It is usually enough to consider the simplified problem of a consumer that budgets in two stages. At the first stage, the consumer must maximize $u = u(\mathbf{x}_{A_1}, \ldots, \mathbf{x}_{A_S})$ subject to the constraint that $\sum_{j=1}^{S} P_j^G \mathbf{x}_{A_j} = m$. The second stage maximization then entails maximizing subject to $\sum_{i=1}^{n_j} p_i x_i = m_{A_j}$ where m_{A_j} is the expenditure allotted to each group from the first stage maximization. The two stage problem will yield the same solution as the consumers single stage problem provided that weak separability holds. But there is an additional consistency requirement that arises as a result of the first stage.

The consistency requirement is that

$$\frac{\partial x_G / \partial p_j}{\partial x_G / \partial p_k} = \frac{\partial P^H / \partial p_j}{\partial P^H / \partial p_k} \tag{2.37}$$

for all possible j, k, G, and H. This condition will hold when weak separability and either homogenous separability or strong separability hold. Precise conditions are given in Green (1964). There are also some considerations to be aware of in the derivation of elasticities from multi-stage budgeting processes. While these concerns are beyond the treatment given in this text, interested readers can find additional information in Edgerton (1997).

The subject of separability and aggregation is considerably more extensive than what we have considered here. There are several other potential motivations for consistent two stage choice models as only one of four sufficient conditions need to be satisfied. These conditions are the Hicks composite commodity theorem, the Leontief composite commodity theorem, homothetically separable production, or the generalized composite commodity theorem. The generalized composite commodity theorem, for instance, allows for aggregation but does not impose any restrictions on preferences. A concise summary of the literature on consistent aggregation can be found in Shumway and Davis (2001).

While this chapter was not exhaustive in its review of economic theory, you now have the necessary theoretical background for applied demand analysis. The next chapter presents several empirical examples that build on the material that we have developed. Special attention is paid to the role of the theory, especially any restrictions or properties of the demand functions that we might want to test. Elasticities are the main object of these studies, and so the examples in the next chapter contain elasticity estimates. We do not focus on the issue of separability and aggregation, but readers should be aware that demand analyses of aggregate commodities implicitly require separability assumptions of one kind or another. In the analyses that follow, we always make the assumption of weak separability. Readers interested in these topics should see Green (1964), George and King (1971), and Uzawa and Goldman (1964).

Chapter 3
Empirical Approaches to Demand Analysis

Contents

3.1	Overview		**23**
3.2	Double Logarithmic Demand Functions		**24**
	3.2.1	The Double Log Form	25
	3.2.2	Empirical Analysis	25
3.3	Rotterdam Model		**29**
	3.3.1	Absolute Price and Relative Price Rotterdam Formulations	30
	3.3.2	Empirical Analysis	33
3.4	Almost Ideal Demand System		**44**
	3.4.1	Full and Linear Approximate AIDS Models	44
	3.4.2	Empirical Analysis	46
3.5	Demand for Differentiated Products		**54**
	3.5.1	Discrete Choice	55
	3.5.2	Logit Models	57
	3.5.3	Empirical Analysis	60
3.6	Conclusion		**74**

3.1 Overview

In the previous chapter, we stated the preference axioms that are sufficient to generate the theory of demand. Some key results of the theory were presented; you will want to take these results into account when conducting empirical studies of demand. Empirical demand analysis has a history that is as long and storied as its theoretical counterpart. In 1699, well before the publication of Adam Smith's *An Inquiry into the Nature and Causes of the Wealth of Nations*, Charles Davenant published a demand schedule for corn using data from Gregory King. Both Davenant and King made statements that roughly correspond to what we now call the Law of Demand (Evans 1967). In this case, empirical observation preceded strictly theoretical developments. Since that time, economists have examined many aspects of demand, including the effects of income on consumption, the effects of prices on consumption, and a number of other important questions.

Much of the early work in demand focused on agricultural commodities. This focus was largely for practical reasons; agricultural goods are mostly homogeneous and consumer preferences for these goods are relatively stable over time. Violation of either of these conditions would complicate statistical analysis and hamper investigation of underlying economic fundamentals. The problems inherent in analyzing heterogeneous goods or goods with unstable preferences have only been partially resolved. Even today, agricultural products remain a popular topic for applied economists. Some of this popularity must also be due to the relative ease with which price and quantity data on agricultural products can be obtained. The United States Department of Agriculture and Bureau of Labor Statistics have a number of data sources that are freely available to the public.

In this chapter, we present and detail a set of commonly used functional forms for demand analysis. The theory of demand says nothing about functional form beyond properties of derivatives. In parametric empirical analyses, it is up to the analyst to choose a functional form which is used to used to estimate elasticities of demand. We provide the derivation of several of the forms and give some account of their development. Readers interested in more technical aspects of demand analysis are advised to check the references in this chapter and at the end of the book. Our main concerns are the ability of these different functional forms to

1. Satisfy restrictions from economic theory

2. Allow for theoretical restrictions to be tested

3. Generate elasticities of demand

The first two items are intimately related to the material developed in the preceding chapter. The last embeds our concerns over the practicality of the proposed methods. It is all well and good if we can test the restrictions from theory, but the estimation of these forms should also be simple. All of the approaches in this chapter can be implemented and extended using SAS. This ease of use will allow you to quickly estimate and test many different models. Different models may be preferred depending on the underlying data, so this flexibility is important in applied analysis.

Apparent in the following applications, the restrictions of economic theory are often rejected. What are the implications of rejection? While there has been some debate on this topic, economists now seem to have widely agreed that rejection of the restrictions implied by economic theory does not constitute a rejection of the law of demand. Nor does rejection in the production context constitute a violation of basic economic concepts in production. Rather, rejection likely represents some underlying aberration in the aggregate data or statistical model. As shown by Kastens and Brester (1996), models with theoretical restrictions imposed can perform better at prediction than those without. As far as out of sample prediction is a valid indicator of the goodness of a model, models with restrictions imposed performed very well. The applied researcher need not be worried upon finding the restrictions of theory rejected. While methodological debates are beyond the scope of this text, an enlightening analysis of these topics can be found in Leontief (1993).

3.2   Double Logarithmic Demand Functions

Elasticities of demand are at the core of almost all applied demand studies. Recognizing that an elasticity is the logarithmic derivative of quantities and prices (or income), it becomes clear that demand functions incorporating logarithmic terms provide an easy way of recovering elasticity estimates. The simplest demand equations of this type are often termed "logarithmic" or "double log" demands. Part of the appeal of the double log form is that the parameters of the estimated equations may immediately be understood as price and income elasticities. Since the equations are linear in parameters, standard statistical techniques can be applied for their estimation.

There are a number of theoretical problems with the double log model, but it continues to be used in applications where a single demand equation is called for. One advantage is that it is easy to incorporate other demand shifters into the double log function. You might consider using double log demand equations when you are interested in analyzing demand for a single good or your data are limited. While your results should only be considered approximate, they can provide a good first look at demand relationships.

3.2.1   The Double Log Form

The double log demand function for good i is

$$\log(x_i) = \alpha_i + \eta_i \log(m) + \sum_{k=1}^{n} \epsilon_{ik} \log(p_k) \tag{3.1}$$

where m is income or expenditure on the set of goods under consideration and p_k denotes the price of good k. The quantity x_i is given in per capita terms, as is the case in almost all demand analyses, so that changes in population do not contaminate empirical results. You can already see that the own price and cross price elasticities are ϵ_{ik} and the expenditure elasticity is given by η_i. This result can be demonstrated by taking the derivative of equation 3.1 with respect to any of the logarithmic variables. Although the single equation double log model is the most applied variant of this form, you could also consider estimating a system of double log demands.

Whether you consider a single equation or system of equations, the double log model cannot satisfy many of the restrictions from demand theory. Even the simple adding–up property is not guaranteed to be satisfied. Deaton and Muellbauer (1980b) go through the short derivations necessary to obtain this result. Adding up will only hold in the unrealistic situation where all of the income elasticities of demand are equal to one. Because of this deficiency, most analysts now choose to use other models in demand analysis.

In fact, the only condition that can be imposed on the double log demands is homogeneity. Homogeneity in a double log demand function implies that

$$\epsilon_{ik} + \cdots + \epsilon_{in} + \eta_i = 0 \tag{3.2}$$

for all $k = 1, \ldots, n$. Two approaches can be pursued to achieve this result. The first is to deflate all prices and income by a single price or income. The second is to restrict the parameters during estimation, instead of deflating the monetary variables. Both methods are easily accomplished using PROC MODEL, but deflating has been more popular historically. The deflator must be one of the monetary variables in the demand equation. As shown in Alston, Chalfant, and Piggott (2002), it is inappropriate to deflate prices and income using a general price index. Using a general price index, the parameters of the demand equation cannot be interpreted as pure elasticities.

3.2.2   Empirical Analysis

We begin with a simple analysis of the demand for dairy products. The data contain information on per capita availability of plain whole milk, butter, cheddar cheese, and processed cheese in the United States. Milk availability is measured in gallons while availabilities of the other goods are measured in pounds. The data set also contains information on the average retail prices of these products across all U.S. cities. Consumption information was obtained from the United States Department of Agriculture's ERS Food Availability (Per Capita) Data System (FADS) while prices were taken from the Bureau of Labor Statistic's Consumer Price Index - Average Price Data. Data are available from 1996 to 2012, and with only sixteen years in the sample, it seems reasonable to assume that consumer preferences are relatively constant over this period.

```
proc print data = dairy(obs = 10);
run;
```

Figure 3.1 U.S. Dairy Consumption Data

Obs	year	cheddar	processed	butter	milk	p_butter	p_cheddar	p_processed	p_milk
1	1996	9.13	5.44	4.3	8.2	2.04675	3.248	3.06550	2.62317
2	1997	9.53	4.92	4.2	8.0	2.16783	3.220	3.33533	2.61400
3	1998	9.57	4.44	4.3	7.7	2.86333	3.548	3.44925	2.70375
4	1999	9.96	4.65	4.6	7.8	2.65300	3.770	3.58992	2.84275
5	2000	9.79	4.86	4.5	7.7	2.51983	3.830	3.81092	2.78067
6	2001	9.94	4.25	4.3	7.4	3.29983	4.027	3.69825	2.88425
7	2002	9.72	4.67	4.4	7.3	3.07283	4.218	3.87142	2.75725
8	2003	9.35	4.61	4.5	7.2	2.81292	3.948	3.88058	2.76108
9	2004	10.33	4.12	4.5	7.0	3.48950	4.273	3.77142	3.15592
10	2005	10.14	4.16	4.5	6.6	3.28142	4.382	3.98433	3.18683

We can see from Figure 3.1 that there is no explicit information on expenditures in this data set. We can form a dairy expenditure variable by calculating and summing the individual expenditures on each product in the category. Because the endogenous variable in the double log demand is the logarithm of quantity, this variable must also be formed in a DATA step before being passed to the MODEL procedure.

```
data dairy;
set dairy;
   expenditures = milk * p_milk + cheddar * p_cheddar + processed * p_processed
               + butter * p_butter;
   log_milk = log(milk);
   log_cheddar = log(cheddar);
   log_processed = log(processed);
   log_butter = log(butter);
run;
```

You now have all the variables necessary to estimate a simple system of double log demands. The following statements use PROC MODEL to estimate each of the four equations without the imposition of homogeneity. We could also estimate these demands using PROC REG, but the flexibility and syntax of PROC MODEL will be useful when we estimate more complicated demand systems later in the chapter.

```
/* Unrestricted Double Log Demands */
proc model data = dairy;
   parameters am bm gmm gmc gmp gmb
              ac bc gcm gcc gcp gcb
              ap bp gpm gpc gpp gpb
              ab bb gbm gbc gbp gbb;
   endogenous log_milk log_cheddar log_processed log_butter;
   exogenous p_milk p_cheddar p_processed p_butter expenditures;

   log_milk      = am + bm * log(expenditures) + gmm * log(p_milk)
                   + gmc * log(p_cheddar) + gmp * log(p_processed)
                   + gmb * log(p_butter);
   log_cheddar   = ac + bc * log(expenditures) + gcm * log(p_milk)
                   + gcc * log(p_cheddar) + gcp * log(p_processed)
                   + gcb * log(p_butter);
   log_processed = ap + bp * log(expenditures) + gpm * log(p_milk)
                   + gpc * log(p_cheddar) + gpp * log(p_processed)
                   + gpb * log(p_butter);
   log_butter    = ab + bb * log(expenditures) + gbm * log(p_milk)
                   + gbc * log(p_cheddar) + gbp * log(p_processed)
                   + gbb * log(p_butter);
```

```
fit log_milk log_cheddar log_processed log_butter / ols
     outest = dairy_estimates;
run;
```

The DATA option specifies the data set that the procedure will utilize. The PARAMETERS statement is used to specify the parameters of the model, the ENDOGENOUS statement specifies the endogenous variables, and the EXOGENOUS statement specifies the exogenous variables. In most cases, SAS will be able to determine the exogenous and endogenous variables from the specified equations. We include these explicit statements for clarity and readability of code. Each equation has $n + 2$ parameters, so that the system as a whole has $n(n + 2)$ parameters.

The system of equations to be estimated is stated in the body of PROC MODEL. The FIT statement tells SAS which equations to estimate. The OLS option accompanies the FIT statement and instructs the procedure to estimate the equations by ordinary least squares. The parameter estimates from the procedure are placed in a data set called dairy_estimates and can be seen in Figure 3.2.

Figure 3.2 Parameter Estimates for Double Log Demands

The MODEL Procedure

Nonlinear OLS Parameter Estimates

Parameter	Estimate	Approx Std Err	t Value	Approx Pr > |t|
am	-4.81513	1.0396	-4.63	0.0007
bm	2.336434	0.2962	7.89	<.0001
gmm	-0.93826	0.1117	-8.40	<.0001
gmc	-1.38695	0.1172	-11.83	<.0001
gmp	-0.57894	0.1599	-3.62	0.0040
gmb	-0.04461	0.0737	-0.61	0.5571
ac	0.478044	1.3565	0.35	0.7312
bc	0.359616	0.3865	0.93	0.3721
gcm	0.248057	0.1457	1.70	0.1167
gcc	-0.45997	0.1530	-3.01	0.0119
gcp	0.411016	0.2086	1.97	0.0745
gcb	0.02284	0.0961	0.24	0.8165
ap	-4.8589	2.1881	-2.22	0.0483
bp	2.106622	0.6234	3.38	0.0061
gpm	-0.64917	0.2350	-2.76	0.0185
gpc	-0.84012	0.2468	-3.40	0.0059
gpp	-0.59288	0.3365	-1.76	0.1058
gpb	-0.46745	0.1550	-3.02	0.0118
ab	1.176331	1.0682	1.10	0.2943
bb	-0.05548	0.3043	-0.18	0.8587
gbm	0.10167	0.1147	0.89	0.3945
gbc	0.718218	0.1205	5.96	<.0001
gbp	-0.19423	0.1643	-1.18	0.2620
gbb	-0.25627	0.0757	-3.39	0.0061

It is encouraging that all of the own-price elasticities are negative with $\epsilon_{mm} = gmm = -0.93826$, $\epsilon_{cc} = gcc = -0.45997$, $\epsilon_{pp} = gpp = -0.59288$, and $\epsilon_{bb} = gbb = -0.25627$. All of the own-price elasticity estimates are also significant at the 5% level except for the own-price elasticity of processed cheese. While all of the goods are own-price inelastic, milk is the most price elastic followed by processed cheese, cheddar cheese, and butter. Milk is a complement for all of the other products, though the relationship is statistically significant only for the two types of cheese.

Many of the cross price elasticities are not statistically significant. There are also some general inconsistencies in the estimates as a result of our inability to impose symmetry. Cheddar cheese is a substitute for processed cheese, but processed cheese is a complement for cheddar cheese. Milk and processed cheese are both classified as luxury goods with respect to income. As there is probably not much income variation in this short time series data, it should not be surprising that only two of the income elasticities are significant.

We should estimate the model with homogeneity to ensure some consistency with theory. Homogeneity is imposed by deflating all prices and expenditure by a single price. The following DATA step deflates all of the prices and expenditures by the price for butter.

```
data dairy;
set dairy;
   expenditures = expenditures / p_butter;
   p_milk = p_milk / p_butter;
   p_cheddar = p_cheddar / p_butter;
   p_processed = p_processed / p_butter;
run;
```

Modifying the demand equations to account for the deflated prices, the following code estimates the same four equations with homogeneity. The price of butter is always one for every observation so the log price of butter is zero. Butter is the numeraire good which means that the relative prices of milk, cheddar, and processed products are all expressed in terms of the price of butter. Notice that the individual equations now have $n + 1$ parameters for a total of $n(n + 1) = 20$ parameters across the system.

```
/* Restricted Double Log Demands */
/* Homogeneity */
proc model data = dairy;
   parameters am bm gmm gmc gmp
              ac bc gcm gcc gcp
              ap bp gpm gpc gpp
              ab bb gbm gbc gbp;
   endogenous log_milk log_cheddar log_processed log_butter;
   exogenous p_milk p_cheddar p_processed p_butter expenditures;

   log_milk      = am + bm * log(expenditures) + gmm * log(p_milk)
                 + gmc * log(p_cheddar) + gmp * log(p_processed);
   log_cheddar   = ac + bc * log(expenditures) + gcm * log(p_milk)
                 + gcc * log(p_cheddar) + gcp * log(p_processed);
   log_processed = ap + bp * log(expenditures) + gpm * log(p_milk)
                 + gpc * log(p_cheddar) + gpp * log(p_processed);
   log_butter    = ab + bb * log(expenditures) + gbm * log(p_milk)
                 + gbc * log(p_cheddar) + gbp * log(p_processed);

   fit log_milk log_cheddar log_processed log_butter / ols
       outest = dairy_estimates;
run;
```

Elasticities for butter can be recovered after the fact using the homogeneity restrictions. The easiest way to do this is to read all of the parameter estimates into PROC IML and then construct a matrix of elasticities. The following code reads in the elasticity estimates, calculates the missing elasticities for butter, constructs a matrix of elasticities, and then prints the matrix of price elasticities.

```
proc iml;
   use dairy_estimates;
   read all var _ALL_;
   close dairy_estimates;

   gmb = 0 - bm - gmm - gmc - gmp;
   gcb = 0 - bc - gcm - gcc - gcp;
   gpb = 0 - bp - gpm - gpc - gpp;
   gbb = 0 - bb - gbm - gbc - gbp;

   price_elasticities = (gmm||gmc||gmp||gmb)//
                        (gcm||gcc||gcp||gcb)//
                        (gpm||gpc||gpp||gpb)//
                        (gbm||gbc||gbp||gbb);

   income_elasticities = (bm||bc||bc||bb);

   factors = {"Milk" "Cheddar" "Processed" "Butter"};

   print price_elasticities[label = "Price Elasticities of Demand"
                            rowname = factors colname = factors format = d7.3],
         income_elasticities[label = "Income Elasticities of Demand"
                             colname = factors format = d7.3];
quit;
```

Figure 3.3 Elasticity Matrix

Price Elasticities of Demand

	Milk	Cheddar	Processed	Butter
Milk	-0.839	-1.835	-0.153	-0.192
Cheddar	0.154	-0.0346	0.00672	0.163
Processed	-0.578	-1.164	-0.285	-0.574
Butter	0.0509	0.948	-0.412	-0.181

Income Elasticities of Demand

Milk	Cheddar	Processed	Butter
3.019	-0.289	-0.289	-0.406

The estimates with homogeneity imposed are also unsatisfactory. It doesn't seem reasonable that all of the dairy products except milk are inferior, or that plain whole milk is a luxury good. Similar inconsistencies arise in substitution relationships as we observed in the unrestricted model. Possibly weak data, coupled with a model that cannot satisfy the requirements of demand theory in general, lead to questionable estimates of elasticities. These weaknesses lead us to consider models that can provide a more satisfactory analysis.

3.3 Rotterdam Model

A major advance in demand system modeling was the development of the Rotterdam model by Theil (1965) and Barten (1964). The name for the model derives from the city of Rotterdam, where both Theil and Barten were stationed for a time. Unlike the double log demand functions, the Rotterdam model is a system-wide approach to demand. Its derivation is firmly rooted in the consumer's maximization problem. For these reasons the Rotterdam model continues to be popular for purposes of demand analysis and testing of economic theory.

In contrast to the linear expenditure system of Stone (1954), the Rotterdam model starts with very general consumer demand functions, and then generalizes up to the consumer's utility function. As Clements and Gao (2015) note, this gives the Rotterdam model a certain type of directness, in the sense that the researcher starts with a basic demand function and at the end of the exercise obtains estimates of demand functions. The form of the utility function is never explicitly given, but work by McFadden (1964) has shown that specific forms for the demand functions may imply restrictions on the consumer's preferences. In spite of the rather minor restrictions on preferences that the Rotterdam model can imply, it is one of the most easily applied and theoretically consistent approaches to the study of demand.

Unlike the double log model, you will see with the Rotterdam model that it is possible to empirically test many implications of economic theory. We saw in the preceding chapter that demand systems must satisfy a host of conditions. The Rotterdam model allows for these conditions to be imposed, or for the system to be estimated without restrictions to test the consistency of economic theory with the data. The Rotterdam model is also specified in terms of first differences of the variables. This makes it a particularly attractive model when time series of prices and income are nonstationary. Early critics of the model noted that its properties hold only in very restrictive cases and this motivated later authors to obtain strong theoretical properties under weaker assumptions. Readers interested in these developments can find additional information in Barnett (1979) and Mountain (1988).

3.3.1   Absolute Price and Relative Price Rotterdam Formulations

There are two distinct versions of the Rotterdam model in use: the Absolute Price model and the Relative Price model. The derivation of either version of the model starts from the consideration of the total differential of a demand function. For this reason, the Rotterdam model and several other approaches to demand analysis have been classified as differential approaches by Barnett and Serletis (2009). Starting from a standard demand function for good i,

$$x_i = x_i(\mathbf{p}, m) \tag{3.3}$$

total differentiation yields

$$dx_i = \frac{\partial x_i}{\partial m} dm + \sum_{k=1}^{n} \frac{\partial x_i}{\partial p_k} dp_k \tag{3.4}$$

The rest of the derivation relies on some of the theoretical developments of the previous chapter. From basic calculus, we know that $\frac{d \log(x)}{dx} = \frac{1}{x}$ which is equivalent to $dx = x d \log(x)$. Substituting for the differentials in the equation above yields

$$x_i d \log(x_i) = \frac{\partial x_i}{\partial m} m d \log(m) + \sum_{k=1}^{n} \frac{\partial x_i}{\partial p_k} p_k d \log(p_k) \tag{3.5}$$

Then dividing the whole equation by x_i gives

$$d \log(x_i) = \frac{\partial x_i}{x_i \partial m} m d \log(m) + \sum_{k=1}^{n} \frac{\partial x_i}{x_i \partial p_k} p_k d \log(p_k) \tag{3.6}$$

You might be concerned that we are moving further and further away from a usable result, but this is not the case. There are several elasticities hiding in equation 3.6. Note that $\frac{\partial x_i}{\partial m} \frac{m}{x_i}$ is the income elasticity of demand and $\frac{\partial x_i}{\partial p_k} \frac{p_k}{x_i}$ is the price elasticity of demand. Simplifying the elasticity terms, the equation can then be written as

$$d \log (x_i) = \eta_i d \log (m) + \sum_{k=1}^{n} \epsilon_{ik} d \log (p_k) \tag{3.7}$$

Substituting for the Slutsky equation,

$$d \log (x_i) = \eta_i \left(d \log (m) - \sum_{k=1}^{n} s_k d \log (p_k) \right) + \sum_{k=1}^{n} \epsilon_{ik}^* d \log (p_k) \tag{3.8}$$

where s_k is the budget share of good k, and ϵ_{ik}^* are the compensated own and cross price elasticities of demand. The model is formulated in continuous time, but we never have economic data in continuous time. In many aggregate demand studies, we will only have data every year or month. Certainly at the time the Rotterdam model was formulated, this was the case. The empirical version of the Rotterdam model approximates the theoretical version in discrete time with $c_{ik} = s_i \epsilon_{ik}^*$, $b_i = p_i \partial f / \partial m$, $s_t = 0.5(s_t + s_{t-1})$, and $\Delta \log \bar{x}_t = \Delta \log x_t - \sum_{k=1}^{n} \bar{s}_t \Delta \log p_{kt}$. The absolute price version of the Rotterdam model can then be stated as

$$\bar{s}_{it} \Delta \log x_{it} = b_i \Delta \log \bar{m}_{it} + \sum_{k=1}^{n} c_{ik} \Delta \log p_{kt} + \epsilon_{it} \tag{3.9}$$

where Δ is a difference operator over time and an error term has been appended for estimation.

The curvature restrictions can then be tested. Homogeneity holds if $\sum_k c_{ik} = 0$ for all i. Negativity if $c_{ii} < 0$ for all i. And symmetry holds if $c_{ik} = c_{ki}$ for all i, k with $i \neq k$. The Rotterdam model is far more useful, at least compared to the double log demands, because it presents an avenue for such tests.

The elasticities of the absolute price version of the Rotterdam model can be calculated directly from the parameters. One assumption inherent in the model is that the parameters are constant. The elasticities must then be evaluated at various points in the sample, most often at the sample average. Budget shares are required for the elasticities that follow, and typically the elasticities are evaluated at the mean budget shares. The income and compensated price elasticities are fairly direct, while the uncompensated price elasticities are calculated using the Slutsky equation.

$$\epsilon_{ik}^* = c_{ik}/s_i \tag{3.10}$$

$$\eta_i = \beta_i / s_i \tag{3.11}$$

$$\epsilon_{ik} = \epsilon_{ij} - s_j \eta_i = c_{ij}/s_i - s_j \beta_i / s_i \tag{3.12}$$

One limitation of the demand system defined by equation 3.9 is that the number of parameters grows rapidly as more goods are added to the model. Partly for this reason, a relative price version of the Rotterdam model was developed. While the absolute price version is linear in parameters, the relative price version is nonlinear. More details on the differences between the two models are given in Barnett and Serletis (2009). Because the estimation of systems of equations with many parameters has been greatly simplified, we do not estimate the relative version of the Rotterdam model in the empirical example that follows. However, it is instructive to show how the model can be derived. From the absolute version of the Rotterdam, and equation 3.10, we know

$$c_{ik} = s_i \epsilon_{ik}^* \tag{3.13}$$

Barten (1964) showed that the substitution effect of a change in the price of good k and demand for good i can be expressed as

$$S_{ik} = \lambda U_{ik}^{-1} - \frac{\lambda}{\partial \lambda / \partial m} \frac{\partial x_i}{\partial m} \frac{\partial x_k}{\partial m} \tag{3.14}$$

where λ is the marginal utility of income. In this case, U_{ij} is the Hessian matrix of the utility function which gives the change in marginal utility as consumption of a good varies. Putting these two elements together

$$c_{ik} = \frac{p_i p_k}{m} S_{ik} = \frac{p_i p_k}{m} [\lambda U_{ik}^{-1} - \frac{\lambda}{\partial \lambda / \partial m} \frac{\partial x_i}{\partial m} \frac{\partial x_k}{\partial m}] \tag{3.15}$$

This can be rewritten as

$$c_{ik} = v_{ik} - \theta b_i b_k \tag{3.16}$$

where:

$$v_{ik} = \frac{p_i p_k}{m} \lambda U_{ik}^{-1}, \quad \theta = \frac{\lambda}{\partial \lambda / \partial m}, \quad b_i = p_i \frac{\partial x_i}{\partial m} \tag{3.17}$$

Now, consider the absolute price version of the Rotterdam:

$$s_i d \ln x_i = b_i d \ln \bar{m} + \sum_k (v_{ik} - \theta b_i b_k) d \ln p_k \tag{3.18}$$

We know that $\sum_k c_{ik} = 0$, and $\sum_k b_k = 1$, which implies that

$$\sum_k v_{ik} = \theta b_i \tag{3.19}$$

Considering again the expression for the Rotterdam

$$s_i d \ln x_i = b_i d \ln \bar{m} + \sum_k (v_{ik} - \theta b_i b_k) d \ln p_k \tag{3.20}$$

Multiply this out and we obtain

$$s_i d \ln x_i = b_i d \ln \bar{m} + \sum_k v_{ik} d \ln p_k - \theta b_i \sum_k b_k d \ln p_k \tag{3.21}$$

Now, the trick—you know that $\sum_k b_k d \ln p_k$ is the same as $\sum_i b_i d \ln p_i$ for any i or k. To prevent confusion, change the subscript in this last summation from k to i and use the fact that $\sum_k v_{ik} = \theta b_i$

$$s_i d \ln x_i = b_i d \ln \bar{m} + \sum_k v_{ik} d \ln p_k - \sum_k v_{ik} \sum_i b_i d \ln p_i, \tag{3.22}$$

which is equivalent to

$$s_i d \ln x_i = b_i d \ln \bar{m} + \sum_k v_{ik}(d \ln p_k - \sum_i b_i d \ln p_i), \tag{3.23}$$

This gives us the relative price version of the Rotterdam model. Equation 3.23 implies that with want independence, demand for a commodity can be expressed as a function of real income and the relative price of good. As opposed to an average price index, the denominator in the relative price is a marginal price index. Likewise, restrictions on preferences can imply restrictions on the coefficients of the model. While it is easier to estimate the relative model, improved computing power has obviated the need for this simplification. With adequate data and currently available statistical software, the absolute version of the model is preferred.

3.3.2 Empirical Analysis

In this application, the Rotterdam model is applied to quarterly meat consumption data from 1975 to 1999. Figure 3.4 shows the first few observations from the data set. The data include variables on U.S. population (in millions of persons), per capita consumption of meats in pounds, average nominal retail prices of meats in cents per pound, the value of the consumer price index, and per capita nominal consumption expenditures on all goods. This is enough data to estimate the Rotterdam model, but not without some minor adjustments. Meat prices in the data set are nominal and must be normalized by the consumer price index in order to obtain an accurate depiction of prices over time. We also need to construct expenditures and expenditure shares for each type of meat. As this is the first true demand system that we have estimated, note that the number of observations in the systems context is equal to the number of observations in the sample multiplied by the number of equations in the system.

```
proc print data = meat(obs = 10);
run;
```

Figure 3.4 Quarterly Meat Consumption Data

Obs	year	qtr	pop	q_beef	q_pork	q_chick	q_turk	p_beef	p_pork	p_chick	p_turk	cpi	pc_exp
1	1975	1	215.132	22.0991	11.8074	9.2631	1.0724	134.833	120.8	58.9000	72.1333	52.43	1143.95
2	1975	2	215.646	21.0304	11.0085	10.1645	1.3916	152.633	129.8	58.9667	70.8333	53.23	1175.19
3	1975	3	216.294	22.2717	9.6583	10.2047	1.8937	163.200	157.4	68.9333	73.8667	54.37	1210.39
4	1975	4	216.851	22.7502	10.4302	9.7381	3.9068	158.167	161.8	66.3000	78.2667	55.23	1240.48
5	1976	1	217.315	23.8753	10.9390	10.3294	1.1450	148.700	149.4	61.9333	78.1000	55.77	1278.21
6	1976	2	217.773	22.8964	10.3597	10.9598	1.5151	148.200	146.3	60.7000	77.0000	56.47	1298.49
7	1976	3	218.337	24.4652	11.0404	11.0310	2.0091	142.800	145.1	60.9000	76.8667	57.37	1329.14
8	1976	4	218.920	23.1085	13.1403	10.1654	4.2247	142.933	126.6	55.1333	78.2333	58.03	1365.91
9	1977	1	219.424	22.9976	11.9593	10.3395	1.2198	142.167	127.2	58.2667	76.0667	59.03	1403.22
10	1977	2	219.953	22.6131	11.4488	11.2841	1.3872	143.933	128.8	60.8000	74.1000	60.33	1432.47

Using PROC MEANS to summarize the meat data, Figure 3.5 shows that over the entirety of the sample, the price for beef has been higher than the price of other meats. Chicken is the cheapest meat. There are 99 observations in the sample corresponding to roughly 25 years of quarterly data.

```
proc means data = meat
   n mean max min range std;
run;
```

Figure 3.5 Summary Statistics for Meat Data

The MEANS Procedure

Variable	N	Mean	Maximum	Minimum	Range	Std Dev
year	99	1986.88	1999.00	1975.00	24.0000000	7.1817125
qtr	99	2.4848485	4.0000000	1.0000000	3.0000000	1.1190706
pop	99	243.4708131	273.5195000	215.1315000	58.3880000	17.0189387
q_beef	99	18.7595734	24.4652000	15.8915000	8.5737000	2.1352497
q_pork	99	12.6880525	14.8637000	9.6583000	5.2054000	0.9764712
q_chick	99	14.4615214	19.9552523	9.2631000	10.6921523	2.8201397
q_turk	99	3.4497231	6.4864000	1.0724000	5.4140000	1.4057030
p_beef	99	242.2377088	300.4000000	134.8333000	165.5667000	45.1326845
p_pork	99	189.8373737	248.1000000	120.8000000	127.3000000	34.5168595
p_chick	99	81.5728949	107.3300000	55.1333000	52.1967000	13.4142885
p_turk	99	95.5736020	109.0000000	70.8333000	38.1667000	9.3858706
cpi	99	113.6405051	167.2300000	52.4300000	114.8000000	34.7966874
pc_exp	99	3232.37	5761.66	1143.95	4617.70	1334.28

The following code uses arrays to simplify the process of constructing expenditures and real prices. The nominal expenditures are quantities of beef multiplied by their prices. Real prices are obtained by dividing nominal prices by the consumer price index (CPI); real expenditures are simply the product of the quantities of meat consumed and their real prices. Total expenditure on meat is obtained by summing expenditures on the individual categories. Because the demand system is expressed in log differences, you also need to create the differenced variables in the DATA step.

```
data meat;
set meat;
   array prices {4} p_beef p_pork p_chick p_turk;
   array quantities {4} q_beef q_pork q_chick q_turk;
   array expenditures {4} exp_beef exp_pork exp_chick exp_turk;
   array shares {4} s_beef s_pork s_chick s_turk;
   array real_prices {4} rp_beef rp_pork rp_chick rp_turk;
   array dlog_quantities {4} dlq_beef dlq_pork dlq_chick dlq_turk;
   array dlog_prices {4} dlp_beef dlp_pork dlp_chick dlp_turk;
   array d_shares {4} ds_beef ds_pork ds_chick ds_turk;
   do i = 1 to 4;
      real_prices{i} = prices{i} / cpi;
      dlog_quantities{i} = dif(log(quantities{i}));
      dlog_prices{i} = dif(log(prices{i}));
   end;
   do i = 1 to 4;
      expenditures{i} = quantities{i} * real_prices{i};
   end;
   exp_meat = sum(exp_beef, exp_pork, exp_chick, exp_turk);
   do i = 1 to 4;
      shares{i} = expenditures{i} / exp_meat;
      d_shares{i} = .5 * (shares{i} + lag(shares{i})) * dlog_quantities{i};
   end;
   dexp_meat = sum(ds_beef, ds_pork, ds_chick, ds_turk);
   date = intnx( 'qtr', '1jan1975'd, _n_-1 );
run;
```

You can use the SGPLOT procedure to examine the behavior of per capita consumption and real price changes over time. When creating the graphs, the VALUESFORMAT option specified that the x axis dates are displayed by year and not another date format.

```
proc sgplot data = meat;
   series x = date y = q_beef / markers markerattrs = (symbol = circle);
   series x = date y = q_pork / markers markerattrs = (symbol = square);
   series x = date y = q_chick / markers markerattrs = (symbol = star);
   series x = date y = q_turk / markers markerattrs = (symbol = diamond);
   title 'Per Capita Consumption of Meats';
   xaxis label = 'Year' valuesformat = year4.;
   yaxis label = 'Pounds';
run;

proc sgplot data = meat;
   series x = date y = rp_beef / markers markerattrs = (symbol = circle);
   series x = date y = rp_pork / markers markerattrs = (symbol = square);
   series x = date y = rp_chick / markers markerattrs = (symbol = star);
   series x = date y = rp_turk / markers markerattrs = (symbol = diamond);
   title 'Average Real Retail Price of Meats';
   xaxis label = 'Year' valuesformat = year4.;
   yaxis label = 'Cents/Pound';
run;
```

One interesting feature of these graphs is the seasonal nature of consumption. Consumption of turkey tends to spike in winter, likely from consumption of whole turkeys at Thanksgiving and Christmas. The average real retail price of meats has gone down over time. The price of turkey and chicken per pound is now equal. Note the dramatic increase in the consumption of chicken over the 25 year period. Consumption has increased from around 10 pounds per quarter to nearly 20 pounds. This increase in the consumption of chicken has been accompanied by a decrease in beef consumption.

Figure 3.6 Changes in Consumption and Prices Over Time

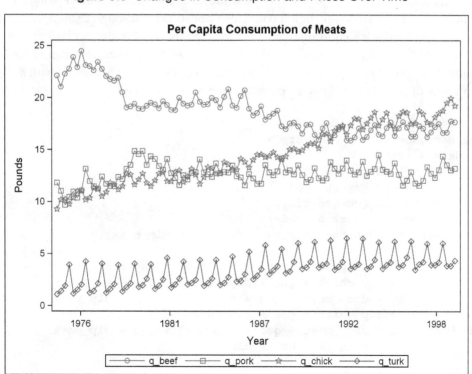

Figure 3.6 *continued*

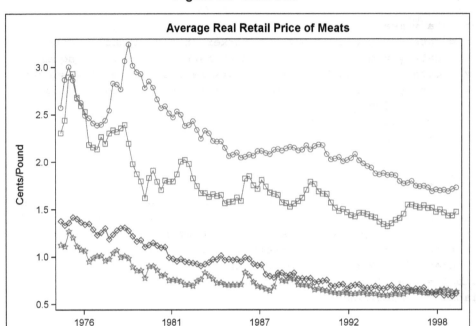

The following code estimates the unrestricted Rotterdam model. Because the error terms are not linearly independent the equation for turkey is dropped. This singularity problem is equivalent to invariance when using maximum likelihood estimation. Barten (1964) shows that the choice of the deleted equation does not affect the parameter values. There are then eighteen parameters to be estimated using the MODEL procedure. The model is estimated using full information maximum likelihood, although it could also be estimated through seemingly unrelated regression techniques. The two approaches are equivalent and, as indicated by Barnett and Seck (2008), it does not matter which method is used. TEST statements specify likelihood ratio tests of the parameter restrictions for homogeneity, symmetry, and joint homogeneity and symmetry. The system consists of three equations with $n + 2$ parameters in each equation, so a total of $(n - 1)(n + 2) = 18$ parameters must be estimated.

```
/* Unrestricted Rotterdam Model */
/* Test for Homogeneity and Symmetry */
proc model data = meat;
   parameters ab bb gbb gbp gbc gbt
              ap bp gpb gpp gpc gpt
              ac bc gcb gcp gcc gct;
   endogenous ds_beef ds_pork ds_chick;
   exogenous dexp_meat dlp_beef dlp_pork dlp_chick dlp_turk;

   ds_beef  = ab + bb * dexp_meat + gbb * dlp_beef + gbp * dlp_pork
              + gbc * dlp_chick + gbt * dlp_turk;
   ds_pork  = ap + bp * dexp_meat + gpb * dlp_beef + gpp * dlp_pork
              + gpc * dlp_chick + gpt * dlp_turk;
   ds_chick = ac + bc * dexp_meat + gcb * dlp_beef + gcp * dlp_pork
              + gcc * dlp_chick + gct * dlp_turk;

   fit ds_beef ds_pork ds_chick / fiml outest = rott_unrest;

   test "Homogeneity"
```

```
        gbb + gbp + gbc + gbt = 0,
        gpb + gpp + gpc + gpt = 0,
        gcb + gcp + gcc + gct = 0, / lr;

    test "Symmetry"
        gbp = gpb,
        gbc = gcb,
        gpc = gcp, / lr;

    test "Joint Homogeneity and Symmetry"
        gbb + gbp + gbc + gbt = 0,
        gpb + gpp + gpc + gpt = 0,
        gcb + gcp + gcc + gct = 0,
        gbp = gpb, gbc = gcb, gpc = gcp, / lr;
  run;
```

Results from the estimation of the unrestricted model, and the likelihood ratio tests are shown in Figure 3.7. All three of the tests for homogeneity, symmetry, and joint homogeneity and symmetry are rejected. As noted in the introduction of the chapter, these rejections should not be viewed as completely invalidating the empirical model.

Figure 3.7 Estimates from Unrestricted Rotterdam Model

The MODEL Procedure

Nonlinear FIML Parameter Estimates

Parameter	Estimate	Approx Std Err	t Value	Approx Pr > |t|
ab	0.361906	0.0488	7.42	<.0001
bb	1.007012	0.0123	81.55	<.0001
gbb	0.07328	0.0877	0.84	0.4053
gbp	0.411893	0.1006	4.09	<.0001
gbc	0.321596	0.0980	3.28	0.0015
gbt	0.469816	0.1007	4.66	<.0001
ap	-0.18463	0.0282	-6.55	<.0001
bp	-0.03926	0.00973	-4.03	0.0001
gpb	-0.17859	0.0487	-3.67	0.0004
gpp	-0.46625	0.0561	-8.31	<.0001
gpc	-0.25703	0.0535	-4.81	<.0001
gpt	-0.33636	0.0537	-6.26	<.0001
ac	-0.05074	0.0427	-1.19	0.2376
bc	-0.0155	0.0121	-1.28	0.2048
gcb	0.147735	0.0640	2.31	0.0233
gcp	0.120819	0.0694	1.74	0.0849
gcc	0.017055	0.0655	0.26	0.7952
gct	-0.0459	0.0726	-0.63	0.5287

Test Results

Test	Type	Statistic	Pr > ChiSq	Label
Homogeneity	L.R.	43.89	<.0001	gbb + gbp + gbc + gbt = 0, gpb + gpp + gpc + gpt = 0, gcb + gcp + gcc + gct = 0
Symmetry	L.R.	41.40	<.0001	gbp = gpb, gbc = gcb, gpc = gcp
Joint Homogeneity and Symmetry	L.R.	81.68	<.0001	gbb + gbp + gbc + gbt = 0, gpb + gpp + gpc + gpt = 0, gcb + gcp + gcc + gct = 0, gbp = gpb, gbc = gcb, gpc = gcp

The homogeneity and symmetry restrictions can be imposed by using RESTRICT statements in the MODEL procedure. The following code is similar to the unrestricted Rotterdam model except for the addition of these statements. Once the restrictions are put in place, there are only 12 free parameters to estimate.

```
/* Restricted Rotterdam Model */
proc model data = meat;
   parameters ab bb gbb gbp gbc gbt
              ap bp gpb gpp gpc gpt
              ac bc gcb gcp gcc gct;
   endogenous ds_beef ds_pork ds_chick;
   exogenous dexp_meat dlp_beef dlp_pork dlp_chick dlp_turk;
   restrict gbb + gbp + gbc + gbt = 0,
            gpb + gpp + gpc + gpt = 0,
            gcb + gcp + gcc + gct = 0,
            gbp = gpb, gbc = gcb, gpc = gcp;

   ds_beef  = ab + bb * dexp_meat + gbb * dlp_beef + gbp * dlp_pork
              + gbc * dlp_chick + gbt * dlp_turk;
   ds_pork  = ap + bp * dexp_meat + gpb * dlp_beef + gpp * dlp_pork
              + gpc * dlp_chick + gpt * dlp_turk;
   ds_chick = ac + bc * dexp_meat + gcb * dlp_beef + gcp * dlp_pork
              + gcc * dlp_chick + gct * dlp_turk;

   fit ds_beef ds_pork ds_chick / fiml outest = rott_rest;

run;
```

The parameter estimates from the restricted Rotterdam model are shown in Figure 3.8 and were stored in the data set rott_rest. As with most demand systems, the elasticities are functions of the parameters. The parameters themselves are usually not of primary interest given their difficult interpretation. Nonetheless, nearly all of the parameters in the restricted model are significant compared to the unrestricted model. This change is particularly evident in the parameters of the chicken demand equation.

Figure 3.8 The Restricted Rotterdam Model

The MODEL Procedure

Model Summary	
Model Variables	8
Endogenous	3
Exogenous	5
Parameters	18
Equations	3
Number of Statements	10

Figure 3.8 *continued*

	Nonlinear FIML Parameter Estimates				
Parameter	Estimate	Approx Std Err	t Value	Approx Pr > |t|	Label
ab	0.406016	0.0433	9.37	<.0001	
bb	1.035698	0.0146	71.17	<.0001	
gbb	-0.22452	0.0233	-9.64	<.0001	
gbp	0.121823	0.0140	8.71	<.0001	
gbc	0.072819	0.0202	3.61	0.0005	
gbt	0.029879	0.00514	5.81	<.0001	
ap	-0.19699	0.0231	-8.53	<.0001	
bp	-0.05206	0.00912	-5.71	<.0001	
gpb	0.121823	0.0140	8.71	<.0001	
gpp	-0.15467	0.0114	-13.52	<.0001	
gpc	0.023187	0.0114	2.04	0.0440	
gpt	0.009663	0.00455	2.12	0.0364	
ac	-0.07623	0.0424	-1.80	0.0755	
bc	-0.03161	0.0112	-2.82	0.0059	
gcb	0.072819	0.0202	3.61	0.0005	
gcp	0.023187	0.0114	2.04	0.0440	
gcc	-0.07755	0.0229	-3.38	0.0010	
gct	-0.01845	0.00703	-2.62	0.0101	
Restrict0	-59.8607	27.9149	-2.14	0.0312	gbb + gbp + gbc + gbt = 0
Restrict1	-5.11839	33.5960	-0.15	0.8799	gpb + gpp + gpc + gpt = 0
Restrict2	179.6788	35.2299	5.10	<.0001	gcb + gcp + gcc + gct = 0
Restrict3	44.25436	44.8651	0.99	0.3266	gbp = gpb
Restrict4	322.6924	51.3303	6.29	<.0001	gbc = gcb
Restrict5	324.3695	71.3950	4.54	<.0001	gpc = gcp

You can evaluate the elasticities of the Rotterdam model at different points in the data. The elasticity formulas require parameter estimates and a budget share; we evaluate the elasticities at the mean budget share over the 25 years of data. The following code calculates elasticities based on the restricted Rotterdam model. First use PROC MEANS to obtain the mean budget shares and then output this data into the data set mean shares.

```
proc means data = meat noprint mean;
   var s_beef s_pork s_chick s_turk;
   output out = meanshares mean = sb sp sc st;
run;
```

The following code uses PROC IML to form the elasticities. Read in the estimates of the parameters, calculate the parameters for the missing turkey equation, and then read in the mean budget shares. The rest of the code uses matrix operations to calculate the elasticities according to equation 3.10 and the following formulas. The elasticities are printed in matrix form.

```
proc iml;
   use rott_rest;
   read all var {gbb gbp gbc gbt gpp gpc gpt gcc gct bb bp bc};
   close rott_rest;

   gtt = 0 - gbt - gpt - gct;
   bt = 1 - bb - bp - bc;

   use meanshares;
```

```
         read all var {sb sp sc st};
   close meanshares;

   s = sb//sp//sc//st;
   b = bb//bp//bc//bt;

   print s;

   gij = (gbb||gbp||gbc||gbt)//
         (gbp||gpp||gpc||gpt)//
         (gbc||gpc||gcc||gct)//
         (gbt||gpt||gct||gtt);

   print gij;

   nk = ncol(gij);
   mi = -1#I(nk);
   uep = j(nk, nk, 0);
   cep = j(nk, nk, 0);
   exe = j(nk, 1, 0);

   do i=1 to nk;
   do j=1 to nk;
      cep[i,j] = (gij[i,j]/s[i]);
      uep[i,j] = (gij[i,j]/s[i]-s[j]#b[i]/s[i]);
      exe[i] = b[i]/s[i];
   end;
   end;

   meats = {"Beef" "Pork" "Chicken" "Turkey"};

   print
      uep[label="Uncompensated Price Elasticities of Demand"
         rowname = meats  colname = meats format = d7.3],
      cep[label="Compensated Price Elasticities of Demand"
         rowname = meats colname = meats format = d7.3],
      exe[label="Expenditure Elasticities" rowname = meats
         format = d7.3];
quit;
```

Figure 3.9 Elasticity Matrices

Uncompensated Price Elasticities of Demand			
	Beef	Pork	Chicken	Turkey
Beef	-1.455	-0.324	-0.135	-0.0188
Pork	0.525	-0.490	0.107	0.0409
Chicken	0.639	0.229	-0.521	-0.123
Turkey	0.108	-0.104	-0.653	-0.594

Figure 3.9 *continued*

Compensated Price Elasticities of Demand				
	Beef	Pork	Chicken	Turkey
Beef	-0.419	0.227	0.136	0.0558
Pork	0.427	-0.542	0.0813	0.0339
Chicken	0.519	0.165	-0.552	-0.131
Turkey	0.774	0.250	-0.478	-0.546

Expenditure Elasticities	
Beef	1.933
Pork	-0.183
Chicken	-0.225
Turkey	1.243

According to the IML output in Figure 3.9, all of the own-price uncompensated and compensated elasticities are negative. According to the uncompensated price elasticities, the only type of meat that is own-price elastic is beef. Beef is also found, somewhat surprisingly, to be a complement to all other forms of meat. Beef and turkey are both classified as luxury goods. You may not be inclined to believe these elasticity estimates because of seasonality in the consumption of the meats, particularly turkey. Turkey consumption increases in winter around the holidays. We have also aggregated all cuts of beef into one category so lower quality cuts are included with high quality cuts. To remove the effects of seasonal behavior, we can append seasonal dummy variables to the model. In SAS, the DATA step is used to create the dummies. A boolean expression constructs the dummies for each quarter. The command creates a variable equal to one when the statement is true, and equal to zero otherwise. The parameter estimate on the first quarter dummy in Figure 3.10 is significant and validates our extension of the model to seasonal consumption behavior.

```
data meat;
set meat;
   qtr1 = (qtr = 1);
   qtr2 = (qtr = 2);
   qtr3 = (qtr = 3);
   qtr4 = (qtr = 4);
run;


/* Restricted Rotterdam Model */
/* Seasonal Dummies          */
proc model data = meat;
   parameters ab ab1 ab2 ab3 bb gbb gbp gbc gbt
              ap ap1 ap2 ap3 bp gpb gpp gpc gpt
              ac ac1 ac2 ac3 bc gcb gcp gcc gct;
   endogenous ds_beef ds_pork ds_chick;
   exogenous dexp_meat dlp_beef dlp_pork dlp_chick dlp_turk
             qtr1 qtr2 qtr3;
   restrict gbb + gbp + gbc + gbt = 0,
            gpb + gpp + gpc + gpt = 0,
            gcb + gcp + gcc + gct = 0,
            gbp = gpb, gbc = gcb, gpc = gcp;

   ds_beef  = ab + ab1 * qtr1 + ab2 * qtr2 + ab3 * qtr3
              + bb * dexp_meat + gbb * dlp_beef + gbp * dlp_pork
              + gbc * dlp_chick + gbt * dlp_turk;
```

```
ds_pork  = ap + ap1 * qtr1 + ap2 * qtr2 + ap3 * qtr3
           + bp * dexp_meat + gpb * dlp_beef + gpp * dlp_pork
           + gpc * dlp_chick + gpt * dlp_turk;
ds_chick = ac + ac1 * qtr1 + ac2 * qtr2 + ac3 * qtr3
           + bc * dexp_meat + gcb * dlp_beef + gcp * dlp_pork
           + gcc * dlp_chick + gct * dlp_turk;

fit ds_beef ds_pork ds_chick / fiml outest = rott_seas;

run;
```

Figure 3.10 The Seasonal Rotterdam Model

The MODEL Procedure

Model Summary	
Model Variables	11
Endogenous	3
Exogenous	8
Parameters	27
Equations	3
Number of Statements	10

Figure 3.10 *continued*

Nonlinear FIML Parameter Estimates

Parameter	Estimate	Approx Std Err	t Value	Approx Pr > |t|	Label
ab	0.169286	0.0448	3.77	0.0003	
ab1	0.075477	0.0102	7.42	<.0001	
ab2	-0.00239	0.00888	-0.27	0.7883	
ab3	0.006438	0.00864	0.74	0.4583	
bb	1.117039	0.0134	83.19	<.0001	
gbb	-0.13134	0.0213	-6.17	<.0001	
gbp	0.10478	0.0117	8.92	<.0001	
gbc	0.001124	0.0164	0.07	0.9454	
gbt	0.025434	0.00356	7.15	<.0001	
ap	-0.12003	0.0241	-4.99	<.0001	
ap1	-0.04588	0.00562	-8.16	<.0001	
ap2	-0.02565	0.00486	-5.28	<.0001	
ap3	-0.02701	0.00453	-5.96	<.0001	
bp	-0.07036	0.00707	-9.95	<.0001	
gpb	0.10478	0.0117	8.92	<.0001	
gpp	-0.15553	0.00743	-20.94	<.0001	
gpc	0.047534	0.00975	4.87	<.0001	
gpt	0.003216	0.00190	1.70	0.0931	
ac	0.059274	0.0349	1.70	0.0926	
ac1	-0.01395	0.00654	-2.13	0.0355	
ac2	0.040722	0.00598	6.81	<.0001	
ac3	0.031891	0.00594	5.37	<.0001	
bc	-0.09055	0.00916	-9.88	<.0001	
gcb	0.001124	0.0164	0.07	0.9454	
gcp	0.047534	0.00975	4.87	<.0001	
gcc	-0.0403	0.0166	-2.43	0.0171	
gct	-0.00836	0.00331	-2.52	0.0134	
Restrict0	5.76821	44.3806	0.13	0.8974	gbb + gbp + gbc + gbt = 0
Restrict1	-55.5392	61.4689	-0.90	0.3691	gpb + gpp + gpc + gpt = 0
Restrict2	298.7035	58.1941	5.13	<.0001	gcb + gcp + gcc + gct = 0
Restrict3	-155.121	78.1106	-1.99	0.0464	gbp = gpb
Restrict4	458.7251	83.4773	5.50	<.0001	gbc = gcb
Restrict5	541.0947	117.1	4.62	<.0001	gpc = gcp

Following its inception, the Rotterdam model has since been applied in a number of different situations and contexts. For instance, Duffy (1987) used a Rotterdam model with advertising to test whether advertising affected demand within industries. Because the incorporation of advertising into the model is fairly simple, it was used by Kinnucan et al. (1997) to investigate the effects of health information on U.S. meat demand. In a similar vein, Marsh, Schroeder, and Mintert (2004) examined the impact of meat recalls on consumer demand and found that elasticity estimates from an absolute price Rotterdam model indicated a shift to non-meat consumption after recalls. Selvanathan (1991) used the model to test whether consumption patterns for alcoholic beverages differed across countries. These studies are only a small subset of the many empirical situations to which the Rotterdam model has been applied. Given the flexibility of the model and its ease of use, it is sure to see application in the future.

3.4   Almost Ideal Demand System

The almost ideal demand system was developed and introduced in a seminal paper by Deaton and Muellbauer (1980a). Since that time, it has become one of the most widely used approaches to demand. The system has several favorable properties that make it "almost ideal". It gives an arbitrary first-order approximation to any demand system, aggregates perfectly over consumers, and satisfies the axioms of choice. As with the Rotterdam model, the AIDS is a system approach to demand where the implications of consumer theory can be tested. We will see that the derivation of the AIDS model begins from the expenditure (cost) function of the consumer and associated assumptions about the form of this function.

Indeed there are several similarities between the AIDS and Rotterdam models. Both models are locally flexible functional forms, possessing sufficient flexibility to approximate elasticities at any point. They are also both linear in parameters (in fact they have the same number of parameters) and thus similar in terms of difficulty of estimation. Because of this similarity a number of studies have tested the suitability of these models, with the aim of identifying a best approach for a given data set. Alson and Chalfant (1993) found that the Rotterdam model was not rejected in an application to meat demand, while the AIDS model was rejected. Later work by Barnett and Seck (2008) concluded that a best approach could not be specified. Like most empirical work, the suitability of any model depends on the application.

3.4.1   Full and Linear Approximate AIDS Models

Our derivation of the almost ideal demand system follows Deaton and Muellbauer (1980a). First consider the following expenditure function

$$\log(e(u, \mathbf{p})) = \ln a(\mathbf{p}) + u \ln b(\mathbf{p}) \tag{3.24}$$

This particular form is an expenditure function that adheres to what are commonly known as PIGLOG preferences or "price-independent, generalized logarithmic" preferences. These preferences have the useful property that they allow exact aggregation over consumers. Several other locally flexible functional forms have PIGLOG preferences, most notably the exactly aggregable translog model found in Christensen, Jorgenson, and Lau (1975). The two price functions are assumed to have the following forms

$$\ln a(\mathbf{p}) = \alpha_0 + \sum_k \alpha_k + \frac{1}{2} \sum_k \sum_j \gamma_{kj}^* \ln p_k \ln p_j \tag{3.25}$$

and

$$\ln b(\mathbf{p}) = \beta_0 \prod_k p_k^{\beta_k} \tag{3.26}$$

Now allow $\gamma_{ij} = \frac{1}{2}(\gamma_{ij}^* + \gamma_{ji}^*)$. Applying Shepherd's lemma results in share equations of the form

$$s_i = \alpha_i + \sum_{j=1}^n \gamma_{ij} \log(p_j) + \beta_i \log(m/P) \tag{3.27}$$

where P is a price index. The price index takes the form

$$\log P = \alpha_0 + \sum_k \alpha_k \ln p_k + \frac{1}{2} \sum_k \sum_j \gamma_{kj} \ln p_k \ln p_j \tag{3.28}$$

The parameters of equation 3.27 have a simple interpretation. The various β_i determine whether the good is a luxury or necessity as they are measures of the response of the expenditure shares to changes in total expenditure. The parameters γ_{ij} measure the change in the budget share to proportional change in the price of good j. Because we started from an expenditure function, the theoretical properties of the expenditure function imply restrictions on the demand functions in equation 3.27. Linear homogeneity holds when $\sum_{k=1} \gamma_{ik} = 0$ for all i and k. Symmetry implies that $\gamma_{ik} = \gamma_{ki}$ for all i and k. Adding up requires that $\sum_{i=1} \alpha_i = 1$ and $\sum_{i=1} \beta_i = 0$.

Let δ_{ik} be the Kronecker delta, which equals 1 when $i = j$ and zero otherwise. The elasticities for the AIDS model are given by

$$\epsilon_{ik} = \frac{\gamma_{ik} - \beta_i [s_k - \beta_k \log (m/P)]}{s_i} - \delta_{ik} \tag{3.29}$$

$$\epsilon_{ik}^h = \frac{\gamma_{ik} - \beta_i [s_k - \beta_k \log (m/P)]}{s_i} - \delta_{ik} + s_j \left(\frac{\beta_i}{s_i} + 1 \right) = \epsilon_{ij} + s_j \eta_i \tag{3.30}$$

$$\eta_i = \frac{\beta_i}{s_i} + 1 \tag{3.31}$$

The elasticity formulas make it more clear that the income elasticities are governed by β_i and the price elasticities are governed by γ_{ij}.

The AIDS model is clearly nonlinear, and while such nonlinearities do not present a problem for today's computing power, it was common to estimate a linear version of the AIDS model. This was achieved by modifying the price index, or approximating the index with a simpler form. One common approach is to use Stone's index where $\log(P) = \sum_i s_i \log p_i$. Then we have

$$s_i = \alpha_i^* + \sum_k \gamma_{ki} \log p_k + \beta_i \log (m/P) \tag{3.32}$$

In fact, if prices are exactly collinear and move proportionally to Stone's index, then the linear approximate model can be used to precisely estimate the parameters of the full AIDS model. In other cases, the relationship between the parameters of the linear approximate model and the AIDS model are not known as the two models are nonnested systems. It is not entirely clear whether the elasticities should be based on the linear approximate model or the full AIDS model. Green and Alston (1990) show that when using the LA/AIDS model, the same formulas for computing elasticities cannot be used. Using theoretically correct formulas for elasticities, they found estimates from AIDS and LA/AIDS models to be similar. Asche and Wessels (1997) later reconciled the AIDS and LA/AIDS models by demonstrating that, where all prices and income are normalized at unity, the two models have the same elasticity formulas.

There has also been debate as to the suitability of the properties of the LA/AIDS model with respect to Stone's price index. Moschini (1995) demonstrated that Stone's index is not invariant to units of measurement in prices, while Eales and Unnevehr (1988) noted that budget shares appear on both sides of the estimated equations when Stone's index is used. Other authors have examined the flexibility of the linear approximate model when constraints from theory are imposed. LaFrance (2004) found the form of the expenditure function in equation 3.24 to be greatly restricted when integrability conditions were imposed. Given the ease of estimating the full AIDS model, concerns with the LA/AIDS model now attract less attention. Nonetheless, the LA/AIDS can be useful as a means of obtaining starting values for the estimation of a full AIDS specification.

As concern over linear approximations to the AIDS decreased, attention has turned to the increasingly popular quadratic almost ideal demand system (QUAIDS). The QUAIDS was derived from the utility function by Banks, Blundell, and Lewbel (1997) and maintains the desirable properties of the AIDS model with increased flexiblity. As its name indicates, quadratic terms are added to the AIDS model to provide this increased flexibility. At the time the QUAIDS was introduced, computing power was already sufficient to allow for nonlinear estimation QUAIDS models of reasonable size. Nonetheless, Matsuda (2006) provides a linear approximation to the QUAIDS and argues that the approximation is particularly useful when working with nonstationary time series data. Applications of the QUAIDS include Moro and Sckokai (2000) who investigated household food consumption and Fisher, Fleissig, and Serletis (2001) who included the QUAIDS in a larger empirical comparison of demand systems.

3.4.2   Empirical Analysis

Our analysis of the almost ideal demand system is based on an annual meat consumption data set. Data is provided on per capita retail quantities of beef, veal, pork, poultry, and fish and seafood in pounds. Consumer price index measurements are available for beef and veal as a composite commodity, pork, poultry, and fish and seafood. Constant dollar per capita retail quantities of the four goods can be computed. Information on the overall consumer price index, U.S. population, and total consumption expenditures are provided. These can be used to derive per capita consumption expenditures on each of the items as well as total per capita consumption expenditure. The data are based on Christensen and Manser (1977).

Because we have time series data, the model that we estimate is a first difference AIDS model. Time series variables are unlikely to be stationary and must first be differenced to be rendered stationary. The model can then be estimated using the differenced variables. After reading in the data, we normalize prices for the meats and then construct differenced quantities and prices. The total expenditure on meat is simply the sum of expenditures on each of the different categories. Mentioned by Barnett and Seck (2008), the LA-AIDS model in first differences has the same dependent variables as an absolute price Rotterdam model.

```
data meat_annual;
set meat_annual;

   bfvlp = (bfvlp / 119.5287457) / 1.0415710;
   porkp = (porkp / 118.1589017) / 1.0278743;
   poultp = (poultp / 124.0272949) / 1.0314877;
   fishp = (fishp / 131.2487286) / 1.0411223;

   lbfvlq = log(bfvlq);
   lporkq = log(porkq);
   lpoultq = log(poultq);
   lfishq = log(fishq);

   lbfvlp = log(bfvlp);
   lporkp = log(porkp);
   lpoultp = log(poultp);
   lfishp = log(fishp);

   dlbfvlq = dif(lbfvlq);
   dlporkq = dif(lporkq);
```

```
   dlpoultq = dif(lpoultq);
   dlfishq = dif(lfishq);


   dlbfvlp = dif(lbfvlp);
   dlporkp = dif(lporkp);
   dlpoultp = dif(lpoultp);
   dlfishp = dif(lfishp);


   xmeat = xbfvl + xpork + xpoult + xfish;


   wbfvl = xbfvl / xmeat;
   wpork = xpork / xmeat;
   wpoult = xpoult / xmeat;
   wfish = xfish / xmeat;


   dwbfvl = dif(wbfvl);
   dwpork = dif(wpork);
   dwpoult = dif(wpoult);
   dwfish = dif(wfish);


   xmeat = (xmeat / 464.7737898)/ 1.0327489;
   dlxmeat = dif(log(xmeat));


run;
```

PROC MEANS can be used to construct the mean shares of the four types of meat. The mean shares are first output to the data set MeanShares. The Stone's price index is then constructed by multiplying the mean shares by their differenced log prices and summing.

```
proc means data = meat_annual noprint;
   variables wbfvl wpork wpoult wfish;
   output out = meanshares mean = wbfvl0 wpork0 wpoult0 wfish0;
run;

data meat_annual;
   if _N_ = 1 then set meanshares(drop = _TYPE_  _FREQ_) ;
set meat_annual;
   dlp = wbfvl0 * dlbfvlp + wpork0 * dlporkp + wpoult0 * dlpoultp
         + wfish0 * dlfishp;
run;
```

The unrestricted linear approximate AIDS model is estimated first. Like the Rotterdam model, one equation is dropped in estimation of the system. In this case, we have chosen to omit the equation for fish. The model thus has 18 free parameters. In the FIT statement, we have instructed SAS to estimate the system using full information maximum likelihood. We can also test the homogeneity, symmetry, and joint restrictions using likelihood ratio tests. The syntax for PROC MODEL remains the same whether estimating an AIDS or Rotterdam model.

```
/* LA/AIDS Model Unrestricted */
proc model data = meat_annual;
   parameters ab bb gbb gbp gbo gbf
              ap bp gpb gpp gpo gpf
              ao bo gob gop goo gof;
   endogenous dwbfvl dwpork dwpoult;
   exogenous dlxmeat dlbfvlp dlporkp dlpoultp dlfishp;

   dwbfvl   = ab + bb * (dlxmeat - dlp) + gbb * dlbfvlp + gbp * dlporkp
```

```
                    + gbo * dlpoultp + gbf * dlfishp;
    dwpork  = ap + bp * (dlxmeat - dlp) + gpb * dlbfvlp + gpp * dlporkp
                    + gpo * dlpoultp + gpf * dlfishp;
    dwpoult = ao + bo * (dlxmeat - dlp) + gob * dlbfvlp + gop * dlporkp
                    + goo * dlpoultp + gof * dlfishp;

    fit dwbfvl dwpork dwpoult / fiml outest = la_aids_unrest;

    test "Homogeneity"
        gbb + gbp + gbo + gbf = 0,
        gpb + gpp + gpo + gpf = 0,
        gob + gop + goo + gof = 0, / lr;

    test "Symmetry"
        gbp = gpb,
        gbo = gob,
        gpo = gop, / lr;

    test "Joint Homogeneity and Symmetry"
        gbb + gbp + gbo + gbf = 0,
        gpb + gpp + gpo + gpf = 0,
        gob + gop + goo + gof = 0,
        gbp = gpb, gbo = gob, gpo = gop, / lr;
run;
```

Figure 3.11 The Unrestricted Linear Approximate AIDS Model

The MODEL Procedure

Model Summary	
Model Variables	8
Endogenous	3
Exogenous	5
Parameters	18
Equations	3
Number of Statements	18

Figure 3.11 *continued*

Nonlinear FIML Parameter Estimates

Parameter	Estimate	Approx Std Err	t Value	Approx Pr > |t|
ab	-0.00229	0.00361	-0.63	0.5300
bb	0.052324	0.0985	0.53	0.5986
gbb	0.077731	0.0265	2.93	0.0060
gbp	0.010424	0.0271	0.38	0.7028
gbo	-0.06242	0.0369	-1.69	0.0998
gbf	-0.03951	0.0379	-1.04	0.3040
ap	-0.00167	0.00227	-0.73	0.4683
bp	-0.00905	0.0917	-0.10	0.9220
gpb	0.008317	0.0225	0.37	0.7145
gpp	0.013281	0.0199	0.67	0.5094
gpo	-0.03133	0.0218	-1.44	0.1591
gpf	0.008097	0.0380	0.21	0.8325
ao	0.003418	0.00140	2.44	0.0200
bo	-0.02573	0.0371	-0.69	0.4927
gob	-0.03466	0.0234	-1.48	0.1483
gop	-0.01774	0.0207	-0.86	0.3972
goo	0.095642	0.0237	4.04	0.0003
gof	-0.04342	0.0259	-1.67	0.1031

Test Results

Test	Type	Statistic	Pr > ChiSq	Label
Homogeneity	L.R.	0.66	0.8821	gbb + gbp + gbo + gbf = 0, gpb + gpp + gpo + gpf = 0, gob + gop + goo + gof = 0
Symmetry	L.R.	3.44	0.3293	gbp = gpb, gbo = gob, gpo = gop
Joint Homogeneity and Symmetry	L.R.	4.60	0.5964	gbb + gbp + gbo + gbf = 0, gpb + gpp + gpo + gpf = 0, gob + gop + goo + gof = 0, gbp = gpb, gbo = gob, gpo = gop

In this case, none of the restrictions implied by theory are rejected but few of the model parameters are significant. As with the Rotterdam model, it's easy to impose the linear restrictions in PROC MODEL. Calculation of the elasticities is omitted for the unrestricted LA/AIDS so we move ahead to the restricted version. The number of free parameters falls from 18 to 12 with six restrictions.

```
/* LA/AIDS Model Restricted*/
proc model data = meat_annual;
    parameters ab bb gbb gbp gbo gbf
               ap bp gpb gpp gpo gpf
               ao bo gob gop goo gof;
    endogenous dwbfvl dwpork dwpoult;
    exogenous dlxmeat dlbfvlp dlporkp dlpoultp dlfishp;
    restrict gbb + gbp + gbo + gbf = 0,
             gpb + gpp + gpo + gpf = 0,
             gob + gop + goo + gof = 0,
             gbp = gpb, gbo = gob, gpo = gop;

    dwbfvl  = ab + gbb * dlbfvlp + gbp * dlporkp + gbo * dlpoultp
              + gbf * dlfishp + bb * (dlxmeat - dlp);
    dwpork  = ap + gpb * dlbfvlp + gpp * dlporkp + gpo * dlpoultp
              + gpf * dlfishp + bp * (dlxmeat - dlp);
    dwpoult = ao + gob * dlbfvlp + gop * dlporkp + goo * dlpoultp
```

```
                + gof * dlfishp + bo * (dlxmeat - dlp);

fit dwbfvl dwpork dwpoult/fiml outest = la_aids_rest;
run;
```

Figure 3.12 The Restricted Linear Approximate AIDS Model

The MODEL Procedure

Model Summary	
Model Variables	8
Endogenous	3
Exogenous	5
Parameters	18
Equations	3
Number of Statements	10

	Nonlinear FIML Parameter Estimates				
Parameter	Estimate	Approx Std Err	t Value	Approx Pr > |t|	Label
ab	-0.0025	0.00138	-1.81	0.0782	
bb	0.091543	0.0500	1.83	0.0753	
gbb	0.0809	0.0251	3.22	0.0027	
gbp	0.010363	0.0129	0.80	0.4282	
gbo	-0.04018	0.0183	-2.19	0.0350	
gbf	-0.05109	0.0167	-3.06	0.0042	
ap	-0.00152	0.000986	-1.54	0.1328	
bp	0.009095	0.0560	0.16	0.8719	
gpb	0.010363	0.0129	0.80	0.4282	
gpp	0.013694	0.0174	0.78	0.4377	
gpo	-0.0215	0.0121	-1.78	0.0840	
gpf	-0.00256	0.0108	-0.24	0.8132	
ao	0.003083	0.000704	4.38	<.0001	
bo	-0.05254	0.0303	-1.73	0.0919	
gob	-0.04018	0.0183	-2.19	0.0350	
gop	-0.0215	0.0121	-1.78	0.0840	
goo	0.086335	0.0188	4.59	<.0001	
gof	-0.02466	0.0108	-2.29	0.0281	
Restrict0	24.75419	42.5354	0.58	0.5679	gbb + gbp + gbo + gbf = 0
Restrict1	8.492706	42.4846	0.20	0.8448	gpb + gpp + gpo + gpf = 0
Restrict2	81.89187	48.9266	1.67	0.0945	gob + gop + goo + gof = 0
Restrict3	-21.4413	38.1585	-0.56	0.5814	gbp = gpb
Restrict4	89.59009	45.4094	1.97	0.0469	gbo = gob
Restrict5	115.4098	53.8786	2.14	0.0301	gpo = gop

Under the restricted LA/AIDS the majority of the coefficient estimates are now significant at the 10% level. The procedure for calculating the elasticities is similar to the Rotterdam model examples and involves the use of PROC IML. The missing parameters of the demand equation for fish are calculated from the estimated parameters. The mean shares for the meats were used in constructing Stone's price index and are used for evaluation of the elasticities. As before, a final print statement gives the elasticities in matrix form.

```
proc iml;
   use la_aids_rest;
   read all var {gbb gbp gbo gbf gpp gpo gpf goo gof bb bp bo};
   close la_aids_rest;

   gff = 0 - gbf - gpf - gof;
   bf = 0 - bb - bp - bo;

   use meanshares;
         read all var {wbfvl0} into wb;
         read all var {wpork0} into wp;
         read all var {wpoult0} into wo;
         read all var {wfish0} into wf;
   close meanshares;

   w = wb//wp//wo//wf;
   b = bb//bp//bo//bf;

   print w;

   gij = (gbb||gbp||gbo||gbf)//
         (gbp||gpp||gpo||gpf)//
         (gbo||gpo||goo||gof)//
         (gbf||gpf||gof||gff);

   print gij;

   nk = ncol(gij);
   mi = -1#I(nk);
   uep = j(nk, nk, 0);
   cep = j(nk, nk, 0);
   exe = j(nk, 1, 0);

   do i=1 to nk;
   do j=1 to nk;
      uep[i,j] = ((gij[i,j]-b[i]#w[j])/w[i]) + mi[i,j];
      cep[i,j] = ((gij[i,j] - b[i] # w[j])/w[i]) + mi[i,j]
                  + w[j] # (1 + (b[i] / w[i]));
      exe[i]   = 1 + b[i] / w[i];
   end;
   end;

   factors = {"Beef/Veal" "Pork" "Poultry" "Fish"};

   print
      uep[label="Uncompensated Price Elasticities of Demand"
          rowname=factors colname=factors format=d7.3],
      cep[label="Compensated Price Elasticities of Demand"
          rowname=factors colname=factors format=d7.3],
      exe[label="Expenditure Elasticities" rowname=factors
          format=d7.3];
quit;
```

Figure 3.13 Elasticity Matrices

Uncompensated Price Elasticities of Demand

	Beef/Veal	Pork	Poultry	Fish
Beef/Veal	-0.918	-0.0253	-0.120	-0.132
Pork	0.0252	-0.953	-0.0952	-0.0149
Poultry	-0.0898	-0.0503	-0.452	-0.106
Fish	-0.246	0.0782	-0.140	-0.279

Compensated Price Elasticities of Demand

	Beef/Veal	Pork	Poultry	Fish
Beef/Veal	-0.360	0.264	0.0882	0.00700
Pork	0.510	-0.701	0.0855	0.106
Poultry	0.236	0.119	-0.330	-0.0252
Fish	0.0281	0.220	-0.0378	-0.211

Expenditure Elasticities

Beef/Veal	1.196
Pork	1.038
Poultry	0.698
Fish	0.587

Interpretation of the elasticities is left to the reader. Our next task is to estimate the full AIDS model and, in any event, we will compare the full model estimates with those of the linear approximate. The AIDS model includes the price index of equation 3.28 and additional restrictions. These statements are added in PROC MODEL and the equation for fish is again omitted. The model has 22 total parameters, but only 15 free parameters after accounting for the seven restrictions. The parameter estimates are suppressed and we move immediately to the elasticity estimates of Figure 3.14.

```
/*AIDS Model Restricted*/
proc model data = meat_annual;
    parameters cb ab bb gbb gbp gbo gbf
               cp ap bp gpb gpp gpo gpf
               co ao bo gob gop goo gof
               cf;
    endogenous dwbfvl dwpork dwpoult;
    exogenous dlxmeat dlbfvlp dlporkp dlpoultp dlfishp;
    restrict gbb + gbp + gbo + gbf = 0,
             gpb + gpp + gpo + gpf = 0,
             gob + gop + goo + gof = 0,
             gbp = gpb, gbo = gob, gpo = gop,
             cb + cp + co + cf = 1;

    dlpindex = cb * dlbfvlp + cp * dlporkp + co * dlpoultp + cf * dlfishp
             + 0.5 * (gbb * dif(lbfvlp * lbfvlp)
             + 2* gbp * dif(lbfvlp * lporkp)
             + 2 * gbo * dif(lbfvlp * lpoultp)
             + 2 * gbf * dif(lbfvlp * lfishp)
             + gpp * dif(lporkp * lporkp)
             + 2 * gpo * dif(lporkp * lpoultp)
             + 2 * gpf * dif(lporkp * lfishp)
             + goo * dif(lpoultp * lpoultp)
             + 2 * gof * dif(lpoultp * lfishp)
```

```
                  - (gbf + gpf + gof) * dif(lfishp * lfishp));

     dwbfvl   = ab + bb * (dlxmeat - dlpindex) + gbb * dlbfvlp
                  + gbp * dlporkp + gbo * dlpoultp + gbf * dlfishp;
     dwpork   = ap + bp * (dlxmeat - dlpindex) + gpb * dlbfvlp
                  + gpp * dlporkp + gpo * dlpoultp + gpf * dlfishp;
     dwpoult = ao + bo * (dlxmeat - dlpindex) + gob * dlbfvlp
                  + gop * dlporkp + goo * dlpoultp + gof * dlfishp;

     fit dwbfvl dwpork dwpoult / fiml outest = aids_rest;
run;

proc iml;
   use aids_rest;
   read all var {gbb gbp gbo gbf gpp gpo gpf goo gof bb bp bo cb cp co cf};
   close aids_rest;

   gff = 0 - gbf - gpf - gof;
   bf = 0 - bb - bp - bo;

   use meanshares;
        read all var {wbfvl0} into wb;
        read all var {wpork0} into wp;
        read all var {wpoult0} into wo;
        read all var {wfish0} into wf;
   close meanshares;

   w = wb//wp//wo//wf;
   b = bb//bp//bo//bf;
   c = cb//cp//co//cf;

   print w;

   gij = (gbb||gbp||gbo||gbf)//
         (gbp||gpp||gpo||gpf)//
         (gbo||gpo||goo||gof)//
         (gbf||gpf||gof||gff);

   print gij;

   nk = ncol(gij);
   mi = -1#I(nk);
   uep = j(nk, nk, 0);
   cep = j(nk, nk, 0);
   exe = j(nk, 1, 0);

   do i=1 to nk;
   do j=1 to nk;
      uep[i,j] = ((gij[i,j]-b[i]#c[j])/w[i])+ mi[i,j];
      cep[i,j] = ((gij[i,j]-b[i]#c[j])/w[i])+ mi[i,j] +w[i]#(1+(b[i]/w[i]));
      exe[i] = 1 + b[i] / w[i];
   end;
   end;

   factors = {"Beef/Veal" "Pork" "Poultry" "Fish"};
```

```
    print
      uep[label = "Uncompensated Price Elasticities of Demand"
         rowname = factors colname = factors format = d7.3],
      cep[label = "Compensated Price Elasticities of Demand"
         rowname = factors colname = factors format = d7.3],
      exe[label = "Expenditure Elasticities" rowname = factors
         format = d7.3];
  quit;
```

Figure 3.14 Elasticity Matrices

Uncompensated Price Elasticities of Demand

	Beef/Veal	Pork	Poultry	Fish
Beef/Veal	-0.822	0.0228	-0.117	-0.110
Pork	0.0273	-0.951	-0.0878	0.00389
Poultry	-0.184	-0.0975	-0.400	-0.335
Fish	-0.495	-0.0482	-0.245	-0.0652

Compensated Price Elasticities of Demand

	Beef/Veal	Pork	Poultry	Fish
Beef/Veal	-0.343	0.502	0.362	0.370
Pork	0.271	-0.707	0.156	0.248
Poultry	-0.0070	0.0797	-0.223	-0.158
Fish	-0.395	0.0510	-0.146	0.0340

Expenditure Elasticities

Beef/Veal	1.026
Pork	1.007
Poultry	1.018
Fish	0.853

The income elasticities for beef, pork, and poultry are all very close to one so a one percent increase in the consumer's income leads to a one percent increase in the quantity demanded of the respective meat. Given that the data used in the analysis are aggregate time series data, these income elasticities seem reasonable. Beef is a substitute for pork, but a complement for poultry and fish. One concern is that the compensated own-price elasticity for fish is positive, though close to zero. It is important to remember that the elasticities are evaluated at a point in the sample and would vary if we were to evaluate them at different shares.

3.5   Demand for Differentiated Products

In the previous sections of this chapter, we have seen examples of demand estimation for homogeneous products or aggregates. When we estimate demand functions for homogeneous goods, a product is usually treated as a single fully integrated entity. Our attention now turns to the estimation of demand for differentiated products. Within the differentiated products framework, the most commonly used approach is often termed the "characteristics space" approach, where a product can be decomposed into several characteristics. In the following sections, we will introduce various estimation methods within the "characteristics space" framework.

Most studies in the characteristics space framework assume that each consumer purchases only one unit of one product on each shopping occasion. For example, a consumer purchases one cell phone every two years. A household with several family members buys one box of cereal per week. A businessman purchases a new suit every six months.

Discrete choice models are appropriate to model these shopping events and types of purchasing behavior. As with our descriptions of demand for homogenous goods, we start with important properties of the theoretical model. Then we define choice probabilities and derive the demand model that is applied in practice.

3.5.1 Discrete Choice

Discrete choice models describe decision makers' choices among alternatives in shopping events. The decision makers could be individual consumers, households, firms, or any other decision making units. The alternatives could be competing products, courses of action, or any other options. The choice set, which is the set of alternatives from which the consumer can select, must satisfy the following three properties.

1. **Mutually exclusive**: the consumer only purchases one unit of one product from the choice set

2. **Exhaustive**: all alternatives are included in the choice set

3. **Finite**: The number of alternatives must be finite

In some cases a consumer may purchase multiple products. Suppose there are three types of mobile phones in the choice set: Android, Apple, and BlackBerry. Some consumers may purchase more than one type of phone in a shopping trip. Instead of defining the choice set to have three products, we can define the alternatives to be Android, Apple, BlackBerry, Android and Apple, Android and BlackBerry, Apple and BlackBerry, and all three products. By re-defining the choice set, the choice set satisfies all three criteria. Theoretically speaking, this method can then be applied to any number of products. However, as the number of products increases, the number of alternatives increases, and so do the practical difficulties of estimating such a model. In the case where a consumer purchases no products, we can define no purchase as an alternative in the choice set. This allows us to answer the following question, what factors determine a consumers' decision between making no purchases and making a purchase?

Discrete choice models are derived under the assumption of utility maximization. We start with the indirect utility function of consumer n, which gives the utility the consumer obtains from product j:

$$U_{nj} = V_{nj} + \epsilon_{nj} \quad j = 1, \ldots, J, n = 1, \ldots, N \tag{3.33}$$

where the utility, U_{nj}, is observed by the decision maker. U_{nj} is decomposed into two parts: V_{nj} and ϵ_{nj}. V_{nj} is revealed to the researcher. ϵ_{nj} is observed to the decision maker, but not the researcher. We assume ϵ_{nj} is a random variable. The probability that consumer n chooses alternative i is then given by

$$\begin{aligned} P_{ni} &= \text{Prob}\left(U_{ni} > U_{nj}, \forall j \neq i\right) \\ &= \text{Prob}\left(\epsilon_{nj} - \epsilon_{ni} > V_{ni} - V_{nj}, \forall j \neq i\right) \\ &= \int I\left(\epsilon_{nj} - \epsilon_{ni} > V_{ni} - V_{nj}, \forall j \neq i\right) f(\epsilon_n) d\epsilon_n, \end{aligned} \tag{3.34}$$

where $f(\cdot)$ is the joint density of the unobserved portion of utility, $\epsilon_{n\cdot}$. Different discrete choice models are obtained by varying the specification for $f(\cdot)$. The total market demand for alternative i can be written as

$$Q_i = \sum_{n=1}^{N} P_{ni}$$

A key concept in econometric analysis is identification: whether we have enough information in the data to estimate the parameters of interest. When we specify a discrete choice model, we need to keep in mind that only differences in utility matter. That is to say, the absolute value of utility is meaningless. The ranking of utilities obtained from different options will not be changed if a constant is added to utilities from these alternatives. Below are three different types of variables that may be present in the data. For each case, problems of identification are considered.

3.5.1.1   Case I: Product Specific Constant Term

In Case I, we assume a very simple model where there are only two products in the choice set. The representative utility has a simple form

$$U_{u1} = C_1 + \epsilon_{n1}$$
$$U_{u2} = C_2 + \epsilon_{n2}$$

where C_1 and C_2 are the product specific constants for the two options. The constant terms do not vary across consumers. We can write the difference between U_{n1} and U_{n2} in the following form:

$$U_{u1} - U_{u2} = C_1 - C_2 + \epsilon_{n1} - \epsilon_{n2}$$

The average of $\epsilon_{n1} - \epsilon_{n2}$ is zero. The average difference in two utility levels identifies the difference between two constant terms, C_1 and C_2. Since the absolute value of utility does not matter, we cannot separately identify these two constant terms. If we normalize $C_1 = 0$, the demand model then becomes

$$U_{u1} = \epsilon_{n1}$$
$$U_{u2} = C_2 + \epsilon_{n2}$$

C_2 should be interpreted as the impact of all factors of alternative 2 that do not vary across decision makers on utility relative to that of all factors of alternative 1 that do not vary across decision makers. In general, if there are J alternatives in the choice set, we can only identify $J - 1$ product specific constants.

3.5.1.2   Case II: Demographic Variables

The demographic variables of decision makers can have an important impact on choices. For example, consumers with high income are more likely to purchase organic food than those with low income. Similar to Case I, we assume there are only two alternatives in the choice set. The utilities obtained from the two options for decision maker n are

$$U_{u1} = x_n \beta_1 + \epsilon_{n1}$$
$$U_{u2} = x_n \beta_2 + \epsilon_{n2}$$

where x_n captures all the demographic variables, such as income, education level, gender, and so on. These demographic variables do not vary across alternatives. However, their impacts can differ across alternatives. The difference in utility is

$$U_{u1} - U_{u2} = x_n(\beta_1 - \beta_2) + \epsilon_{n1} - \epsilon_{n2}$$

Since only the differences in utility matter, only the difference between β_1 and β_2 can be identified. However, β_1 and β_2 cannot be separately identified. Usually we normalize $\beta_1 = 0$. The interpretation of β_2 is the impact of x_n on utility of alternative 2 relative to the impact of x_n on utility of alternative 1.

If the demographic variables are believed to have the same impacts on utilities of the two alternatives, the model is written as

$$U_{u1} = x_n \beta + \epsilon_{n1}$$
$$U_{u2} = x_n \beta + \epsilon_{n2}$$

and the difference in utility is

$$U_{u1} - U_{u2} = \epsilon_{n1} - \epsilon_{n2}$$

In this case, no parameter can be identified. Therefore, only the demographic variables that are assumed to have different impacts on utilities of alternatives can enter the discrete choice model.

3.5.1.3   Case III: Decision Maker and Product Specific Variables

Some variables vary across both alternatives and decision makers. For example, an individual may choose to go to a park near his home. The distance variable then varies across both individuals and alternatives.

Assuming there are two alternatives in the choice set, utility is written as

$$U_{u1} = x_{n1} \beta_1 + \epsilon_{n1}$$
$$U_{u2} = x_{n2} \beta_2 + \epsilon_{n2}$$

where $x_n.$ varies across choices. The difference in utility is

$$U_{u1} - U_{u2} = x_{n1} \beta_1 - x_{n2} \beta_2 + \epsilon_{n1} - \epsilon_{n2}$$

In this case, both β_1 and β_2 can be separately identified. β_1 can be interpreted as the impact of x_n on utility of alternative 1 and β_2 is interpreted as the impact of x_n on utility of alternative 2.

3.5.2   Logit Models

Different specifications of discrete choice models are generated from different distributions of the error term. These differences can be important and are discussed in more detail in Greene (2018). If we assume the error term, ϵ_{nj} is independently and identically distributed and follows a type-I extreme value distribution (also called the Gumbel distribution), the discrete choice model is a multinomial logit model. The density of the distribution is

$$f(\epsilon_{nj}) = e^{-\epsilon_{nj}} e^{-e^{-\epsilon_{nj}}}, \tag{3.35}$$

and its cumulative distribution function is

$$F(\epsilon_{nj}) = e^{-e^{-\epsilon_{nj}}} \tag{3.36}$$

Using the Gumbel form for the distribution of the error terms, the probability in equation 3.34 can then be calculated. The probability for consumer n to choose alternative i is

$$
\begin{aligned}
P_{ni} &= \int_{-\infty}^{+\infty} I\left(\epsilon_{nj} - \epsilon_{ni} > V_{ni} - V_{nj}, \forall j \neq i\right) f(\epsilon_n) d\epsilon_n \\
&= \int_{-\infty}^{+\infty} I\left(\epsilon_{nj} > V_{ni} - V_{nj} + \epsilon_{ni}, \forall j \neq i\right) f(\epsilon_n) d\epsilon_n \\
&= \int_{-\infty}^{+\infty} \prod_{j \neq i} \int_{-\infty}^{+\infty} I\left(\epsilon_{nj} > V_{ni} - V_{nj} + \epsilon_{ni}\right) f(\epsilon_{nj}) d\epsilon_{nj} f(\epsilon_{ni}) d\epsilon_{ni} \\
&= \int_{-\infty}^{+\infty} \prod_{j \neq i} F\left(V_{ni} - V_{nj} + \epsilon_{ni}\right) f(\epsilon_{ni}) d\epsilon_{ni} \\
&= \int_{-\infty}^{+\infty} \prod_{j \neq i} e^{-e^{-\left(V_{ni} - V_{nj} + \epsilon_{ni}\right)}} e^{-\epsilon_{ni}} d\epsilon_{ni}
\end{aligned}
\tag{3.37}
$$

With some algebraic manipulation, the logit probability becomes

$$P_{ni} = \frac{e^{V_{ni}}}{\sum_j e^{V_{nj}}} \tag{3.38}$$

You may notice that we have not specified a functional form for representative utility, V_{nj}. Representative utility is typically given a linear specification, that is, $V_{nj} = x'_{nj}\beta$, where x_{nj} is a vector of characteristics variables of alternative j. The multinomial logit formula has desirable properties. First, it guarantees the value of choice probability, P_{ni} is between 0 and 1. Second, the sum of choice probabilities for all alternatives, $\sum^J P_{j=1} P_{nj}$, is equal to 1. This is consistent with the exhaustiveness property of discrete choice models.

3.5.2.1 Elasticities

One important purpose of demand estimation is to calculate price elasticities. As explained in chapter 2, the own price elasticity measures the percentage change in quantity demanded for a product when its own price changes by one percent. The cross price elasticity measures the responsiveness of the quantity demanded for a good to a change in the price of another good, all else being equal. Assume that the representative utility for individual n obtaining from product i is $V_{ni} = \alpha p_{ni} + x'_{ni}\beta$, where α is the coefficient for the price variable, and β is a vector of coefficients for all the product characteristics other than price, x_{ni}. From the previous section, we know the quantity demanded of product i for consumer n can be written as

$$q_{ni} = 1 * P_{ni} = \frac{e^{V_{ni}}}{\sum_j e^{V_{nj}}} = \frac{e^{\alpha p_{ni} + x'_{ni}\beta}}{\sum_j e^{\alpha p_{nj} + x'_{nj}\beta}}$$

where P_{ni} is the probability for consumer n to choose product i. The own price elasticity of product i for consumer n can then be calculated as

$$e_{n,ii} = \frac{p_i \partial q_{ni}}{q_{ni} \partial p_i} = \alpha p_i (1 - P_{ni}) \tag{3.39}$$

Since the price coefficient α is negative, the own price elasticity is negative. This is consistent with the law of demand. The cross price elasticity of product i can be calculated as

$$e_{n,ij} = \frac{p_j \partial q_{ni}}{q_{ni} \partial p_j} = -\alpha p_j P_{nj} \tag{3.40}$$

Since α is negative, cross price elasticity is positive. It is interesting to point out that i does not enter this formula; for a one percent decrease in the probability of product j, the probabilities of all other alternatives increase by one percent. This property is by construction of the logit model.

3.5.2.2 Consumer Welfare

Researchers are often interested in measuring how consumer welfare responds to a change in policies. For example, we expect consumer welfare to increase when a more energy efficient vehicle enters the car market. When the market becomes more competitive, car producers may decrease prices to attract more customers. Or car producers may invest more resources into research and development (R&D) and try to adapt to new technology and provide better quality. Another example is mergers and acquisitions. The merger of two cable companies may bring synergy and cut costs. However, the merger could significantly reduce market competition if both firms are big players in the market and have high market shares. Economists and policy makers are often interested in predicting how a merger will affect consumer welfare.

Consumer welfare is the area below the demand curve and above the market price. After we estimate expected demand using the logit model, we can calculate the consumer welfare. The consumer chooses the product that yields the highest utility. Consumer welfare is $CS_n = (1/\alpha_n)\max_i(U_{ni})$, where α_n is the marginal utility of income of consumer n. The division of α allows us to convert welfare into dollars. The monetary term that shows up in the utility is $\alpha_n(I_n - p_i)$, where I_n is the income of consumer n and drops out of the specification because it is a demographic variable that does not vary across products.

Since we observe the representative utility, V_{ni} but not U_{ni}, we can calculate the expected consumer welfare in the following way:

$$E(CS_n) = \frac{1}{\alpha_n} E\left[\max_i(V_{ni} + \epsilon_{ni})\right] \tag{3.41}$$

where the expectation is with respect to the error term ϵ_{ni}. When ϵ_{ni} is i.i.d. type-I extreme value distributed and α_n does not vary with respect to income, Small and Rosen (1981) show that the expected consumer welfare can be written as

$$E(CS_n) = \frac{1}{\alpha_n} ln\left(\sum_i e^{V_{ni}}\right) + C \tag{3.42}$$

where C is an unknown constant. Therefore, we don't know the exact value of $E(CS_n)$. Because utility and welfare are ordinal measures, we are not interested in knowing their absolute values. We are normally interested in the change of welfare due to a change in policy or the market structure. The change in consumer welfare can be calculated as

$$E(CS_n^1) - E(CS_n^0) = \frac{1}{\alpha_n} \left[ln\left(\sum_j^{J^1} e^{V_{nj}^1}\right) - ln\left(\sum_j^{J^0} e^{V_{nj}^0}\right) \right] \tag{3.43}$$

where 0 stands for the old policy environment and 1 stands for the new policy environment. It is then possible to conduct counterfactual analysis.

3.5.3   Empirical Analysis

Using the discrete choice models developed in the previous section, we can model individual shopping choices. The purpose of the following empirical applications is to use simple model and data analysis commands in SAS to estimate discrete choice models. We do not cover data cleaning, assumption verification, and other research processes relevant to the research enterprise. The applied researcher would, however, be required to complete these steps on their own.

3.5.3.1   An Example with Individual Data

In this example, an individual has three choices of where to shop: a department store, a luxury department store, and an outlet mall. Individuals' choices may be influenced by their income status and age. In reality, there are other factors that affect individuals' decisions, but for simplicity, we only consider these two predictors: age and income.

We start with model specification and identification. The utility of individual i choosing each option can be written as

$$\begin{aligned}
U_{i,\text{dept}} &= C_{\text{dept}} + \alpha_{\text{dept}} age_i + \beta_{dept}^2 (inc_i = 2) + \beta_{\text{dept}}^3 (inc_i = 3) + \epsilon_{i,\text{dept}} \\
U_{i,\text{lux}} &= C_{\text{lux}} + \alpha_{\text{lux}} age_i + \beta_{\text{lux}}^2 (inc_i = 2) + \beta_{\text{lux}}^3 (inc_i = 3) + \epsilon_{i,\text{lux}} \\
U_{i,\text{out}} &= C_{\text{out}} + \alpha_{\text{out}} age_i + \beta_{\text{out}}^2 (inc_i = 2) + \beta_{\text{out}}^3 (inc_i = 3) + \epsilon_{i,\text{out}}
\end{aligned} \tag{3.44}$$

where $U_{i,\text{dept}}$ is the utility of individual i choosing a department store as a shopping location. Note that the demographic variables, age and income status, do not vary across different choices. age_i is the age of individual i. $\epsilon_{i,\text{dept}}$ is the error term of individual i choosing a department store and is type I extreme value distributed. inc_i is a dummy variable with three different values, 1, 2, and 3, with 1 being the lowest and 3 being the highest income status. Because this dummy variable has three values, it can be defined with two variables. Here we choose $inc_i = 1$ as our reference, and write it as a row vector $[0\,0]$. $inc_i = 2$ and $inc_i = 3$ can be written as $[1\,0]$ and $[0\,1]$, respectively.

Before we run the regression, it is important to understand which parameters can actually be identified in our model. Since the scale of utility does not matter, we have to choose one option to be our base when we use the logistic regression. In this example the luxury department store is chosen as the reference. The system of equations can be written as

$$\begin{aligned}
U_{i,\text{dept}}^* &= C_{\text{dept}}^* + \alpha_{\text{dept}}^* age_i + \beta_{\text{dept}}^{*2} (inc_i = 2) + \beta_{\text{dept}}^{*3} (inc_i = 3) + \epsilon_{i,\text{dept}}^* \\
U_{i,\text{out}}^* &= C_{\text{out}}^* + \alpha_{\text{out}}^* age_i + \beta_{\text{out}}^{*2} (inc_i = 2) + \beta_{\text{out}}^{*3} (inc_i = 3) + \epsilon_{i,\text{out}}^*
\end{aligned} \tag{3.45}$$

where

$$U^*_{i,\text{dept}} = U_{i,\text{dept}} - U_{i,\text{lux}}$$

$$U^*_{i,\text{out}} = U_{i,\text{out}} - U_{i,\text{lux}}$$

$$C^*_{\text{dept}} = C_{\text{dept}} - C_{\text{lux}}$$

$$C^*_{\text{out}} = C_{\text{out}} - C_{\text{lux}}$$

$$\alpha^*_{\text{dept}} = \alpha_{\text{dept}} - \alpha_{\text{lux}}$$

$$\alpha^*_{\text{out}} = \alpha_{\text{out}} - \alpha_{\text{lux}}$$

$$\beta^{*2}_{\text{dept}} = \beta^2_{\text{dept}} - \beta^2_{\text{lux}}$$

$$\beta^{*2}_{\text{out}} = \beta^2_{\text{out}} - \beta^2_{\text{lux}}$$

$$\beta^{*3}_{\text{dept}} = \beta^3_{\text{dept}} - \beta^3_{\text{lux}}$$

$$\beta^{*3}_{\text{out}} = \beta^3_{\text{out}} - \beta^3_{\text{lux}}$$

$$\epsilon^*_{i,\text{dept}} = \epsilon_{i,\text{dept}} - \epsilon_{i,\text{lux}}$$

$$\epsilon^*_{i,\text{out}} = \epsilon_{i,\text{out}} - \epsilon_{i,\text{lux}}$$

Since the demographic variables do not vary across choices, we can only identify the relative impact of the change in a predictor on the choice of department store relative to the luxury department store (or outlet store to luxury department store). Therefore, the coefficients that can be estimated are C^*_{dept}, C^*_{out}, α^*_{dept}, α^*_{out}, β^{*2}_{dept}, β^{*2}_{out}, β^{*3}_{dept}, and β^{*3}_{out}. By applying the logit fomula, the final estimated equations are

$$\ln\left(\frac{P(\text{shop} = \text{department store})}{P(\text{shop} = \text{luxury store})}\right) = C^*_{\text{dept}} + \alpha^*_{\text{dept}} age_i + \beta^{*2}_{\text{dept}}(inc_i = 2) + \beta^{*3}_{\text{dept}}(inc_i = 3) + \epsilon^*_{i,\text{dept}}$$

$$\ln\left(\frac{P(\text{shop} = \text{outlet store})}{P(\text{shop} = \text{luxury store})}\right) = C^*_{\text{out}} + \alpha^*_{\text{out}} age_i + \beta^{*2}_{\text{out}}(inc_i = 2) + \beta^{*3}_{\text{out}}(inc_i = 3) + \epsilon^*_{i,\text{out}}$$

(3.46)

The data are read into SAS from a comma-separated text file using the IMPORT procedure. The output data set is named shopping and the CONTENTS procedure is used to view information on the variables.

```
proc import datafile = "shopping.csv" out = shopping
dbms = csv replace;
getnames = yes;
run;

proc contents data = shopping;
run;
```

Figure 3.15 Contents

The CONTENTS Procedure

Data Set Name	WORK.SHOPPING	Observations	200
Member Type	DATA	Variables	4
Engine	V9	Indexes	0
Created	03/01/2018 12:59:22	Observation Length	32
Last Modified	03/01/2018 12:59:22	Deleted Observations	0
Protection		Compressed	NO
Data Set Type		Sorted	NO
Label			
Data Representation	WINDOWS_32		
Encoding	wlatin1 Western (Windows)		

Alphabetic List of Variables and Attributes

#	Variable	Type	Len	Format	Informat
4	age	Num	8	BEST12.	BEST32.
1	id	Num	8	BEST12.	BEST32.
2	income	Num	8	BEST12.	BEST32.
3	store	Num	8	BEST12.	BEST32.

The data set contains 4 variables on 200 individuals. The choice variable is $store$, store type. This is a categorical variable. If an individual chooses a department store to shop, the value of $store = 1$. Choice of a luxury store is denoted by $store = 2$ and choice of an outlet is denoted by $store = 3$. $income$ is also a categorical variable, the value of which can be 1, 2, or 3, with 1 being the lowest and 3 the highest. age is the age of each individual and is the single continuous variable. We start with PROC FREQ to obtain summary statistics on the variables of interest. The FREQ procedure is useful for obtaining crosstabulation tables that can be used to summarize association between variables. The TABLES statement specifies a crosstabulation of store with income.

```
proc freq data = shopping;
    tables store * income / chisq norow nocol nofreq;
run;
```

Figure 3.16 Frequency of Shopping Choices

The FREQ Procedure

Percent	Table of store by income			
		income		
store	1	2	3	Total
1	8.00	10.00	4.50	22.50
2	9.50	22.00	21.00	52.50
3	6.00	15.50	3.50	25.00
Total	47	95	58	200
	23.50	47.50	29.00	100.00

Figure 3.16 shows that 29 percent of the sample is in the highest income category while 25.5 percent of the sample is in the lowest income category. The majority of the sample chooses to shop in the luxury department store. For all three income groups, the most popular store type is the luxury store. Curiously, middle income individuals constitute the greatest share of consumers shopping at outlets. The same information can be displayed graphically using PROC GCHART. The vbar3d statement asks for a 3d bar chart for each store showing the shopping choices of different

income groups.

```
proc format;
   value incomeform 1='1-Low Income'
                    2='2-Medium Income'
                    3='3-High Income';

   value storeform 1='1-Department Store'
                   2='2-Luxury Store'
                   3='3-Outlet Store';
run;

proc sgplot data = shopping;
   format income incomeform.;
   format store storeform.;
   styleattrs datacolors=('#7f9896' '#abc3d4' '#d7e5f3') datacontrastcolors=(black) ;
   vbar income /group=store seglabel seglabelattrs=(size=12);
   label store = 'Choice of Store:';
   xaxis display=(nolabel);
run;
```

Figure 3.17 Income Grouped by Shopping Choice

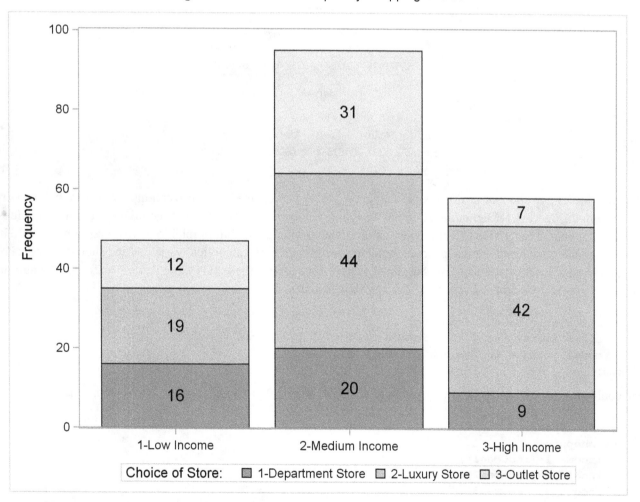

We have not said anything about the relationship between age and shopping choice. Through the use of PROC MEANS, and a BY statement, we can easily obtain summary statistics by store type. The data are first sorted according to store type and then the relevant call to the MEANS procedure is given.

```
proc sort data = shopping;
   by store;
run;

proc means data = shopping;
   var age;
   by store;
run;
```

Figure 3.18 Summary Statistics by Store

The MEANS Procedure

store=1

		Analysis Variable : age		
N	Mean	Std Dev	Minimum	Maximum
45	51.3333333	9.3977754	31.0000000	67.0000000

store=2

		Analysis Variable : age		
N	Mean	Std Dev	Minimum	Maximum
105	56.2571429	7.9433433	33.0000000	67.0000000

store=3

		Analysis Variable : age		
N	Mean	Std Dev	Minimum	Maximum
50	46.7600000	9.3187544	31.0000000	67.0000000

The maximum age shopper at every store category is 67 years of age, but the mean age does vary by category. According to Figure 3.18, the outlet store has the youngest average shopper while the luxury store has the oldest average shopper. The LOGISTIC procedure can be used to estimate a multinomial logistic regression model. The choice variable $store$ and the independent variable $income$ are both categorical variables and should be indicated as such in the CLASS statement. The baseline category for $store$ is the luxury store ($store = 2$). For the dummy variable $income$, we choose $income = 1$ as our baseline case.

```
proc logistic data = shopping;
   class store (ref = "2") income (ref = "1") / param = ref;
   model store = income age / link = glogit;
run;
```

We could also manually create dummy variables for the categorical predictors using a DATA step.

```
data shopping;
set shopping;
   income_1=(income=1);
   income_2=(income=2);
   income_3=(income=3);
run;
```

Since income is now indicated by dummy variables, instead of a single categorical variable, the corresponding CLASS statement can be dropped. However, the MODEL statement has to be adjusted to include the additional predictors. In any event, both of these approaches will produce the same results.

```
proc logistic data = shopping;
   class store (ref = "2") / param = ref;
   model store = income_2 income_3 age / link = glogit;
run;
```

In the output shown in Figure 3.19, we can see that

1. a one unit increase in *age* is associated with a 0.058 decrease in the relative log odds of choosing a department store versus a luxury store.

2. a one unit increase in *age* is associated with a 0.1136 decrease in the relative log odds of choosing an outlet store versus a luxury store.

3. moving from the lowest income group ($income = 1$) to the highest income group ($income = 3$) leads to a decrease in relative log odds of shopping in a department store vs. a luxury store.

Figure 3.19 Logit Model Estimates

The LOGISTIC Procedure

Model Information	
Data Set	WORK.SHOPPING
Response Variable	store
Number of Response Levels	3
Model	generalized logit
Optimization Technique	Newton-Raphson

Analysis of Maximum Likelihood Estimates							
Parameter	store	DF	Estimate	Standard Error	Wald Chi-Square	Pr > ChiSq
Intercept	1	1	2.8522	1.1664	5.9790	0.0145
Intercept	3	1	5.2182	1.1635	20.1128	<.0001
income	2 1	1	-0.5333	0.4437	1.4444	0.2294
income	2 3	1	0.2914	0.4764	0.3742	0.5407
income	3 1	1	-1.1628	0.5142	5.1137	0.0237
income	3 3	1	-0.9827	0.5956	2.7224	0.0989
age	1	1	-0.0579	0.0214	7.3200	0.0068
age	3	1	-0.1136	0.0222	26.1392	<.0001

Odds Ratio Estimates				
Effect	store	Point Estimate	95% Wald Confidence Limits	
income 2 vs 1	1	0.587	0.246	1.400
income 2 vs 1	3	1.338	0.526	3.404
income 3 vs 1	1	0.313	0.114	0.856
income 3 vs 1	3	0.374	0.116	1.203
age	1	0.944	0.905	0.984
age	3	0.893	0.855	0.932

In the logit model, we assume that consumers' tastes for product characteristics, as presented by the coefficients β, do not vary across consumers. A more general model allows β to vary across consumers, that is, $\beta_n \neq \beta_{n'}$ when $n \neq n'$.

The ratio between the probability of choosing product i and j can be written as

$$\frac{P_{ni}}{P_{nj}} = e^{V_{ni} - V_{nj}}$$

This ratio only depends on the characteristics of product j and i, but does not depend on characteristics of any other products. This property called the Independence of Irrelevant Alternatives (IIA) property.

While the IIA property is realistic in some choice situations, this type of substitution patterns is restrictive. Consider the case where a new product enters the market. If the characteristics of this new product are very similar to those of product j but not so close to product i, the relative odd of choosing product i and j should be affected.

The restriction of the IIA property is also reflected by the cross price elasticity that we derived in the previous section. Recall the cross price elasticity of product i derived from the logit model does not depend on the characteristics of product i. This implies that when there is a change in the price of product j, the demand for all other products will change by the same percentage. This is not realistic in many cases because the demand for close substitutes of product j should be affected more than those that are not close substitutes of product j.

3.5.3.2   An Example with Aggregate Level Data

In the previous section, we showed how consumer demand can be estimated when we observe choices made by each individual. It is sometimes difficult for researchers to collect micro level data in reality. Aggregate level data, however, is more widely available. We only need to observe choices made by consumers at the aggregate level, that is, the market share of products. This section contains a brief introduction to the estimation of discrete choice models when only aggregate level data is available. We first discuss model specification and identification and then present an example to show how estimation can be realized in SAS.

Suppose there are J products in the market and each individual consumer buys at most one unit of product. The utility function of consumer i for product j is specified as

$$
\begin{aligned}
U_{ij} &= X_j \beta - \alpha p_j + \eta_j + \epsilon_{ij} \\
&= \delta_j + \epsilon_{ij}
\end{aligned}
\tag{3.47}
$$

where the mean utility level of product j can be written as

$$\delta_j = X_j \beta - \alpha p_j + \eta_j \tag{3.48}$$

X_j is a vector of characteristics of product j, where $j = 0, 1, 2..., J$. p_j is the price of product j and α is the regression coefficient of price. β is a vector of regression coefficients for X_j. For example, X_j can be fuel efficiency, number of seats, etc, for a car. Unobserved time-invariant product characteristics are denoted by η_j. η_j can be thought of as the mean of the consumers' valuation of the unobserved product characteristics of product j. ϵ_{ij} is i.i.d. across products and consumers and follows the extreme value distribution.

Since consumer i chooses the product that yields the highest utility, the probability for consumer i to choose product j can be written as

$$
\begin{aligned}
s_{ij} &= \text{Prob}\left(U_{ij} > U_{il}, l = 0, 1, ..., j - 1, j + 1, ..., J\right) \\
&= \frac{e^{\delta_{ij}}}{e^{\delta_0} + \sum_{k=1}^{J} e^{\delta_k}}
\end{aligned}
\tag{3.49}
$$

where $\delta_0 = 0$ for the outside option, product 0. The outside option is a failure to purchase any of the available alternatives, thus spending the entire income of the consumer on goods outside of the analysis. Integrating over individual consumers, a formula for the market share of each product can be obtained.

$$
\begin{aligned}
s_j &= \frac{\sum_i s_{ij}}{\sum_k \sum_i s_{ik}} \\
&= N * \frac{e^{\delta_{ij}}}{1 + \sum_{k=1}^{J} e^{\delta_k}} \\
&= \frac{e^{\delta_j}}{1 + \sum_{k=1}^{J} e^{\delta_k}}
\end{aligned}
\tag{3.50}
$$

Next we convert the demand functions to obtain estimates of the mean utility level, δ_j as a function of the market share, s_j

$$
\begin{aligned}
\frac{s_j}{s_0} &= \frac{e^{\delta_j}}{1 + \sum_{k=1}^{J} e^{\delta_k}} \left(\frac{e^{\delta_0}}{1 + \sum_{k=1}^{J} e^{\delta_k}} \right)^{-1} \\
&= e^{\delta_j}
\end{aligned}
\tag{3.51}
$$
$$
\ln(s_j) - \ln(s_0) = \delta_j
$$

Therefore, the demand estimation can be specified as

$$
\ln(s_j) - \ln(s_0) = X_j \beta - \alpha p_j + \eta_j
\tag{3.52}
$$

Similar to the previous section, we can derive the own price elasticity and cross price elasticity of a product as follows.

$$
\frac{\partial s_j}{\partial p'_j} = \frac{e^{\delta_j} e^{\delta'_j}}{\left[1 + \sum_{k=1}^{J} e^{\delta_k} \right]^2}
\tag{3.53}
$$

where j and j' can be any two choices. The own price elasticity of product j can be calculated as

$$
e_{jj} = \frac{\partial s_j}{\partial p_j} \frac{p_j}{s_j} = -\alpha p_j (1 - s_j)
\tag{3.54}
$$

Similarly, the cross price elasticity can be calculated as

$$
e_{jj'} = \frac{\partial s_j}{\partial p'_j} \frac{p'_j}{s_j} = \alpha s_{j'} p_{j'}
\tag{3.55}
$$

The own price elasticity of demand is negative, which is consistent with law of demand. The cross price elasticity of demand is also negative. Because product j does not enter this formula, a change in price of product j has the same effect on all the other products. It may not be appropriate in some cases because closer competitors of product j should have a larger impact. This is the IIA critique that simple logit models suffer.

The difficulty in estimating demand models lies in endogeneity. Some of the product characteristics are unobserved (to the researcher) and these characteristics may be correlated with the independent variables. For example, we want to estimate demand for cereal. Researchers can observe how much sugar, fat, and calories per 100 gram of each brand. But researchers cannot observe the taste of each brand. Intuitively, taste should be positively correlated with price. Therefore, estimating this equation by ordinary least squares (OLS) would yield biased estimates.

To deal with endogeneity, we need to find instrumental variables (IVs). A good IV should be uncorrelated with the unobserved product characteristic, η_j, but highly correlated with the endogenous variable, in our case, p_j. The first strategy is to assume product characteristics, X_j are exogenous and to use X_j (or functions of X_j) as IVs. X_j is obviously correlated with p_j because firms set their prices based on these characteristics. However, for some products, the unobserved characteristics, η_j are correlated with X_j. For example, how good the cereal tastes may depend on the amount of sugar it contains.

The second strategy is to use the average characteristics of all competing products as IVs to control for p_j. For example, we can use the average price of all other products which should be positively correlated with p_j because the price of product j is likely to increase if all its competitors increase their prices. This IV is unlikely to be correlated with the unobserved characteristics of product j. For instance, the taste of cereal is not likely to be associated with the average price of its rivals.

In this example, we estimate consumer preferences for cereal using aggregate level data. The data set includes product information of the top selling 50 brands of cereal in 1992, such as the market share of each brand, average retail price, level of sugar, fat, and calories. Two dummy variables indicate whether the brand targets families and whether the flavor is child or adult oriented. The market shares are shares of total cereal purchased during 1992. For simplicity, we assume that the outside option is the composite basket of all other brands in the market.

3.5.3.3   Model Specification

The utility specification for individual i of choosing brand j can be written as

$$u_{ij} = X_j\beta - \alpha p_j + \eta_j + \epsilon_{ij} \tag{3.56}$$

where X_j are characteristics of brand j, η_j is unobserved characteristics of product j. ϵ_{ij} is i.i.d. type I extreme value. The mean utility level of product j can then be written as

$$\delta_j = X_j\beta - \alpha p_j + \eta_j$$

The estimation equation is then

$$\ln(s_j) - \ln(s_0) = X_j\beta - \alpha p_j + \eta_j$$

where s_0 is the market share of the outside option. As discussed in the previous section, the price variable, p_j is endogenous and OLS estimation can lead to bias. In the estimation, we will use different sets of IVs to estimate consumer demand and potentially correct for the endogeneity bias. We begin by reading the data into SAS using the IMPORT statement.

```
proc import out = WORK.cereal datafile= "Cereal1"
   dbms = xls replace;
   getnames = yes;
run;
```

The market share of the outside option is 24.29 percent and the average price of the outside option is 2.68. We construct the dependent variable and deflate the prices using a DATA step.

```
data cereal;
set cereal;
   Y = log(Mkt_share) - log(24.29);
   price = Avg_Trans_Price/2.68;
run;
```

We can start with OLS estimation implement in PROC REG.

```
proc reg data=cereal;
   model Y = FAM_Dummy Kids_Dummy Cals Fat Sugar price;
run;
```

Although OLS gives the correct sign for the price parameter, endogeneity could be an issue. To improve our estimation, we use several sets of IVs and compare these results with the OLS results.

Figure 3.20 OLS Parameter Estimates

The REG Procedure
Model: MODEL1
Dependent Variable: Y

Parameter Estimates

Variable	Label	DF	Parameter Estimate	Standard Error	t Value	Pr > |t|
Intercept	Intercept	1	-2.80294	0.60455	-4.64	<.0001
Fam_Dummy	Fam_Dummy	1	0.57541	0.17768	3.24	0.0023
Kids_Dummy	Kids_Dummy	1	0.07034	0.20915	0.34	0.7383
Cals	Cals	1	0.00246	0.00275	0.90	0.3753
Fat	Fat	1	0.01125	0.05168	0.22	0.8288
Sugar	Sugar	1	-0.04231	0.01556	-2.72	0.0094
price		1	-0.21037	0.37430	-0.56	0.5770

IV Method 1

The first set of IVs are constructed using average characteristics of all the other brands produced by the same company. These IVs are likely to be correlated with the price variable but unlikely to be correlated with the unobserved product characteristics. To obtain the sum of the characteristics for each company, we use PROC SUMMARY and the CLASS statement. This instructs PROC SUMMARY to compute the statistics by company. After obtaining the output data set sum, this data is merged with the original data set.

```
proc summary data = cereal;
   var price cals fat sugar;
   class company_id;
   output out = sum_company
   n = count_company
   sum=;
run;
```

```
proc print data = sum_company;
run;

/*Generate sum of characteristics variables*/
data sum_company;
set sum_company;
   if _TYPE_ = 0 then DELETE;
   rename price = sum_price_company
               cals = sum_cals_company
               fat = sum_fat_company
               sugar = sum_sugar_company
               count_identifier = count_company;
run;

/*Merge sum table to main table*/
data cereal;
   merge cereal sum_company(keep=company_id count_company sum_price_company
       sum_cals_company sum_fat_company sum_sugar_company);
   by company_id;
run;

/*Generate averages of characteristics of other products
  produced by the same company*/
data cereal;
set cereal;
   ave_price_company = (sum_price_company -price) / (count_company - 1);
   ave_cals_company = (sum_cals_company -cals) / (count_company - 1);
   ave_fat_company = (sum_fat_company - fat) / (count_company - 1);
   ave_sugar_company = (sum_sugar_company - sugar) / (count_company - 1);
run;

proc print data = cereal;
run;
```

There are a number of ways to implement two stage least squares (2SLS) in SAS; in this instance we use PROC SYSLIN. The 2SLS option statement specifies the 2SLS method. The ENGOGENOUS statement specifies which regressor is endogenous. The first stage predicted values are substituted for this variable. Note that the dependent variable, market share, is endogenous. But the dependent variable is not used as a regressor in this type of model, and hence should not be included in the ENDOGENOUS statement. The INSTRUMENT statement specifies the instrumental variables that are used to control for the right-hand side endogenous variable. In our case, we should include the average characteristics of all the other brands produced by the same company, including ave_price_company, ave_cals_company, ave_fat_company, and ave_sugar_company. We also need to include the other independent variables in the second stage, including Cals, Fat, Sugar, FAM_Dummy, and KIDS_Dummy.

```
/*2SLS using average characteristics of other products produced by same company*/
proc syslin data = cereal 2sls ;
   endogenous price ;
   instruments ave_price_company ave_cals_company ave_fat_company
                   ave_sugar_company FAM_Dummy  Kids_Dummy Cals Fat Sugar;
   model Y = FAM_Dummy Kids_Dummy Cals Fat Sugar price;
run ;
```

Figure 3.21 Estimates from PROC SYSLIN

The SYSLIN Procedure
Two-Stage Least Squares Estimation

Model	Y
Dependent Variable	Y

Parameter Estimates

Variable	DF	Parameter Estimate	Standard Error	t Value	Pr > |t|	Variable Label
Intercept	1	-4.17869	0.977925	-4.27	0.0001	Intercept
Fam_Dummy	1	0.684948	0.201118	3.41	0.0014	Fam_Dummy
Kids_Dummy	1	0.043367	0.227200	0.19	0.8495	Kids_Dummy
Cals	1	0.004429	0.003154	1.40	0.1674	Cals
Fat	1	-0.00024	0.056357	-0.00	0.9966	Fat
Sugar	1	-0.04811	0.017142	-2.81	0.0075	Sugar
price	1	0.817732	0.677375	1.21	0.2340	

Another way to implement 2SLS estimation is to use the MODEL procedure. In the PARAMETERS statement, the parameters to be estimated are specified. In this case, they are the constant term, parameters for Cals, Fat, Sugar, FAM_Dummy, and KIDS_Dummy. The EXOGENOUS statement specifies the exogenous independent variables and the ENDOGENOUS statement specifies the endogenous variables. The estimation method selected comes after the slash in the FIT statement. The INSTRUMENTS statement follows the FIT statement and in this case we include the average characteristics of all the other brands produced by the same manufacturer, as well as all the exogenous variables as instruments with the _EXOG_keyword. PROC MODEL and PROC SYSLIN return the same parameter estimates.

```
proc model data=cereal;
    parameters b0 a1 a2 a3 a4 a5 a6;
    exogenous FAM_Dummy Kids_Dummy Cals Fat Sugar;
    endogenous price;
    Y = b0 + a1 * FAM_Dummy + a2 * Kids_Dummy
             + a3 * Cals + a4 * Fat + a5 * Sugar + a6 * price;
    fit Y / 2sls;
    instruments _exog_ ave_price_company ave_cals_company ave_fat_company
    ave_sugar_company;
run;
```

Figure 3.22 Estimates from PROC MODEL

The MODEL Procedure

Model Summary	
Model Variables	7
Endogenous	1
Exogenous	5
Parameters	7
Equations	1
Number of Statements	1

Model Variables	Fam_Dummy Kids_Dummy Cals Fat Sugar price Y
Parameters	b0 a1 a2 a3 a4 a5 a6
Equations	Y

Figure 3.22 *continued*

Nonlinear 2SLS Parameter Estimates				
Parameter	Estimate	Approx Std Err	t Value	Approx Pr > |t|
b0	-4.17869	0.9779	-4.27	0.0001
a1	0.684948	0.2011	3.41	0.0014
a2	0.043367	0.2272	0.19	0.8495
a3	0.004429	0.00315	1.40	0.1674
a4	-0.00024	0.0564	-0.00	0.9966
a5	-0.04811	0.0171	-2.81	0.0075
a6	0.817732	0.6774	1.21	0.2340

IV Method 2

The second set of IVs can be constructed by using the average characteristics of products produced by rivals. The construction of similar to the first method.

```
/*Calculate the sum of all variables*/
proc summary data = cereal;
  var price cals fat sugar;
  output out = sum n=count sum = sum_price sum_cals sum_fat sum_sugar;
run;

proc print data = sum;
run;

/*Merge sum of characteristics to every observation*/
data cereal;
   if _N_ = 1 then set sum(keep = count sum_price sum_cals sum_fat sum_sugar);
set cereal;
   ave_price_rival = (sum_price - sum_price_company) / (count - count_company);
   ave_cals_rival = (sum_cals - sum_cals_company) / (count - count_company);
   ave_fat_rival = (sum_fat - sum_fat_company) / (count - count_company);
   ave_sugar_rival = (sum_sugar - sum_sugar_company) / (count - count_company);
run;

proc print data = cereal;
run;
```

Both PROC SYSLIN and PROC MODEL can be used to implement the estimation and, again, produce the same results.

```
proc syslin data = cereal 2sls ;
   endogenous price ;
   instruments ave_price_rival ave_cals_rival ave_fat_rival ave_sugar_rival
                  FAM_Dummy Kids_Dummy Cals Fat Sugar ;
   model Y = FAM_Dummy Kids_Dummy Cals Fat Sugar price;
run ;

proc model data=cereal;
   parameters b0 a1 a2 a3 a4 a5 a6;
   exogenous FAM_Dummy Kids_Dummy Cals Fat Sugar;
      endogenous price;
   Y = b0 + a1 * FAM_Dummy + a2 * Kids_Dummy
             + a3 * Cals + a4 * Fat + a5 * Sugar + a6 * price;
```

```
fit Y / 2sls;
   instruments _exog_ ave_price_rival ave_cals_rival ave_fat_rival ave_sugar_rival;
run;
```

Figure 3.23 Logit Estimates Using Rival Char. IV

The MODEL Procedure

Model Variables	Fam_Dummy Kids_Dummy Cals Fat Sugar price Y
Parameters	b0 a1 a2 a3 a4 a5 a6
Equations	Y

Nonlinear 2SLS Parameter Estimates

Parameter	Estimate	Approx Std Err	t Value	Approx Pr > |t|
b0	-3.61667	0.8683	-4.17	0.0001
a1	0.640199	0.1893	3.38	0.0015
a2	0.054387	0.2158	0.25	0.8022
a3	0.003625	0.00296	1.22	0.2273
a4	0.004453	0.0535	0.08	0.9340
a5	-0.04574	0.0162	-2.82	0.0073
a6	0.397737	0.5942	0.67	0.5069

Lastly, the average characteristics of all other products could be used as IVs.

```
data cereal;
set cereal;
   ave_price_other = (sum_price - price) / (count - 1);
   ave_cals_other = (sum_cals - cals) / (count - 1);
   ave_fat_other = (sum_fat - fat) / (count - 1);
   ave_sugar_other = (sum_sugar - sugar) / (count - 1);
run;

/*Using average characteristics of all other products as IVs to run 2SLS*/
proc syslin data = cereal 2sls ;
endogenous price ;
instruments ave_price_other ave_cals_other ave_fat_other ave_sugar_other
                FAM_Dummy Kids_Dummy Cals  Fat Sugar ;
model Y = FAM_Dummy Kids_Dummy Cals Fat Sugar price;
run ;
```

Figure 3.24 Logit Estimates Using Avg. Char. IV

The SYSLIN Procedure
Two-Stage Least Squares Estimation

Model	Y
Dependent Variable	Y

		Parameter Estimates				
Variable	DF	Parameter Estimate	Standard Error	t Value	Pr > |t|	Variable Label
Intercept	1	-2.80294	0.604554	-4.64	<.0001	Intercept
Fam_Dummy	1	0.575408	0.177680	3.24	0.0023	Fam_Dummy
Kids_Dummy	1	0.070342	0.209147	0.34	0.7383	Kids_Dummy
Cals	1	0.002461	0.002747	0.90	0.3753	Cals
Fat	1	0.011246	0.051680	0.22	0.8288	Fat
Sugar	1	-0.04231	0.015556	-2.72	0.0094	Sugar
price	1	-0.21037	0.374297	-0.56	0.5770	

3.6 Conclusion

We have only examined some of the functional forms in use for demand analysis. We would be remiss if we did not note some of the forms that we have not discussed. Several of these forms are used in later chapters on the derived demand of producers. We have not treated the translog model, the generalized Leontief model, the fourier flexible form, the miniflex laurent, the normalized quadratic, or the asymptotically ideal model. Many discrete choice models have also been omitted. However, the important concepts surrounding applied demand analysis have been addressed. Likewise, the use of several SAS procedures has been demonstrated.

Chapter 4
Theory of Supply

Contents

4.1	Overview	**75**
4.2	The Production Function	**76**
4.3	The Cost Function and Derived Factor Demands	**77**
4.4	The Profit Function	**79**
	4.4.1 Profit Derived Factor Demands	80
	4.4.2 Elasticities	80
4.5	Concepts of Time in Production	**81**
4.6	Separability and Aggregation	**81**

4.1 Overview

The study of markets is usually approached from one of two perspectives: the demand side or the supply side. In either case, we must model the decision making processes of economic actors. On the supply side, our model is a simplified representation of the real world production of goods and services by firms. A firm may be a private business, partnership, or corporation, and the term can be extended to productive units in areas that may not commonly be thought of as economic markets. Becker (1973, 1983) demonstrated the relevance of supply and demand analysis to areas as diverse as the household and political regulation. Regardless of whether the market is economic, political, or social, the firm is always an economic decision maker whose chief function is the supply of a good or service as broadly understood.

To analyze market interactions, we must be able to characterize the choices that the firm makes as it responds to various incentives. A firm takes scarce inputs and produces outputs that are then consumed by other firms or consumers. There are two behavioral principles that underlie this process. Just as consumers seek to maximize their utility, firms seek to maximize their profits. And just as consumers seek to minimize their expenditures, firms seek to minimize their costs. In pursuing maximum profit and minimum cost, firm decisions are constrained by available technologies, the nature of the input market, and the nature of the output market. While the firm decision making process is enormously complex in reality, producer behavior can be modeled in a parsimonious way by appealing to the complementary ideas of cost and profit.

One of the advantages of modeling firm behavior is that firm outputs are most often real. Whether a commodity good or service, firm products can be directly observed. The profit maximization problem gives an optimum that can be stated in dollars or whatever the currency of choice might be. This is in contrast to the consumer's problem of utility maximization. Utility is, in some sense, an indirectly observed output of consumer choice. For more information about the ordinality of utility, see chapter 2. This chapter does not need to make similar concessions.

The problems of separability and aggregation in production are also somewhat reduced when compared with their demand counterparts. Whereas the modern consumer has an almost unfathomable set of consumption possibilities, the firm's production process is often more amenable to simplification. We will examine empirical examples that extend concepts of individual firm behavior to aggregate production, by considering industry-wide production functions, for instance. Nonetheless, with the increasing availability of firm-level data, studies of individual firm behavior are becoming more common. While simplifying assumptions of separability and aggregation are still maintained in almost every supply or production analysis, their justification may be more plausible.

Like chapter 2 of this text, this theoretical exposition provides basic foundations for empirical analysis. We would again be deficient if we did not list more comprehensive treatments of some of the developments in supply, production, and cost theory. Cornes (1992) deals with producer problems in a compact way and takes great pains to link ideas of consumer and producer duality. An in-depth discussion of applied production analysis is provided by Chambers (1988). Note that many of the concepts that have been discussed under the heading of consumer theory apply to producer theory as well, although the nomenclature is often changed. You will find that this chapter is more succinct than the first due to this carryover.

4.2   The Production Function

The producer takes individual inputs to production, which can be represented by the scalar x_i, bundles them into a vector of inputs $\mathbf{x}_i$, and produces a single–scalar valued output y. This process can be represented by the production function

$$y = f(\mathbf{x}) \tag{4.1}$$

where we impose the common condition that the production function returns the maximum level of output available from the bundle of inputs.

The production function is an engineering concept. It is a mathematical representation of the production processes available to the firm and says little about the pure economic behavior of the producer. Many authors refer to the production function as the production technology. This is because the function represents a particular state of technology that the firm has at its disposal. There are two interesting extensions to the scalar-valued production function that are not pursued here, but are worth nothing. We could consider a firm that produces multiple outputs in accordance with a vector-valued production function, although this yields little economic content and is covered in detail in other texts. Consideration can also be given to firms with access to multiple production plants, with each plant thought to have access to its own production function.

As we have seen, for the firm undertaking production of a single output, production proceeds according to a given technology as embodied in the production function. A natural question is whether any structure can be placed on this function. If this simplified representation of production is to adequately approximate reality, several assumptions must be imposed the on the production function. To be clear, these properties are maintained assumptions. Unlike the expenditure function in demand theory or the cost function in producer theory, the production function is not the solution to a problem of maximization or minimization. As a consequence, any properties taken by the production technology do not arise naturally.

The production function is assumed to have the properties of:

1. **Essentiality**: If any of the inputs to the production function are missing, then zero output can be produced. Remember that - at the most basic level - economics is concerned with the use of scarce inputs. If output could be produced with zero inputs, then the inputs would not be scarce in production. There are two kinds of essentiality: strong and weak. Weak essentiality, defined as $f(0) = 0$, simply says that with zero of every input no output can be produced. Strong essentiality implies that $f(\mathbf{x}) = 0$, so that output is zero when a single input is missing. We will typically assume strong essentiality as most of our analyses deal with aggregate inputs. But, there are some products where relaxation of strong essentially is warranted.

2. **Monotonicity**: Adding additional inputs will never decrease the amount of output. Given two bundles of inputs x_j and x_k, with $x_j \geq x_k$, $f(x_j) \geq f(x_k)$. The marginal product with respect to any input is always nonnegative. Even if we could conceive of a production process where the addition of inputs might cause output to fall, the use of such technologies is unlikely to ever be observed.

3. **Concavity**: Concavity holds for the inputs to the production function. Thus $f((1 - \alpha)x_i + \alpha x_j) \geq (1 - \alpha)f(x_i) + \alpha f(x_j)$ for any input vectors i and j and any $0 \leq \alpha \leq 1$. The practical result of this assumption is that if two bundles of inputs can produce a certain level of output, some average of these two bundles can produce the same amount. The second derivative of the production function with respect to any input will also be nonpositive. This is a mathematical statement of the law of diminishing marginal productivity. With the property of monotonicity, it implies that the production function increases at a decreasing rate in its inputs.

4.3 The Cost Function and Derived Factor Demands

Mathematical models are often used in the social sciences as a means of approximating or describing a real world system. One advantage of formulating a model mathematically is that the model can be tailored so that it is both a realistic and manageable representation of reality. Econometric analysis usually begins by identifying relevant theory, constructing a model, and then applying the model and theory to data. It is then possible to compare the behaviors implied by theory to facts embodied in the data.

Let y be a single scalar-valued output and x an n-dimensional vector of nonnegative inputs. The cost function dual to the production function of the firm can be defined as

$$C(w, y) \equiv min_x(wx | f(x) \geq y, x \geq 0_N) \tag{4.2}$$

where w is a vector of factor prices for the inputs of the firm's production process. The production function, $f(x)$, represents the technologies or production plans available to the producer. Given a certain level of output y, and taking input prices w and the production function $f(x)$ as given , the producer chooses the input mix x that minimizes cost.

There are several properties that the cost function must satisfy from a theoretical perspective. Each of these properties has an intuitive behavioral interpretation.

1. **Nondecreasing**: The cost function must be nondecreasing in w, and nondecreasing in y. The assumption that the function is nondecreasing in w and y simply means that as input prices rise or the level of output is increased, the cost to the firm increases.

2. **Concavity**: The cost function is concave and continuous in w. Thus, $C((1 - \alpha)w_i + \alpha w_j) \geq (1 - \alpha)C(w_i) + \alpha C(w_j)$ where y is omitted for the sake of brevity. The concavity property follows from the definition of the cost function as the solution to a problem of minimization. One consequence of concavity is that certain restrictions are placed on the substitution possibilities of inputs.

3. **Homogeneity**: Only relative prices of inputs matter to firm decisions, so the cost function is homogeneous of degree one in w. Homogeneity of the first degree in w implies that if input prices increase by a certain percentage, total cost must increase by the same relative amount. If the input prices change, but relative prices remain the same, then the input bundle that minimized cost will not change.

Often we are interested not only in explicit cost relationships but in a firm's demand for various inputs. Shepherd's Lemma provides a link between the cost function and factor demand functions. As long as the cost function is differentiable in **w**, the partial derivative of the cost function with respect to a single factor price is the unique cost minimizing factor demand for the given input. In other words, if we can specify a well behaved cost function, we can also generate factor demand functions. The cost function and factor demands contain similar information. From an empirical standpoint it is possible to completely characterize production behavior from the cost function and its associated factor demands. Through application of Shepherd's Lemma, the derived demand for input i can be written as

$$\frac{\partial C(\mathbf{w}, y)}{\partial w_i} = x_i(\mathbf{w}, y) \tag{4.3}$$

Comparative statics provide a convenient mechanism for understanding the impact of a shift in an exogenous variable on an economic system. We might, for instance, be interested in how the firm changes its demand for input i when the price of input j increases and all else is held constant. This change in quantity demanded given a change in price can be found by taking the partial derivative of the factor demand function.

$$\frac{\partial x_i(\mathbf{w}, y)}{\partial w_j} \tag{4.4}$$

Later when we specify functional forms for the cost function, parameters of the functional forms will embody comparative static effects. One of our goals in estimating cost functions is to capture these effects in order to better understand the impact of changes in the exogenous variables (e.g. input prices) on firm behavior. All of the equations used in constructing the theory of cost have been general functions so far. In applying these models to real data, it is necessary to specify functional forms. Stochastic disturbance terms are appended to each equation to take randomness in the data and imperfections in the model into account. It is then possible to apply standard techniques of statistical inference to the system of equations.

The benefits and costs of appending error terms to deterministic cost and profit functions are discussed by Kumbhakar and Tsionas (2011). They also derive primal and dual cost systems that have a stochastic specifications based on the optimizing behavior of the firm. This follows work by McElroy (1987) and others who have argued that the stochastic specification is a fundamental component of the specification of the production model. Chavas and Segerson (1987) showed that the results of statistical inference for these models is highly dependent on the stochastic approach chosen by the researcher. The applications that follow assume that there are no implications from the theory for the stochastic elements of the behavioral equations. This is, admittedly, a simplified approach and readers interested in additive general error and multiplicative general error models are directed to Kumbhakar and Tsionas (2011).

Because economic theory suggests a number of properties for the cost function, much attention has been focused on discovering functional forms that adhere to these theoretical properties. However, the functional forms must also be estimable; the goal is, after all, to make use of real data. These developments have led to a class of functional forms that have been termed "flexible." For a form to be "flexible", it must be capable of providing a second order differential approximation to an arbitrary twice continuously differentiable cost function that is homogeneous of degree one in prices. There are several functional forms that meet this requirement including the translog cost function and the generalized Leontief cost function. Note that this definition of flexibility says nothing of concavity, an interesting feature of the cost function mentioned earlier.

4.4   The Profit Function

A dual problem is also encountered in the theory of supply. Consider the producer who, instead of minimizing cost, aims to maximize profit. This is the common notion of a firm's responsibility: the maximization of profits. The prices of the firms inputs and its output are again taken as given. The producer will $\max py - \mathbf{w}\mathbf{x}$ subject to $y = f(\mathbf{x})$. The profit function can then be stated as

$$\pi(p, \mathbf{w}) \equiv max(py - \mathbf{w}\mathbf{x} | y = f(\mathbf{x})) \tag{4.5}$$

As usual the problem can be solved by the method of Lagrange multipliers with

$$L = py - \mathbf{w}\mathbf{x} + \lambda(f(\mathbf{x}) - y) \tag{4.6}$$

with the first order conditions

$$w_i = \lambda \frac{\partial f}{\partial x_i} \quad i = 1, \ldots, n \tag{4.7}$$

$$f(x) = y \tag{4.8}$$

$$p = \lambda \tag{4.9}$$

leading to a system of n+2 equations in n+2 unknowns. Remember that n is the number of inputs, and the firm must simultaneously select quantities of n inputs and the single output. Substitution of the solutions into the objective function leads to the profit function which satisfies the following properties:

1. **Monotonicity**: The monotonicity of the profit function differs whether we are considering the output price or the input prices. For the price of the output, profit will of course be monotonically increasing in p. In other words, with $p_j \geq p_k$, then $\pi(p_j, \mathbf{w}) \geq \pi(p_k, \mathbf{w})$. As you may expect the profit function will be monotonically decreasing in the input prices $\mathbf{w}$ so that $\mathbf{w}_j \geq \mathbf{w}_k$, then $\pi(p, \mathbf{w}_j) \geq \pi(p, \mathbf{w}_k)$.

2. **Homogeneity**: The profit function is homogeneous of degree one in both the output price p and the input price vector $\mathbf{w}$. This property is a restatement of the absence of money illusion. If all prices are scaled by some factor then the resulting profit is scaled by the same factor. Another way of stating this is to say that if nominal prices are changed, but relative prices are the same, then relative profit will be unchanged. It does not matter if we price inputs and outputs in dollars, yen, or any other currency. Real profit is the same.

3. **Convexity**: Convexity holds for p and $\mathbf{w}$ for the profit function. If the profit function is convex in output price, and strictly increasing in the output price, then the supply function for the competitive firm cannot slope downwards. It can similarly be shown that the input demand functions for the competitive firm cannot slope upwards.

4.4.1 Profit Derived Factor Demands

In a result similar to Shephard's lemma, Hotelling showed that if the profit function is differentiable then it will yield supply and demand functions. This result is now known as Hotelling's lemma. It formally says that

$$s(p, \mathbf{w}) = \frac{\partial \pi(p, \mathbf{w})}{\partial p} \tag{4.10}$$

$$x_i(p, \mathbf{w}) = \frac{\partial \pi(p, \mathbf{w})}{\partial w_i} \tag{4.11}$$

If we begin with a well behaved profit function, then it is simple to determine the associated supply and input demand functions. Likewise, should we have unique supply and demand functions, then there must exist a profit function that satisfies this behavior.

You may have noticed that in deriving factor, or input demands, we have arrived at two different functions. In equation 4.3 the factor demands are a function of input prices and output, while in equation 4.11 the factor demands are a function of input prices and the output price. Because of the dual relationship between cost minimization and profit maximization, factor demands will be equivalent at the optimum.

4.4.2 Elasticities

Having defined the production function, cost function, and given some basic assumptions, there are several quantities that we may wish to measure. These quantities provide information on the structure of the technology. They measure technical relationships, but have relevance for the decision making of the firm and in discussions of public policy. The first notion is the elasticity of scale, which describes the relationship between the output y and the entire vector of inputs $\mathbf{x}$. The elasticity of scale is

$$\epsilon = \frac{\partial \ln f(\lambda x)}{\partial \ln \lambda} \tag{4.12}$$

The elasticity of scale measures how output responds to the simultaneous change of all inputs. If we scale all of the inputs by a given factor, what will be the percentage change in output? The elasticity of scale provides the answer. The production function has the property of constant returns to scale if $\epsilon = 1$. For production functions with constant returns, if we increase all inputs by a given percentage (or scale them by the same factor), then output will increase by the same percentage. When $\epsilon < 1$ the production function has decreasing returns to scale; when $\epsilon > 1$ the production function has increasing returns to scale.

As with all elasticity measures, the elasticity of scale is local. It varies depending on the input bundle over which it is evaluated. Because the elasticity will vary, we cannot expect that characterizations of returns to scale will hold across all possible bundles of inputs. When confronted with data for empirical analysis the elasticity of scale is often evaluated at the mean of the sample inputs. The typical finding is that the production process is constant or decreasing returns to scale, which aligns with the concavity of the production function.

Just as we defined elasticities of substitution in consumption, elasticities of substitution can also be defined for the production process. The formulas for these elasticities are virtually unchanged from what was encountered in chapter 2. If you think of consumption as a process of production, whereby consumers use inputs to produce utility, the connection is obvious.

The Allen–Uzawa Elasticity is given by

$$\omega_{ij}^A = \frac{C_{ij}(y\mathbf{w})c(y, \mathbf{w})}{C_i(y\mathbf{w})C_j(y, \mathbf{w})} \tag{4.13}$$

The Morishima Elasticity is

$$\omega_{ij}^M = w_i \left(\frac{C_{ij}(y, \mathbf{w})}{C_j(y, \mathbf{w})} - \frac{C_{ii}(y, \mathbf{w})}{C_i, \mathbf{w}} \right) \tag{4.14}$$

where the subscripts of the cost function denote partial derivatives. The Morishima elasticity of substitution can also be stated as a function of price elasticities of demand for the inputs. A revealing discussion of the differences between various elasticities of substitutions in production contexts can be found in Blackorby, Primont, and Russell (2007).

4.5   Concepts of Time in Production

An important distinction in production analysis is that of the long run and the short run. These concepts of time are defined by the inputs that the firm uses in production. In the short run the amount of one or more inputs that the firm uses in the production process is fixed. In the long run, all inputs are freely variable. Because the concepts are defined by fixity of inputs, the short run could end up being a nominally long amount of time, and the long run a short period. This dichotomy is a practical way of introducing input fixity into economic analysis without having to explicitly introduce time into the model.

The difference between the short run and long run has implications for both the cost and profit functions. Suppose that the inputs $\mathbf{x}$ are divided into two sets. We allow $\mathbf{x}_1$ to be variable inputs and constrain $\mathbf{x}_2$ to be fixed. The cost function of the firm can now be given by

$$C(\mathbf{w}_1, y, \mathbf{x}_2) \equiv min_{\mathbf{x}_1} (\mathbf{w}_1 \mathbf{x}_1 | f(\mathbf{x}) \geq y, \mathbf{x}_1 \geq 0_N) \tag{4.15}$$

In this instance, $\mathbf{w}_1$ are the input prices associated with the variable inputs. If the production function satisfies the properties given in previous sections, a well-defined short-run cost function results. The principle result, which illustrates the major difference between the short run and long run cost functions, is that fixed inputs do not always minimize cost. However, variable costs are always minimized. Similar results can be obtained for the variable profit function.

Some authors have incorporated fixed inputs into models of firm behavior. These models have tended to be more complex than fully variable approaches where inputs and output adjust instantaneously. An interesting empirical example is Morrison (1988) who developed a model from a generalized Leontief cost function. The model was applied to manufacturing data from the United States and Japan and allowed for quasi-fixed inputs that adjust, but at a slow rate. While our empirical applications do not consider restricted cost and profit functions, they can usually be implemented in SAS through the MODEL or IML procedures.

4.6   Separability and Aggregation

Similar to the case of demand, problems of separability and aggregation also arise in supply analysis. The problems are again a result of the realities of economic data and the limitations of computational ability. Data on inputs and outputs is usually aggregated before it ever reaches the economist. Inputs are often compartmentalized as capital, labor, energy, materials, and services. Nevermind the fact that capital may include machines, real estate, or other more specific inputs. Labor may consist of line workers, managers, or others, all of which receive a different wage for their contributions to the production process. Leonard Read's famous essay "I, Pencil" is both testament to the power of prices to coordinate economic activity and the vast complexity of production processes for even seemingly simple products. Whole fields of study have arisen to deal with supply chains and their management.

The computational burden of modeling complex production processes may exceed available resources. Suppose that we are interested in modeling a firm that produces a number of distinct products using a multitude of inputs which may or may not differ according to the output. A natural problem might again be that the number of observations in the data is exceeded by the number of relevant variables.

Separability in production can be defined in terms of both the cost function and the profit function. Both results are presented here. The n inputs to the producer's problem are divided into S different aggregates that are denoted with capital letters A. B. C, etc. The vector of inputs in each group can be given by $X_G = [x_1, ..., x_{nG}]$ and the vector of input prices can be given as $w_G = [w_1, ..., w_{nG}]$ where n_G is the number of inputs in each partition.

Weak Separability Weak separability holds if and only if the cost function can be written in the form

$$c(w, y) = c(y, c_1(y, w_1), ...c_S(y, w_S))$$ (4.16)

and the profit function takes the form

$$\pi(p, w) = \pi(p, \pi_1(p, w_1), ...\pi_S(p, w_S))$$ (4.17)

The consequence of weak separability is that

$$\frac{\partial[(\partial c/\partial w_i)/(\partial c/\partial w_k)]}{\partial w_j} = 0$$ (4.18)

for $i, k \in G$, $j \in H$, and $G \neq H$. and

$$\frac{\partial[(\partial \pi/\partial w_i)/(\partial \pi/\partial w_k)]}{\partial w_j} = 0$$ (4.19)

for $i, k \in G$, $j \in H$, and $G \neq H$.

Strong Separability Strong separability holds if and only if the cost function can be written in the form

$$c(w, y) = c(y, c_1(y, w_1), ...c_S(y, w_S))$$ (4.20)

and the profit function takes the form

$$\pi(p, w) = \pi(p, \sum)$$ (4.21)

The consequence of strong separability is that

$$\frac{\partial[(\partial c/\partial w_i)/(\partial c/\partial w_k)]}{\partial w_j} = 0$$ (4.22)

for $i, k \in G$, $j \in H$, and $G \neq H$. and

$$\frac{\partial[(\partial \pi/\partial w_i)/(\partial \pi/\partial w_k)]}{\partial w_j} = 0$$ (4.23)

for $i, k \in G$, $j \in H$, and $G \neq H$.

The major result of weak separability is that the cost and profit function can be written as functions of price indices for aggregate inputs. Instead of having to specify a cost function over prices for different types of labor, a composite price for labor can be constructed, and all analysis can proceed using this composite price. Similarly, the profit function can be estimated based on various price indices. As in the demand chapters, we assume weak separability in the analyses that follow.

Chapter 5
Empirical Approaches to Supply Analysis

Contents

5.1	Overview	**83**
5.2	Cobb–Douglas Production	**84**
	5.2.1 Econometric Analysis	85
5.3	Translog Functional Form	**91**
	5.3.1 Empirical Analysis	93
5.4	Frontier Production Functions	**104**
	5.4.1 Empirical Analysis	107

5.1   Overview

Applied production analysis is concerned with the way that real firms make choices in using inputs to supply outputs. Additionally, economists often want to be able to describe certain technological characteristics of the production process. In the previous chapter we saw mention of elasticities that can be used to characterize such relationships. A typical research question might relate to the scale elasticities of the production function. If the production function is constant returns to scale, then a one percent increase in all inputs will lead to a one percent increase in output. Whether we observe such properties in the data is an empirical question.

Just as the study of demand evolved from use of aggregate data to use of household level data, so has the study of supply moved to lower levels of aggregation. Much of the work in production over the middle to late twentieth century was conducted at the industry level. The analyst usually had access to information on aggregate inputs, outputs, and prices. Because the variables were measured at an industry level, a great deal of research was directed toward the appropriate construction of these aggregate variables. This led, in part, to an approach to productivity measurement known as the index number approach (Diewert 1976; Diewert and Nakamura 2003). As time has gone on, firm level data has been made available. This data is typically panel data where information on multiple firms is measured over a number of years.

Instead of measuring and describing a static production process, we often would like to know how a production process has changed over time. Changes in production are central to economic growth. Using results from production theory, econometric techniques can be put to good use disentangling the story of technological advancement. Otherwise, we might confuse technological change with increased input use or a host of other policy shocks. A classic paper in this area is Griliches (1957) who studied the adoption and effects of hybrid corn in the United States. In his paper, Griliches found that the rate of adoption was influenced by a number of different profitability variables. Aggregate productivity growth is caused not only by the adoption of technologies by individual firms, but also by shuffling of firms within an industry. Market forces drive inefficient firms from the sector, with their resources shifting to new entrants or high productivity firms. In a study of tobacco farms in the United States, Kirwan, Uchida, and White (2012) found changes both within firms and between firms to be significant factors in determining overall productivity growth.

The primary purpose of this chapter is to provide examples of functional forms that

1. Satisfy restrictions from economic theory

2. Allow for theoretical restrictions to be tested

3. Generate elasticities of supply

Our objectives are then closely related to the empirical studies of chapter 2.

The approaches contained herein are structural, in the sense that they use economic theory as the basis for relationships between variables. The relationships are often linear functions with certain constraints on the parameters of the functions. Those parameters can be estimated from the data. The model should be capable of obtaining all of the outcomes that are possible given the theory. This is just another way of saying that we desire flexible functional forms.

5.2   Cobb–Douglas Production

You encountered the Cobb–Douglas utility function in chapter 2. We now consider revisiting this common functional form in the case of production. The Cobb-Douglas production function for a firm producing one output, using n inputs, is

$$y = A \sum_{i=1}^{n} x_i^{\alpha_i} \tag{5.1}$$

where it is usually assumed that $0 < \alpha_i < 1$ and $\sum_{i=1}^{n} \alpha_i = 1$. To maintain positivity $A > 0$. The restrictions on the α's result in linear homogeneity of the production function. If all of the inputs increase in a given proportion, then the single output will increase in the same proportion. We defined this property in the previous chapter as constant returns to scale. A defines total factor productivity.

An interesting history of the development of the Cobb-Douglas production function is given in Douglas (1976). It provides another fine example of empirical research driving the economic enterprise. Douglas plotted various production data on a chart and sought out his colleague Cobb to determine a functional form that might fit the data. Thus the Cobb-Douglas production function was born. Since that time the Cobb-Douglas form has been extensively studied and used in empirical research. It remains a basic component of every economist's toolbox.

The form has several appealing mathematical properties. The marginal product is given by $MP_i = \frac{\partial y}{\partial x_i} = \alpha_i \frac{y}{x_i}$. Using results from the producer's maximization problem, namely that $MP_i = w_i/p$, we arrive at

$$\alpha_i = \frac{w_i x_i}{py} \tag{5.2}$$

The Cobb-Douglas production function has α_i parameters that can be interpreted as factor shares. You can also consider the ratio of two parameters

$$\frac{\alpha_i}{\alpha_j} = \frac{w_i x_i}{w_j x_j} \tag{5.3}$$

which is the relative factor share. Equation 5.3 shows that proportional changes in relative factor prices and relative inputs result in constant relative factor shares.

The cost function and profit functions can be derived using the techniques of the previous chapter. Substituting into the standard formula for revenue, then revenue for the Cobb-Douglas production function is given by

$$\text{Revenue} = pA \sum_{i=1}^{n} x_i^{\alpha_i} \tag{5.4}$$

For profit maximization the objective function is then

$$\pi = pA \sum_{i=1}^{n} x_i^{\alpha_i} - \sum_{i=1}^{n} w_i x_i \tag{5.5}$$

where w_i is the input price for good i. The first order conditions from the profit maximization are

$$\frac{\partial \pi}{\partial x_i} = p\alpha_i \frac{y}{x_i} - w_i = 0 \quad i = 1, \ldots, n \tag{5.6}$$

which can be solved to yield the input demand functions. Note that the condition implies that at the optimum the marginal revenue product of an input must be equal to the input price, a fact we used in deriving equation 5.2. The use of the Cobb-Douglas form implies several assumptions. The production of the output requires positive amounts of all inputs and the marginal productivity of an input corresponds to the level of production per unit of the input. It also implies that the output elasticities of the inputs are constant over time. In a given empirical scenario, the analyst may have good reason to question the suitability of the Cobb-Douglas given these considerations.

5.2.1 Econometric Analysis

This empirical example is based on Nerlove (1963), which was one of the first studies to consider estimating features of a parameterized cost function. Nerlove's specific question relates to returns to scale in the regulated United States power industry. At the time the study was conducted, power in the U.S. was regulated, with prices set by government regulators. We have cross section data on 145 electric power suppliers in 1955. The data includes measurements of total cost, output, and input prices for labor, capital, and fuel. This data set is somewhat unique for the time as it was partially gathered at the firm level.

Nerlove (1963) receives attention in Hayashi (2000) as well, and is cited as a good example of the basic techniques of ordinary least squares. Nerlove considers the case of electricity generation, where firm i's production follows a three input Cobb–Douglas production function given as

$$y_i = A_i l_i^{\alpha_l} c_i^{\alpha_c} f_i^{\alpha_f} \tag{5.7}$$

The labor input is denoted by l, the capital input by c, and the fuel input by f. The A_i term is unique for each firm, and thus captures differences in firm technologies. The degree of returns to scale is $r = \alpha_1 + \alpha_2 + \alpha_3$ which is not assumed to be constant, thus departing from one of the original assumptions made on the Cobb-Douglas form.

The log cost function duel to this production function is

$$\log C_i = \mu_i + \frac{1}{r} \log(y_i) + \frac{\alpha_1}{r} \log(w_{l,i}) + \frac{\alpha_2}{r} \log(w_{c,i}) + \frac{\alpha_3}{r} \log(w_{f,i}) \tag{5.8}$$

with $\mu_i = \log(r(A_i l_i^{\alpha_1} c_i^{\alpha_2} f_i^{\alpha_3})^{-1/r})$. Because the production function is Cobb-Douglas, the cost function is also Cobb-Douglas, with a different constant out front. By letting $\mu = E(\mu_i)$ and $\epsilon_i = \mu_i - \mu$, an error term can be appended to the log cost function. The log cost function can then be estimated using the following parameterization

$$\log C_i = \mu + \beta_1 \log(y_i) + \beta_2 \log(w_l) + \beta_3 \log(w_c) + \beta_4 \log(w_f) + \epsilon_i \tag{5.9}$$

The cost function to be estimated is in logarithms, so a DATA step is used to transform the inputs for the REG procedure. First load the data and print the first ten observations to verify that we have the necessary information.

```
proc print data = nerlove(obs=10);
run;
```

Figure 5.1 Nerlove's Firm Data

Obs	totcost	output	plabor	pfuel	pkap
1	0.08200	2	2.09000	17.9000	183
2	0.66100	3	2.05000	35.1000	174
3	0.99000	4	2.05000	35.1000	171
4	0.31500	4	1.83000	32.2000	166
5	0.19700	5	2.12000	28.6000	233
6	0.09800	9	2.12000	28.6000	195
7	0.94900	11	1.98000	35.5000	206
8	0.67500	13	2.05000	35.1000	150
9	0.52500	13	2.19000	29.1000	155
10	0.50100	22	1.72000	15.0000	188

```
data nerlove;
set nerlove;
   ltcost = log(totcost);
   ly     = log(output);
   lpl    = log(plabor);
   lpf    = log(pfuel);
   lpk    = log(pkap);
run;
```

Since the problem is one of estimating a single equation, PROC REG can be used to both estimate the parameters of the equation and test for homogeneity. That is, we can test the restriction $\alpha_l + \alpha_c + \alpha_f = 1$. The MODEL statement specifies the regression equation while a TEST statement gives the homogeneity criteria that we would like to test.

```
proc reg data = nerlove;
   model ltcost = ly lpl lpf lpk;
   homogeneity: test lpl + lpf + lpk = 1;
run;
```

Estimates of the parameters of the cost function are given in Figure 5.2. Given the log-log parameterization of the cost function, the coefficient estimates can be interpreted as elasticities. Note that the sign on the capital coefficient is wrong. In the data, the capital rent is imputed and measured with some inaccuracy, possibly leading to this result. According to the output from the REG procedure, the F statistic on the homogeneity test is 0.57 and we fail to reject the null hypothesis of homogeneity.

Figure 5.2 Unrestricted Cost Function Estimates

The REG Procedure
Model: MODEL1
Dependent Variable: ltcost

Root MSE	0.39236	R-Square	0.9260
Dependent Mean	1.72466	Adj R-Sq	0.9238
Coeff Var	22.74969		

Figure 5.2 *continued*

		Parameter	Standard		
Variable	DF	Estimate	Error	t Value	Pr > |t|
Intercept	1	-3.52650	1.77437	-1.99	0.0488
ly	1	0.72039	0.01747	41.24	<.0001
lpl	1	0.43634	0.29105	1.50	0.1361
lpf	1	0.42652	0.10037	4.25	<.0001
lpk	1	-0.21989	0.33943	-0.65	0.5182

Parameter Estimates

The REG Procedure
Model: MODEL1

Test homogeneity Results for Dependent Variable ltcost

Source	DF	Mean Square	F Value	Pr > F
Numerator	1	0.08831	0.57	0.4501
Denominator	140	0.15394		

Given the failure to reject homogeneity, we can comfortably impose this restriction on the cost function. One approach is to divide total cost and input prices by a given numeraire. Nerlove (1963) uses capital as the numeraire input, but we choose to use fuel. The choice is arbitrary. We might consider testing constant returns to scale as well. Constant returns to scale holds only if the coefficient on output is equal to one, that is if $\beta_1 = 1$. A statement testing for constant returns to scale is added to the call to PROC REG.

```
data nerlove;
set nerlove;
   resttcost = log(totcost/pfuel);
   restpl = log(plabor/pfuel);
   restpk = log(pkap/pfuel);
run;


proc reg data = nerlove;
   model resttcost = ly restpl restpk;
   crs: test ly = 1;
run;
```

The test statistic in Figure 5.3 is exceptionally large, so that we can confidently reject the null hypothesis of constant returns to scale in the electricity industry. We also have somewhat more sensible elasticity estimates.

Figure 5.3 Restricted Cost Function Estimates

The REG Procedure
Model: MODEL1
Dependent Variable: resttcost

Root MSE	0.39176	R-Square	0.9316
Dependent Mean	-1.48420	Adj R-Sq	0.9301
Coeff Var	-26.39558		

Figure 5.3 *continued*

Parameter Estimates

Variable	DF	Parameter Estimate	Standard Error	t Value	Pr > |t|
Intercept	1	-4.69079	0.88487	-5.30	<.0001
ly	1	0.72069	0.01744	41.33	<.0001
restpl	1	0.59291	0.20457	2.90	0.0044
restpk	1	-0.00738	0.19074	-0.04	0.9692

The REG Procedure
Model: MODEL1

Test crs Results for Dependent Variable resttcost

Source	DF	Mean Square	F Value	Pr > F
Numerator	1	39.38634	256.63	<.0001
Denominator	141	0.15348		

The fit diagnostics in Figure 5.4 for the restricted regression expose some potential problems in this analysis. We can see in the first plot that there appears to be evidence of heteroskedasticity. The distribution of residuals may not be normally distributed. Plotting residuals by log output, the residuals are all positive and large for electricity producers with small levels of output. Medium size power companies have negative residuals, and the largest electricity generators have positive residuals.

Figure 5.4 Fit Diagnostics

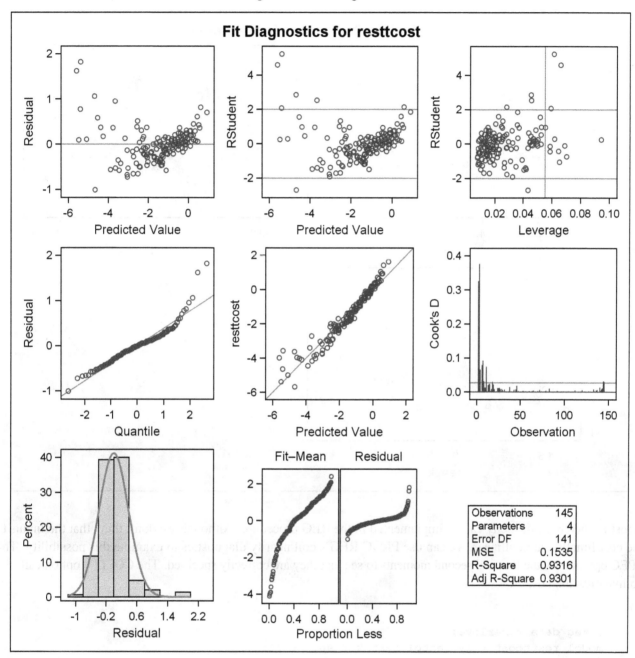

Figure 5.4 *continued*

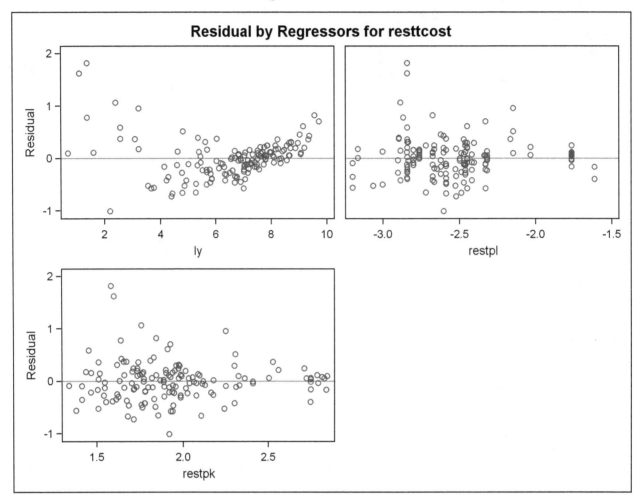

A test for heteroskedasticity can be implemented in the REG procedure. Although we don't think that the inputs to the cost function are collinear, we can use PROC REG's collinearity diagnostics to examine this possibility. The SPEC option tests the first and second moments to see that they are correctly specified. The COLLIN option calls the collinearity diagnostics.

```
proc reg data = nerlove;
   model resttcost = ly restpl restpk / spec collin;
run;
```

Oddly enough, the specification test fails to reject the null hypothesis of homoskedastic errors. The collinearity diagnostics in Figure 5.5 show little evidence of collinearity problems. In further analysis, Nerlove splits the sample into five groups based on levels of output. His results indicate that the degree of returns to scale varies with the level of output. One way to account for such a possibility is to use a functional form that allows for different degrees of returns to scale among firms. A form that meets this criteria is the translog, which is discussed and applied in the next section.

Figure 5.5 Specification and Collinearity Diagnostics

The REG Procedure
Model: MODEL1
Dependent Variable: resttcost

Collinearity Diagnostics

			Proportion of Variation			
Number	Eigenvalue	Condition Index	Intercept	ly	restpl	restpk
1	3.89276	1.00000	0.00008872	0.00471	0.00024762	0.00047541
2	0.06188	7.93157	0.00170	0.80208	0.01604	0.00004150
3	0.04446	9.35738	0.00000608	0.15047	0.02333	0.10702
4	0.00090246	65.67727	0.99820	0.04274	0.96038	0.89246

The REG Procedure
Model: MODEL1
Dependent Variable: resttcost

Test of First and Second
Moment Specification

DF	Chi-Square	Pr > ChiSq
9	13.09	0.1588

5.3   Translog Functional Form

The translog cost function is

$$C = a_0 y^{a_y} \prod_{i=1}^{N} w_i^{a_i} \, y^{\frac{1}{2}a_{yy} \ln y} \prod_{i=1}^{N} w_i^{a_{iy} \ln y} \prod_{i=1}^{N} w_i^{\frac{1}{2}\sum_{j=1}^{N} a_{ij} \ln w_j} \qquad (5.10)$$

Just as in the theory of cost, this functional form for the cost function takes **w** and y as its inputs and returns minimum cost. N is the total number of inputs to production and the a's are the parameters of the function. It may not be apparent from equation 5.10, but the translog form nests the Cobb-Douglas form. If all a_{ij} and a_{iy} are zero, then the translog form reduces to

$$C = a_0 y^{a_y} \prod_{i=1}^{N} w_i^{a_i} \qquad (5.11)$$

This is simply a Cobb-Douglas cost function. As the Cobb-Douglas is nested within the translog form, we can think of the translog as a more general and more flexible version of the Cobb-Douglas.

One disadvantage of 5.10 is that the function is not linear in its parameters. Because of this, it is rather difficult to interpret the effects of the parameters. A standard technique when dealing with power functions like the translog cost function is to take logarithms. The resulting function is linear in parameters and standard statistical techniques can be used for estimation.

$$\ln C = a_0 + \sum_{i=1}^{N} a_i \ln w_i + a_y \ln y + \frac{1}{2} \sum_{i=1}^{N} \sum_{j=1}^{N} a_{ij} \ln w_i w_j + \sum_{i=1}^{N} a_{iy} \ln w_i \ln y + \frac{1}{2} a_{yy} \ln y \ln y \qquad (5.12)$$

While it is possible to include terms to account for technological progress in the translog cost function, the specification given in equation 5.12 implies that cost is independent of time. Using Shepherd's lemma, the factor demand equations can be derived as

$$s_i = a_i + a_{iy} \ln y + \sum_{j=1}^{N} a_{ij} \ln w_j \qquad (5.13)$$

where $s_i = \frac{w_i x_i}{C}$ is the cost share of the ith input. The result of this derivation is a system of $N + 1$ equations consisting of N derived demand equations and one cost function.

Several theoretical restrictions can be imposed on this functional form; these restrictions are often curvature constraints. We assumed the cost function was continuous and one restriction, via Young's Theorem, is that symmetry of second derivatives implies $a_{ij} = a_{ji}$. Homogeneity of the first degree requires $\sum_{i=1}^{N} a_i = 1$, $\sum_{j=1}^{N} a_{ij} = 0$, and $\sum_{i=1}^{N} a_{iy} = 0$ for all i. It is also possible to impose constant returns to scale – equivalent to imposing homogeneity in y – and details of this procedure can be found in Diewert and Wales (1987). Global concavity can also be imposed on this specification by forcing the matrix of $[a_{ij}]$ to be negative semidefinite. A technique for accomplishing this is given by Jorgenson (1986). This procedure tends to restrict the price elasticities in an undesirable way and destroys the flexibility of the form. Because of these drawbacks, it is rare to find applications of the translog cost function where concavity has been imposed.

The aim of econometric analysis is often to evaluate various elasticities. Depending on the functional form chosen, formulas for elasticities of substitution and price elasticities will depend on certain parameters of the model. Price elasticities of demand are

$$\eta_{ij} = \frac{a_{ij}}{s_i} + s_j \qquad (5.14)$$

for all $i \neq j$ and

$$\eta_{ii} = \frac{a_{ii}}{s_i} + s_i - 1 \qquad (5.15)$$

for all i.

Hicks-Allen elasticities of substitution are given by

$$\sigma_{ij} = \frac{1}{s_i s_j} a_{ij} + 1 \qquad (5.16)$$

for all $i \neq j$ and

$$\sigma_{ii} = \frac{1}{s_i^2} a_{ii} s_i^2 - s_i \qquad (5.17)$$

for all i.

Morishima elasticities of substitution are simply computed as

$$\sigma_{ij}^{M} = \eta_{ij} - \eta_{jj} \tag{5.18}$$

To complete the econometric model, an error term is appended to the N+1 equations of the system. At first glance, it may seem that the factor demands are completely unrelated. If this was the case, each equation could be estimated by ordinary least squares under standard assumptions. However, the fact that the cost shares of the factor demand equations must add to one restricts the sum of the error terms to zero. The errors are not independently distributed in this case and one of the basic assumptions of ordinary least squares is violated. This correlation among errors suggests that an efficient way to estimate the system is through the use of seemingly unrelated regression.

5.3.1 Empirical Analysis

Economic theory was used in formulating our econometric model and an appropriate statistical method for estimation has been suggested. To complete our econometric analysis, the model must be applied to data. In this example, the translog cost function is used to study production relationships in the United States textiles manufacturing sector (standard industrial classification code 22). The goal is to obtain price elasticities, Hicks-Allen elasticities of substitution, and Morishima elasticities of substitution for five different aggregate inputs. These elasticities capture information about how the industry's input use changes as the price of an input is varied or the use of another input is varied. The data is a subset of the Multifactor Productivity Data set available from the Bureau of Labor Statistics. The time series runs from 1949 to 2001 and contains real quantity indices, real price indices, and real cost measures for a single aggregate industry output and five aggregate inputs: capital (K), labor (L), energy (E), materials (M), and services (S). The original data set, and information on other industrial sectors, can be obtained from the Multifactor Productivity Home Page at http://www.bls.gov/mfp/.

To check that the data has been read correctly, the PRINT procedure is used to print the data set.

```
proc print data = klems(obs = 10);
run;
```

Figure 5.6 shows the first 10 observations of the KLEMS data for textile manufacturing in the United States. In each year, we have information on various quantity indices and price indices for the output and five inputs. Both the quantity and price indices are normalized to a value of 100 in 1996. The final six variables correspond, respectively, to the total value of production and individual factor costs as measured in billions of current dollars.

Figure 5.6 The Data

Obs	year	y	k	l	e	m	s	py	pk	pl	pe	pm	ps	vy	vk	vl	ve	vm	vs
1	1949	26.5	67.1	179.3	50.1	39.2	26.4	43.8	23.7	9.4	17.1	21.8	13.6	6.978	1.047	3.271	0.198	2.279	0.183
2	1950	29.6	70.0	198.6	53.5	45.8	34.9	47.0	21.7	10.0	17.6	24.8	13.9	8.336	0.996	3.847	0.217	3.030	0.247
3	1951	30.0	72.0	192.0	54.5	48.7	36.5	52.9	30.3	10.1	16.6	29.6	14.7	9.506	1.432	3.743	0.208	3.850	0.272
4	1952	30.7	71.6	181.7	56.8	49.3	34.1	46.5	21.3	10.6	16.9	25.3	15.7	8.552	1.004	3.729	0.221	3.326	0.272
5	1953	31.5	69.3	180.4	56.0	52.7	35.2	45.0	18.1	11.1	18.1	23.3	16.6	8.495	0.824	3.853	0.234	3.287	0.297
6	1954	29.0	68.5	159.7	50.8	45.3	32.0	43.0	5.9	12.3	17.1	24.2	17.0	7.480	0.264	3.808	0.200	2.930	0.278
7	1955	32.7	68.1	167.9	56.4	52.7	37.0	43.2	19.9	11.3	16.7	23.8	17.5	8.461	0.889	3.670	0.217	3.355	0.329
8	1956	32.6	68.3	163.4	56.6	51.9	36.9	43.0	20.2	11.8	17.2	23.3	18.2	8.421	0.908	3.716	0.224	3.232	0.342
9	1957	31.8	67.1	152.5	53.2	49.1	37.0	42.8	18.6	12.3	17.8	24.0	18.7	8.165	0.820	3.633	0.218	3.142	0.353
10	1958	31.3	64.6	141.8	53.0	47.2	35.8	41.5	19.7	12.7	17.1	23.0	19.7	7.790	0.837	3.490	0.208	2.898	0.358

Now that the data has been verified, it is necessary to manipulate and transform the data to meet the requirements of the translog specification. We need to use the individual factor costs and total cost to calculate the cost shares as required.

```
data klems;
set klems;
   array values {5} vk vl ve vm vs;
   array costshares {5} sk sl se sm ss;
   cost = sum(vk,vl,ve,vm,vs);
   do i = 1 to 5;
     costshares{i} = values{i}/cost;
   end;
run;
```

Data manipulation is typically accomplished in a DATA step as shown above. A number of functions are available to assist users in transforming their data. The SUM function is used to return the sum of its arguments. Array operations can be used to efficiently compute the cost shares and are generally a concise means of performing repeated calculations.

Plotting the quantity indices, price indices, and cost shares over time will give us a sense of the dynamics of the U.S. textiles sector. The SGPLOT procedure enables SAS users to produce and customize a variety of statistical graphics.

```
proc sgplot data = klems;
   series x = year y = k / markers markerattrs =(symbol=circle);
   series x = year y = l / markers markerattrs =(symbol=square);
   series x = year y = e / markers markerattrs =(symbol=star);
   series x = year y = m / markers markerattrs =(symbol=diamond);
   series x = year y = s / markers markerattrs =(symbol=hash);
   title 'Factor Quantities';
   yaxis label = 'Quantity';
run;

proc sgplot data = klems;
   series x = year y = pk / markers markerattrs =(symbol=circle);
   series x = year y = pl / markers markerattrs =(symbol=square);
   series x = year y = pe / markers markerattrs =(symbol=star);
   series x = year y = pm / markers markerattrs =(symbol=diamond);
   series x = year y = ps / markers markerattrs =(symbol=hash);
   title 'Factor Prices';
   yaxis label = 'Price';
run;

proc sgplot data = klems;
   series x = year y = sk / markers markerattrs =(symbol=circle);
   series x = year y = sl / markers markerattrs =(symbol=square);
   series x = year y = se / markers markerattrs =(symbol=star);
   series x = year y = sm / markers markerattrs =(symbol=diamond);
   series x = year y = ss / markers markerattrs =(symbol=hash);
   title 'Factor Cost Shares';
   yaxis label = 'Cost Share';
run;
```

The SERIES statement in this procedure instructs SAS to construct a line plot, while the MARKERS option adds data point markers to the plot. Producing multiple line plots on a single graph is as easy as adding additional SERIES statements. To ensure readability when graphics are printed in black and white, it is advisable to use different symbols to mark each series. The TITLE statement specifies the title of the graphic that PROC SGPLOT produces and you can specify a label for either axis with a simple label option. The graphs produced by our code can be seen in Figure 5.7.

Figure 5.7 Changes in Variables Over Time

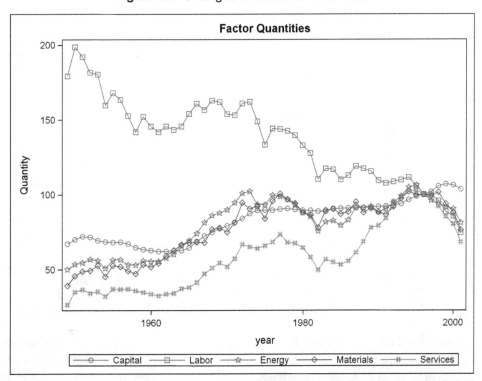

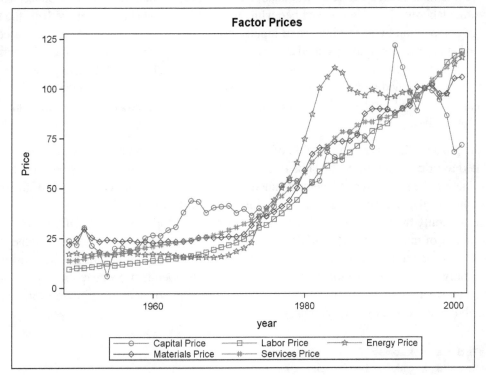

Figure 5.7 *continued*

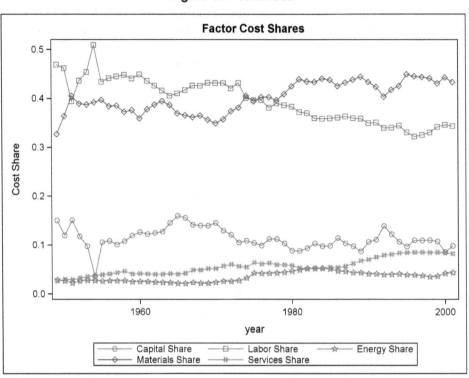

This initial exploration of the data indicates that the sector has seen significant changes in input use over time. Textiles manufacturing was once a significant part of total manufacturing output in the United States. As international trade increased, many textile mills moved overseas where labor costs are lower than in the United States. The first graph in Figure 5.7 shows that labor use has steadily declined while use of other inputs has grown. Perhaps the textile industry adjusted to foreign competition by increasing use of inputs besides labor. The price of energy increased rapidly in the 1970s, reflecting what has commonly been called the "energy crisis." Note that as energy prices increased, energy use remained flat or declined slightly. The result of these two movements is a higher cost share for energy in general. As labor use and cost shares declined in the sector, there were nearly coincident increases in the quantity indices and cost shares of capital and purchased services. This relationship suggests that capital and services may substitute for labor in the production of textiles.

Unfortunately, the plots produced are not capable of providing complete answers to our questions of interest. How is input use related to price? Can inputs be substituted for one another and to what degree? Both of these can be answered by estimating the parameters of the cost function and factor demands. One benefit of the translog form is that the factor demands give nearly the same information as the cost function. It is not necessary to estimate both sets of equations and only the factor demands are estimated in what follows. The MODEL procedure is capable of estimating a variety of models and is particularly useful when estimating systems of equations. In this case, the MODEL procedure is used to fit four factor demand equations. One of the equations has been arbitrarily dropped from estimation; only $N - 1$ of the factor demands are linearly independent because the dependent variables are cost shares which must sum to one. The parameters of the dropped factor demand equation can be recovered after estimation through the homogeneity and symmetry restrictions.

```
proc model data = klems;
    parameters a_k gkk gkl gke gkm gks gky
               a_l glk gll gle glm gls gly
               a_e gek gel gee gem ges gey
               a_m gmk gml gme gmm gms gmy;
    endogenous sk sl se sm;
```

```
exogenous pk pl pe pm ps y;

sk = a_k + gkk*log(pk) + gkl*log(pl) + gke*log(pe) + gkm*log(pm) + gks*log(ps)
         + gky*log(y);
sl = a_l + glk*log(pk) + gll*log(pl) + gle*log(pe) + glm*log(pm) + gls*log(ps)
         + gly*log(y);
se = a_e + gek*log(pk) + gel*log(pl) + gee*log(pe) + gem*log(pm) + ges*log(ps)
         + gey*log(y);
sm = a_m + gmk*log(pk) + gml*log(pl) + gme*log(pe) + gmm*log(pm) + gms*log(ps)
         + gmy*log(y);

fit sk sl se sm / itsur;

label a_k = "SK Intercept"
      a_l = "SL Intercept"
      a_e = "SE Intercept"
      a_m = "SM Intercept"
      gkk = "SK K Price"
      gkl = "SK L Price"
      gke = "SK E Price"
      gkm = "SK M Price"
      gks = "SK S Price"
      gky = "SK Output"
      glk = "SL K Price"
      gll = "SL L Price"
      gle = "SL E Price"
      glm = "SL M Price"
      gls = "SL S Price"
      gly = "SL Output"
      gek = "SE K Price"
      gel = "SE L Price"
      gee = "SE E Price"
      gem = "SE M Price"
      ges = "SE S Price"
      gey = "SE Output"
      gmk = "SM K Price"
      gml = "SM L Price"
      gme = "SM E Price"
      gmm = "SM M Price"
      gms = "SM S Price"
      gmy = "SM Output";
run;
```

The DATA= option specifies the data set that the procedure should utilize. The next three statements specify the parameters and variables of the model. The PARAMETERS statement is used to specify the parameters of the model, the ENDOGENOUS statement specifies the endogenous variables, and the EXOGENOUS statement specifies the exogenous variables. (In fact there are several ways to make these statements. PARMS could be used instead of PARAMETERS for example.)

Next, the system of equations that is estimated is explicitly stated in the body of PROC MODEL. The FIT statement tells SAS which equations to estimate. The ITSUR option on the FIT statement specifies the estimation method as iterated seemingly unrelated regression. A method that was suggested by our consideration of the relationship between the error terms of the system.

It is common for factor demand systems to be estimated both with and without restrictions. Tests can then be undertaken to determine whether the estimates adhere to such restrictions. A TEST statement can be used in the body of the MODEL procedure to specify a wide variety of statistical tests for linear hypotheses. The relationship being tested (the hypothesis) is stated explicitly and the LR option specifies that the type of test to be performed is a likelihood ratio test. The first two TEST statements below are individual tests of homogeneity and symmetry respectively. The final TEST statement is a joint test of these hypotheses.

```
test "Homogeneity"
        gkk+gkl+gke+gkm+gks=0,
        glk+gll+gle+glm+gls=0,
        gek+gel+gee+gem+ges=0,
        gmk+gml+gme+gmm+gms=0, / lr;

    test "Symmetry"
        gkl-glk=0,
        gke-gek=0,
        gkm-gmk=0,
        glm-gml=0,
        gle-gel=0,
        gem-gme=0, / lr;

    test "Joint Homogeneity and Symmetry"
        gkk+gkl+gke+gkm+gks=0,
        glk+gll+gle+glm+gls=0,
        gek+gel+gee+gem+ges=0,
        gmk+gml+gme+gmm+gms=0,
        gkl-glk=0,
        gke-gek=0,
        gkm-gmk=0,
        glm-gml=0,
        gle-gel=0,
        gem-gme=0, / lr;
```

Most of the output of immediate interest is contained in the ITSUR estimation summary. Some of this information can be found in the model summary as well, but the results presented here are crucial to the analysis of our model. To form estimated elasticities, you need parameter estimates. To evaluate the fit of the share equations, we will also need fit statistics.

The summary of residual errors provides fit statistics for each of the estimated demand equations and is shown in Figure 5.8. In this case, our model achieves a good fit to the data based on R-squared values. It is common to find high values of the coefficient of determination when fitting a model to time series data.

Figure 5.8 Residual Summary

The MODEL Procedure

			Nonlinear ITSUR Summary of Residual Errors					
Equation	DF Model	DF Error	SSE	MSE	Root MSE	R-Square	Adj R-Sq	Label
sk	7	46	0.00118	0.000026	0.00506	0.9519	0.9457	Capital Share
sl	7	46	0.00449	0.000098	0.00988	0.9565	0.9508	Labor Share
se	7	46	0.000079	1.724E-6	0.00131	0.9847	0.9827	Energy Share
sm	7	46	0.00436	0.000095	0.00973	0.9146	0.9035	Materials Share

Because the form of the elasticities is somewhat complicated, it can be difficult to interpret the meaning for the values and signs of parameter estimates. It is far easier to proceed by computing the elasticities themselves, an approach that will be taken shortly.

Figure 5.9 Parameter Estimates

Nonlinear ITSUR Parameter Estimates

Parameter	Estimate	Approx Std Err	t Value	Approx Pr > |t|	Label
a_k	0.265024	0.0436	6.08	<.0001	SK Intercept
gkk	0.077342	0.00346	22.33	<.0001	SK K Price
gkl	0.056493	0.0219	2.57	0.0133	SK L Price
gke	-0.01476	0.00445	-3.31	0.0018	SK E Price
gkm	-0.03719	0.0108	-3.46	0.0012	SK M Price
gks	-0.05723	0.0208	-2.75	0.0084	SK S Price
gky	-0.05793	0.0106	-5.45	<.0001	SK Output
a_l	0.837496	0.0851	9.84	<.0001	SL Intercept
glk	-0.03843	0.00677	-5.68	<.0001	SL K Price
gll	0.11056	0.0429	2.58	0.0132	SL L Price
gle	0.007116	0.00871	0.82	0.4179	SL E Price
glm	-0.07052	0.0210	-3.35	0.0016	SL M Price
gls	-0.10667	0.0406	-2.63	0.0117	SL S Price
gly	-0.01126	0.0208	-0.54	0.5906	SL Output
a_e	-0.00481	0.0113	-0.43	0.6728	SE Intercept
gek	-0.00296	0.000899	-3.29	0.0019	SE K Price
gel	-0.01281	0.00570	-2.25	0.0294	SE L Price
gee	0.030617	0.00116	26.47	<.0001	SE E Price
gem	-0.01889	0.00279	-6.76	<.0001	SE M Price
ges	0.004105	0.00539	0.76	0.4506	SE S Price
gey	0.009433	0.00276	3.41	0.0013	SE Output
a_m	-0.19096	0.0839	-2.28	0.0275	SM Intercept
gmk	-0.03517	0.00667	-5.28	<.0001	SM K Price
gml	-0.25166	0.0422	-5.96	<.0001	SM L Price
gme	-0.00433	0.00858	-0.50	0.6161	SM E Price
gmm	0.136081	0.0207	6.57	<.0001	SM M Price
gms	0.218672	0.0400	5.47	<.0001	SM S Price
gmy	0.072446	0.0205	3.54	0.0009	SM Output

The tests results in Figure 5.10 indicate that both symmetry and homogeneity are rejected. This result is not unusual and many studies proceed by imposing these constraints. This only requires a slight adjustment of the MODEL procedure.

Figure 5.10 Tests of Symmetry and Homogeneity

Test Results

Test	Type	Statistic	Pr > ChiSq	Label
Homogeneity	L.R.	114.22	<.0001	gkk+gkl+gke+gkm+gks=0, glk+gll+gle+glm+gls=0, gek+gel+gee+gem+ges=0, gmk+gml+gme+gmm+gms=0
Symmetry	L.R.	109.72	<.0001	gkl-glk=0, gke-gek=0, gkm-gmk=0, glm-gml=0, gle-gel=0, gem-gme=0
Joint Homogeneity and Symmetry	L.R.	240.80	<.0001	gkk+gkl+gke+gkm+gks=0, glk+gll+gle+glm+gls=0, gek+gel+gee+gem+ges=0, gmk+gml+gme+gmm+gms=0, gkl-glk=0, gke-gek=0, gkm-gmk=0, glm-gml=0, gle-gel=0, gem-gme=0

The following code introduces both symmetry and homogeneity restrictions to the underlying model.

```
proc model data = klems;
    parameters a_k gkk gkl gke gkm gks gky
               a_l glk gll gle glm gls gly
               a_e gek gel gee gem ges gey
               a_m gmk gml gme gmm gms gmy;
    endogenous sk sl se sm;
    exogenous pk pl pe pm ps y;
    restrict gks=0-gkk-gkl-gke-gkm,
             gls=0-gkl-gll-gle-glm,
             ges=0-gke-gle-gee-gem,
             gms=0-gkm-glm-gem-gmm,
             gkl=glk, gke=gek, gkm=gmk, gle=gel, glm=gml, gem=gme;

    sk = a_k + gkk*log(pk) + gkl*log(pl) + gke*log(pe) + gkm*log(pm) + gks*log(ps)
             + gky*log(y);
    sl = a_l + glk*log(pk) + gll*log(pl) + gle*log(pe) + glm*log(pm) + gls*log(ps)
             + gly*log(y);
    se = a_e + gek*log(pk) + gel*log(pl) + gee*log(pe) + gem*log(pm) + ges*log(ps)
             + gey*log(y);
    sm = a_m + gmk*log(pk) + gml*log(pl) + gme*log(pe) + gmm*log(pm) + gms*log(ps)
             + gmy*log(y);

    fit sk sl se sm / itsur chow = (24) outest=est;

    test "Constant Returns to Scale"
        gky=0,
        gly=0,
        gey=0,
        gmy=0, / lr;
run;
```

The linear restrictions are imposed with a RESTRICT statement. The symmetry restriction shrinks the number of parameters of the model considerably. This is particularly useful in cases where the time series is not long and we wish to conserve degrees of freedom. Linear homogeneity has also been imposed. Figure 5.11 shows the primary results of the MODEL procedure.

Figure 5.11 The Restricted Model

The MODEL Procedure

Model Summary	
Model Variables	10
Endogenous	4
Exogenous	6
Parameters	28
Equations	4
Number of Statements	20

Figure 5.11 *continued*

Parameter	Estimate	Approx Std Err	t Value	Approx Pr > |t|	Label
a_k	0.109996	0.0219	5.02	<.0001	SK Intercept
gkk	0.062014	0.00357	17.38	<.0001	SK K Price
gkl	-0.01898	0.00725	-2.62	0.0118	SK L Price
gke	-0.00179	0.000836	-2.15	0.0369	SK E Price
gkm	-0.03872	0.00610	-6.35	<.0001	SK M Price
gks	-0.00252	0.00342	-0.74	0.4648	SK S Price
gky	-0.00104	0.00496	-0.21	0.8354	SK Output
a_l	0.865473	0.0903	9.58	<.0001	SL Intercept
glk	-0.01898	0.00725	-2.62	0.0118	SL K Price
gll	-0.00999	0.0360	-0.28	0.7826	SL L Price
gle	-0.00106	0.00420	-0.25	0.8013	SL E Price
glm	-0.06766	0.0248	-2.73	0.0087	SL M Price
gls	0.097692	0.0214	4.57	<.0001	SL S Price
gly	-0.11488	0.0200	-5.74	<.0001	SL Output
a_e	0.012747	0.00984	1.30	0.2013	SE Intercept
gek	-0.00179	0.000836	-2.15	0.0370	SE K Price
gel	-0.00106	0.00420	-0.25	0.8013	SE L Price
gee	0.029876	0.00112	26.76	<.0001	SE E Price
gem	-0.01954	0.00275	-7.12	<.0001	SE M Price
ges	-0.00748	0.00325	-2.30	0.0257	SE S Price
gey	0.005808	0.00217	2.68	0.0101	SE Output
a_m	-0.08173	0.0701	-1.17	0.2492	SM Intercept
gmk	-0.03872	0.00610	-6.35	<.0001	SM K Price
gml	-0.06766	0.0248	-2.73	0.0087	SM L Price
gme	-0.01954	0.00275	-7.12	<.0001	SM E Price
gmm	0.146849	0.0222	6.62	<.0001	SM M Price
gms	-0.02092	0.0103	-2.03	0.0477	SM S Price
gmy	0.113729	0.0157	7.27	<.0001	SM Output
Restrict0	-563.453	242.8	-2.32	0.0187	gks=0-gkk-gkl-gke-gkm
Restrict1	82.23307	193.0	0.43	0.6747	gls=0-gkl-gll-gle-glm
Restrict2	321.7446	689.2	0.47	0.6455	ges=0-gke-gle-gee-gem
Restrict3	-279.71	211.0	-1.33	0.1879	gms=0-gkm-glm-gem-gmm
Restrict4	-261.228	196.3	-1.33	0.1860	gkl=glk
Restrict5	-1041.84	755.0	-1.38	0.1700	gke=gek
Restrict6	-27.855	219.3	-0.13	0.9005	gkm=gmk
Restrict7	-880.821	742.7	-1.19	0.2396	gle=gel
Restrict8	259.513	215.6	1.20	0.2326	glm=gml
Restrict9	1103.343	320.8	3.44	0.0003	gem=gme

The majority of the parameter estimates are significant. Remember however that insignificant parameters are statistically equivalent to zero. When the g_{ij} are all zero, we saw that the translog cost function reduced to the Cobb-Douglas cost function. Statistically insignificant parameter estimates imply that corresponding elasticities of substitution are equal to the Cobb-Douglas value of one.

A TEST statement is used to determine whether this industry exhibits constant returns to scale in the range of the sample. A CHOW option has also been added to the FIT statement. This option tells SAS to perform a Chow Test for a structural break occuring at the twenty-fourth year of the sample. The twenty-fourth year of the sample is 1973; in

October of that year OPEC declared an oil embargo. Markets were affected by significant shocks to oil prices and in the United States gasoline was rationed. The results of the two tests can be seen in Figure 5.12.

Figure 5.12 CRS and Chow Test Results

	Test Results			
Test	Type	Statistic	Pr > ChiSq	Label
Constant Returns to Scale	L.R.	74.27	<.0001	gky=0, gly=0, gey=0, gmy=0

	Structural Change Test				
Test	Break Point	Num DF	Den DF	F Value	Pr > F
Chow	24	23	2	0.28	0.9560

The null hypothesis of constant returns to scale is rejected. The null hypothesis of the Chow Test cannot be rejected. Even with the turmoil of the oil embargo, there is no evidence of a structural break in 1973.

To generate elasticities, the IML procedure is used. Because the elasticities will be evaluated at the sample mean, the MEANS procedure is first used to produce a data set containing the sample means of the cost shares. The first two blocks of code tell SAS to open a given SAS data set and then read all instances of a given variable or parameter value into a vector. Because the quantities of interest have unique values, each instance is read into a 1×1 matrix.

Because some of the parameters were not estimated, their values can be backed out through application of the homogeneity restrictions. Just like a DATA step, there are a number of functions available to the user in PROC IML. The NCOL function is used to return the number of columns of the gij matrix. DO loops are used to assign specific values to matrices for the elasticities.

```
proc means data = klems noprint mean;
   var sk sl se sm ss;
   output out = meanshares mean = ;
run;


proc iml;
   use est;
   read all var {gkk gkl gke gkm gks gll gle glm gls gee gem ges gmm gms};
   close est;

   gss=0-gks-gls-ges-gms;

   use meanshares;
   read all var {sk sl se sm ss};
   close meanshares;

   w = sk//sl//se//sm//ss;

   print w;


   gij = (gkk||gkl||gke||gkm||gks)//
         (gkl||gll||gle||glm||gls)//
         (gke||gle||gee||gem||ges)//
         (gkm||glm||gem||gmm||gms)//
         (gks||gls||ges||gms||gss);
```

```
print gij;

nk=ncol(gij);
mi = -1#I(nk);
eos = j(nk,nk,0);
mos = j(nk,nk,0);
ep  = j(nk,nk,0);

do i=1 to nk;
do j=1 to nk;
    eos[i,j] = (gij[i,j]+w[i]#w[j]+mi[i,j]#w[i])/(w[i]#w[j]);
    ep[i,j] = w[j]#eos[i,j];
end;
end;

i=1;
do i=1 to nk;
j=1;
do j=1 to nk;
    mos[i,j] = ep[i,j]-ep[j,j];
end;
end;

factors = {"Capital" "Labor" "Energy" "Materials" "Services"};
print
    ep[ label="Price Elasticities of Demand" rowname=factors
        colname=factors format=d7.3],
    eos[label="Hicks-Allen Elasticities of Substitution" rowname=factors
        colname=factors format=d7.3],
    mos[label="Morishima Elasticities of Substitution" rowname=factors
        colname=factors format=d7.3];

quit;
```

The last piece of IML code prints the matrices containing price elasticities and elasticities of substitution which are shown in Figure 5.13. All of the own price elasticities have a negative sign. Services are particularly elastic, while energy is relatively inelastic. In other words, the factor demand for services is more responsive to changes in own-price than the factor demand for energy. As we saw, the formula for the elasticities of substitution depends on the cost share of the factor as well. Substitution relationships can then most easily be determined by examining the Hicks-Allen and Morishima elasticities directly.

With the Hicks-Allen measure, substitutability holds for all of the inputs except energy and services and energy and materials. By design, the matrix of Hicks-Allen elasticities is symmetric. In general, the degree of substitution is not particularly high except in the case of labor and services. This indicates that the textile industry has responded to increased competition from foreign firms with low labor cost by substituting away from labor to greater use of services. The Morishima elasticities support this interpretation, but the magnitudes of these elasticities seem more reasonable. Virtually all inputs are substitutes under this measure.

Figure 5.13 Elasticity Matrices

Price Elasticities of Demand				
	Capital	Labor	Energy	Materials	Services
Capital	-0.338	0.227	0.0183	0.0593	0.0335
Labor	0.0650	-0.630	0.0315	0.231	0.303
Energy	0.0606	0.364	-0.0915	-0.170	-0.163
Materials	0.0167	0.227	-0.0145	-0.233	0.00367
Services	0.0679	2.148	-0.1000	0.0265	-2.142

Hicks-Allen Elasticities of Substitution				
	Capital	Labor	Energy	Materials	Services
Capital	-2.993	0.575	0.536	0.148	0.600
Labor	0.575	-1.594	0.921	0.574	5.435
Energy	0.536	0.921	-2.679	-0.423	-2.925
Materials	0.148	0.574	-0.423	-0.579	0.0658
Services	0.600	5.435	-2.925	0.0658	-38.437

Morishima Elasticities of Substitution				
	Capital	Labor	Energy	Materials	Services
Capital	0	0.857	0.110	0.292	2.176
Labor	0.403	0	0.123	0.463	2.445
Energy	0.399	0.994	0	0.0627	1.979
Materials	0.355	0.857	0.0771	0	2.146
Services	0.406	2.778	-0.0084	0.259	0

5.4   Frontier Production Functions

A number of caveats apply to standard empirical models of production. Production functions estimated by standard ordinary least squares techniques may suffer from important specification biases that result from, among other factors, the treatment of inputs (e.g., inputs that are risk reducing rather than mean increasing) and from the characterization of technology. More specifically, production functions define an efficient frontier, with individual observations being on or beneath this frontier. The technical factors that underlie the characterization of the relationships among inputs and outputs generally define the maximum possible output that may be derived from a given set of inputs. In recent years, an extensive literature has developed to consider departures from an efficient frontier representing maximum possible output and determinants of such deviations. Much of this discussion draws heavily from the survey of Battese (1992). An extensive review of applications in agricultural economics is presented in his work.

A convenient pedagogical tool for considering frontier production functions can be derived by considering the production function for a single output (holding other factors constant) or equivalently through a unit isoquant. Battese (1992) presents both such expositions. Figure 5.14 illustrates production conditions for two inputs–K and L. The unit isoquant represents the technical frontier in terms of the maximum output that can be obtained from various combinations of K and L. Observed combinations of input/output ratios above the isoquant reflect inefficient levels of production in that more inputs per unit of output are being used than would be technically efficient. For any combination of K/Y and L/Y, a ray from the origin through the point provides an obvious measure of the degree of technical inefficiency. At combination B, the level of technical efficiency (as defined by Farrell (1957)) is $0B/0A$. A fully efficient use of inputs would be represented by combinations on the unit isoquant, which would in turn reflect full technical efficiency with a value of 1.0.

Figure 5.14 Production with Two Inputs

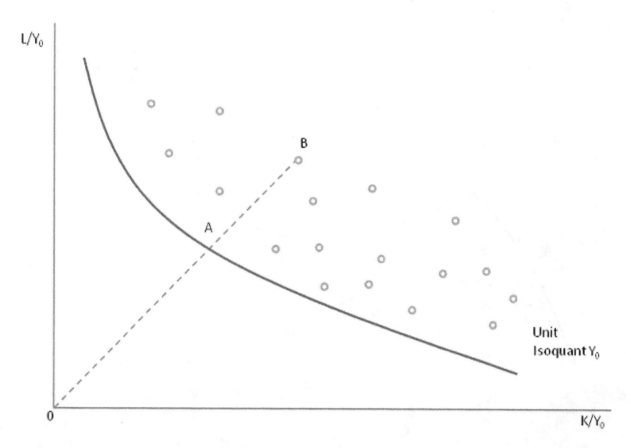

An analogous representation of technical efficiency can be illustrated for a single input by considering the technically-efficient production frontier. Figure 5.15 illustrates the production frontier and observed levels of input usage. In this case, inefficient use of inputs is reflected by levels of corresponding output that are below the frontier. The level of technical efficiency in this case is represented by the ratio of actual output to possible output for a given level of input usage $L^{o}B/L^{o}A$.

Figure 5.15 Production Frontier and Observed Input Use

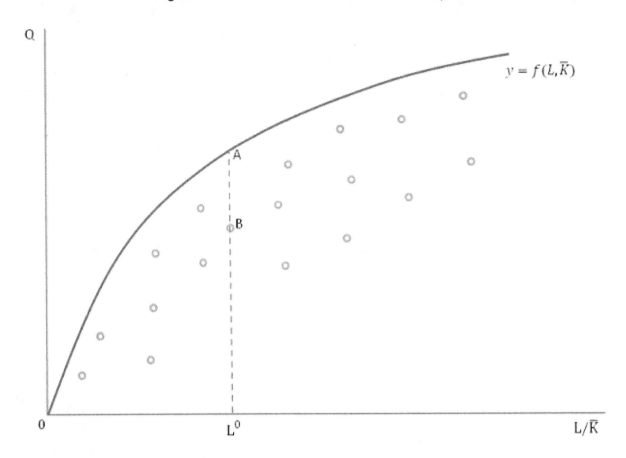

When the randomness of production conditions is considered, departures from the efficient frontier may also arise from stochastic factors such as weather. Stochastic frontier models were initially introduced by Aigner, Lovell, and Schmidt (1977). A standard stochastic production function for firm i is typically defined as

$$Y_i = f(K_i, L_i, \beta) \exp(V_i - U_i) \tag{5.19}$$

where V_i is a mean-zero random error representing stochastic production shocks and U_i is a non-negative random variable that represents the level of technical inefficiency of the firm. In this case, $Y_i = f(K_i, L_i, \beta)$ represents the deterministic production frontier for which $Y_i \leq f(K_i, L_i, \beta)$ must hold. This implies that $exp(-U_i)$ represents a metric of technical (in)efficiency. In Figure 2, this is represented as the ratio of actual output to possible output

$$f(K_i, L_i, \beta)exp(-U_i)/f(K_i, L_i, \beta) = exp(-U_i) = L^o B/L^o A. \tag{5.20}$$

Stochastic frontier models are typically applied to production and cost function estimation. The implications for technical inefficiency are analogous although the efficient frontier is defined as a minimum for a cost function. Extensions to distance functions, as in Atkinson and Dorfman (2005), have also been considered. Alternative specifications for the truncated distribution of the technical efficiency term are commonly applied. The random element of departures from the efficient frontier, V_i, is typically assumed to be normally distributed with a mean of zero and a variance of σ_V^2. The inefficiency term is identified by applying a truncated parametric distribution. Common examples include the half-normal, the exponential, and the truncated normal distribution. PROC QLIM in SAS offers each of these alternatives.

A common analysis often undertaken in conjunction with estimation of a stochastic frontier production or cost function involves an evaluation of the determinants of the estimates of technical efficiency (TE_i). This is usually undertaken using a two-stage analysis whereby the first stage estimates the stochastic frontier and TE_i terms and a second stage estimates a regression of TE_i on observable firm or individual characteristics. Alternatively, a more efficient approach to estimation involves specification of a full likelihood function that incorporates both steps in a single stage. Other extensions include applications of stochastic frontier methods to panel data with fixed and random effects.

5.4.1 Empirical Analysis

We consider an empirical application to panel data collected from Philippine rice farmers. The data were taken from 43 smallholder rice producers in the Tarlac region of the Philippines between 1990 and 1997. These data are presented as a supplement to the text of Coelli et al. (2005). In this case, the data are a balanced panel because each unit of analysis (or farmer in this case) is observed in each year. The data are stored in what is often referred to as long format. Each row of the data set contains one unit of aalysis per unit of time. This is in contrast to wide format, where each row contains information on one unit of analysis at all points in time. First read the data using the IMPORT procedure.

```
proc import file = "ricedata.csv"
   dbms = csv out = rice replace;
   getnames = YES;
run;
```

Variables in the data set are as follow: YEARDUM is a dummy variable for the time period (1= 1990, ..., 8 = 1997); FMERCODE is the individual code for the farm household (1, ..., 43); PROD is output in tons of freshly threshed rice; AREA is the area planted in hectares; LABOR is the labor used in terms of man-days of household and hired labor; NPK is fertilizer used in kilograms of active ingredients; OTHER captures all other inputs using a Laspeyres index which is normalized to 100 for firm 17 in 1991; PRICE which is the output price in pesos per kilogram; AREAP is the renal price of land in pesos per hectare; LABORP is the labor price in pesos per hired man-day, NPKP is fertilizer price in pesos per kilogram of active ingredients, OTHERP is an implicit price index for other inputs; AGE is the age of the household head in years; EDYRS is the education of the household head in years; HHSIZE is the household size; NADULT is the number adults in the household; and BANRAT is the percentage of area classified as bantog (upland) fields. The following code prints the first ten observations.

```
proc print data = rice(obs = 10);
run;
```

The printed data in Figure 5.16 makes the long format evident. Each observation contains information on a different farmer from the first year of the series. Were we to print the whole data set, we could see that the panel data in long format is nothing more than a series of stacked cross-sections. Using PROC MEANS, we obtain summary statistics on this sample of Philippine rice farmers.

```
proc means data = rice;
run;
```

Figure 5.16 Data on Philippine Rice Farmersl

Obs	VAR1	YEARDUM	FMERCODE	PROD	AREA	LABOR	NPK	OTHER	PRICE	AREAP
1	1	1	1	7.87	2.5	161	207.5	52.86376342	5	3821.768014
2	2	1	2	10.35	3.8	184	303.5	284.441761	5	3029.267172
3	3	1	3	9.98	3.4	170	252	77.61649475	5	3413.691547
4	4	1	4	4.83	1.4	68	88	14.2976741	5	4438.461225
5	5	1	5	8.74	3.6	130	149.8	82.67570272	5	2527.746788
6	6	1	6	1.84	0.5	34	21	5.991925653	5	4937.49464
7	7	1	7	7.36	1.75	91	243	37.42882364	5	6173.491997
8	8	1	8	6.67	1.7	114	154.6	34.91877177	5	5493.559363
9	9	1	9	9.2	3	211	166.4	55.46225928	5	3663.165533
10	10	1	10	9.29	3.4	192	253.8	67.53230012	5	3044.593136

Obs	LABORP	NPKP	OTHERP	AGE	EDYRS	HHSIZE	NADULT	BANRAT
1	66.23403727	14.0726747	44.77945945	37	10	7	4	1
2	80.43	15.23901153	10.52802862	35	6	5	2	0.93
3	70.40329412	13.80952381	41.50158215	48	10	5	5	0.58
4	68.50588235	9.886363636	61.17833065	37	6	3	2	0.36
5	81.89538462	13.0670227	31.52229229	48	6	4	4	0.72
6	51.74823529	13.81714286	54.24925455	49	10	3	3	1
7	87.97714286	16.56395062	47.45776545	25	10	3	2	1
8	47.74736842	11.86959897	41.22395855	52	6	8	8	1
9	45.5442654	15.38653846	41.89260914	54	10	6	4	0.5
10	53.60625	13.04113475	31.87092072	62	6	4	2	0.93

A stochastic production frontier is estimated using logarithmic transformations of output and inputs under the assumption that the production function has a log-linear Cobb-Douglas form. We posit a production model where PROD is determined by AREA, LABOR, NPK, and OTHER. As usual, a DATA step is used to take logarithms of the relevant variables.

```
data rice;
set rice;
    lPROD = log(PROD);
    lAREA = log(AREA);
    lLABOR = log(LABOR);
    lNPK = log(NPK);
    lOTHER = log(OTHER);
run;
```

The following code uses PROC QLIM to estimate the stochastic production frontier. The syntax is similar to other procedures but includes a few important options. The MODEL statement confirms that the log of production is being modeled as a linear function of log area, log labor, log fertilizer, and log other (other inputs). The ENDOGENOUS statement specifies that the log of production is the dependent variable and all independent variables are treated as exogenous. The log of production follows a production frontier model, and the TYPE option designates a model with an exponential error term. PROC QLIM also supports stochastic production function models with half-normal and truncated normal errors.The output data set, te, contains two estimates of technical efficiency for every household in the model. Estimates according to Battese, Harter, and Fuller (1988) are stored as te1 and estimates following Jondrow et al. (1982) are stored as te2.

```
proc qlim data = rice;
   model lprod = larea llabor lnpk lother;
   endogenous lprod ~ frontier (type = exponential production);
   output out = te te1 te2;
run;
```

Output from the QLIM procedure is shown in Figure 5.17. Summary statistics for the continuous response variable are displayed along with statistics of fit and other optimization criteria.

Figure 5.17 Stochastic Output

The QLIM Procedure

Summary Statistics of Continuous Responses

Variable	Mean	Standard Error	Type
IPROD	1.55167	0.876518	Frontier (Prod)

Model Fit Summary

Number of Endogenous Variables	1
Endogenous Variable	IPROD
Number of Observations	344
Log Likelihood	-79.75210
Maximum Absolute Gradient	1.29829E-7
Number of Iterations	18
Optimization Method	Quasi-Newton
AIC	173.50420
Schwarz Criterion	200.38870
Sigma	0.32989
Lambda	1.47538

Parameter Estimates

Parameter	DF	Estimate	Standard Error	t Value	Approx Pr > |t|
Intercept	1	-1.193197	0.245085	-4.87	<.0001
IAREA	1	0.325756	0.059923	5.44	<.0001
ILABOR	1	0.333217	0.059914	5.56	<.0001
INPK	1	0.259414	0.034331	7.56	<.0001
IOTHER	1	0.033133	0.017148	1.93	0.0533
_Sigma_v	1	0.185089	0.017356	10.66	<.0001
_Sigma_u	1	0.273076	0.026706	10.23	<.0001

The signs of the coefficients are all positive, in line with what we would expect, and all of the estimates except the coefficient on LOTHER are statistically significant at the 5% level.

Having obtained an estimate of the stochastic frontier model in the preceding code, regression analysis can be used to evaluate those factors affecting technical efficiency. PROG REG can be used for the second stage estimation where technical efficiency is modeled as a function of the farmer age, years of education of the household head, the number of adults in the household, and the percentage of farm area classified as upland fields. In this case, we use the Battese, Harter, and Fuller (1988) estimate as our measure of technical efficiency.

```
proc reg data=te;
   model te1 = AGE EDYRS HHSIZE NADULT BANRAT;
run;
```

The output displayed in Frefsreg1out has several interesting features. The coefficients on AGE, NADULT, and BANRAT are all significant at the 5% level.

Figure 5.18 Regression 1

The REG Procedure
Model: MODEL1
Dependent Variable: TE1 Technical Efficiency Estimate #1

Number of Observations Read	344
Number of Observations Used	344

Root MSE	0.14051	R-Square	0.0474
Dependent Mean	0.78542	Adj R-Sq	0.0333
Coeff Var	17.88957		

Parameter Estimates

Variable	Label	DF	Parameter Estimate	Standard Error	t Value	Pr > |t|
Intercept	Intercept	1	0.79413	0.05931	13.39	<.0001
AGE		1	-0.00176	0.00082804	-2.12	0.0345
EDYRS		1	0.00073531	0.00431	0.17	0.8646
HHSIZE		1	-0.00945	0.00621	-1.52	0.1291
NADULT		1	0.01404	0.00702	2.00	0.0461
BANRAT		1	0.09035	0.02863	3.16	0.0017

The dependent variable in the previous regression, te1, is bounded between 0 and 1. As such, it is preferable to recognize the truncation of this variable when working with the second stage regression. This can be accomplished in PROC QLIM which provides methods for truncated regression, accounting for the bias that is introduced when ordinary least squares is used with truncated data. The MODEL statement specifies the Battese, Harter, and Fuller (1988) estimate of technical efficiency as a linear function of the same independent variables. The TRUNCATED option tells SAS that the dependent variable is truncated at a lower bound of 0 and upper bound of 1.

```
proc qlim data=te;
   model te1 = AGE EDYRS HHSIZE NADULT BANRAT / truncated (lb=0 ub=1);
run;
```

Output in Figure 5.19 provides summary statistics for the continuous response variable, or technical efficiency. Mean technical efficiency in the sample is 0.78 and the variable is truncated between 0 and 1. Accounting for bias related to truncation, the estimates from PROC QLIM shows statistically significant coefficients at the 5% level only for AGE and BANRAT. The coefficients on age indicate that older farmers are less technically efficiency while farms with significant amounts of land classified as upland are more technically efficient.

Figure 5.19 Regression 2

The QLIM Procedure

Summary Statistics of Continuous Responses

Variable	Mean	Standard Error	Type	Lower Bound	Upper Bound	N Obs Lower Bound	N Obs Upper Bound
TE1	0.785419	0.142905	Truncated	0	1		

Model Fit Summary

Number of Endogenous Variables	1
Endogenous Variable	TE1
Number of Observations	344
Log Likelihood	230.04610
Maximum Absolute Gradient	0.00205
Number of Iterations	17
Optimization Method	Quasi-Newton
AIC	-446.09219
Schwarz Criterion	-419.20770

Parameter Estimates

Parameter	DF	Estimate	Standard Error	t Value	Approx Pr > |t|
Intercept	1	0.881696	0.107373	8.21	<.0001
AGE	1	-0.003144	0.001494	-2.10	0.0353
EDYRS	1	0.000953	0.007849	0.12	0.9034
HHSIZE	1	-0.016168	0.010924	-1.48	0.1388
NADULT	1	0.024384	0.012612	1.93	0.0532
BANRAT	1	0.156162	0.051544	3.03	0.0024
_Sigma	1	0.186506	0.013749	13.56	<.0001

The preceding analysis does not account for technical change or time-varying changes in efficiency. In this sense, we have not taken full advantage of the time dimension in the data. As shown in Battese and Coelli (1995), one approach is to include the time dummy as a covariate in the stochastic frontier production function. This accounts for Hicks neutral technological change (change that does not affect the proportion of different inputs in the production function). When the time dummy is also included in the efficiency regressions, changes in inefficiency effects over time can be identified. The following code includes the year dummy in the stochastic frontier estimation to account for technical change.

```
proc qlim data = rice;
   model lprod = larea llabor lnpk lother YEARDUM;
   endogenous lprod ~ frontier (type = exponential production);
   output out = te te1 te2;
run;
```

There is, of course, no guarantee that any technological change has occurred. Figure 5.20 shows that output has tended to increase over time. However, the coefficient on the year dummy is not significant. In light of this lack of significance, we should not be surprised that the other coefficient estimates are similar to those of Figure 5.18. The panel model has a lower value of the Akaike Information Criterion but a larger value for the Schwarz Criterion. The simple model without the time trend appears to be sufficient for our analysis of technical efficiency.

Figure 5.20 Stochastic Output

The QLIM Procedure

Summary Statistics of Continuous Responses			
Variable	Mean	Standard Error	Type
IPROD	1.55167	0.876518	Frontier (Prod)

Model Fit Summary	
Number of Endogenous Variables	1
Endogenous Variable	IPROD
Number of Observations	344
Log Likelihood	-78.44827
Maximum Absolute Gradient	2.29716E-7
Number of Iterations	21
Optimization Method	Quasi-Newton
AIC	172.89654
Schwarz Criterion	203.62168
Sigma	0.32974
Lambda	1.50959

Parameter Estimates					
Parameter	DF	Estimate	Standard Error	t Value	Approx Pr > |t|
Intercept	1	-1.245794	0.244580	-5.09	<.0001
IAREA	1	0.331556	0.059463	5.58	<.0001
ILABOR	1	0.349019	0.060124	5.81	<.0001
INPK	1	0.253257	0.034313	7.38	<.0001
IOTHER	1	0.023790	0.017969	1.32	0.1855
YEARDUM	1	0.011057	0.006811	1.62	0.1045
_Sigma_v	1	0.182100	0.017188	10.59	<.0001
_Sigma_u	1	0.274897	0.026515	10.37	<.0001

Thus ends our treatment of the theory of supply; it may also be called the theory of production. We have covered empirical models using both aggregate and firm level data. The applications made use of the Cobb-Douglas and translogarithmic functional forms. As with our empirical examples related to demand, the reader would be well-advised to consider alternate functional forms beyond those discussed here. Economists have been able to move closer to ideal forms and consider interesting new empirical questions. One example is the two-stage production technology of Pollak and Walkes (1987). Another is the relationship between aggregate productivity growth and firm level productivity as examined in Petrin and Levinsohn (2012). In any event, the theory and empirical methods presented in this chapter form the basis of much contemporary work in production analysis.

Chapter 6
Empirical Approaches to Risk

Contents

6.1	Overview	**113**
6.2	Frequency and Severity Modeling	**114**
	6.2.1 Compound Distribution Model	115
	6.2.2 Empirical Analysis	116
6.3	Agricultural Insurance	**124**
	6.3.1 Yield Insurance	125
	6.3.2 Empirical Analysis	125
	6.3.3 Revenue Insurance	142
	6.3.4 Dependence and Copulas	143
	6.3.5 Empirical Analysis	146

6.1 Overview

At its core, all econometric analysis deals with relationships among stochastic variables. A central paradigm of the behavior of individuals acting under conditions of uncertainty is risk aversion. Individual agents facing uncertainty are typically assumed to undertake actions or positive expenditures to avoid risk. Much of the recent research in applied agricultural economics addresses the evaluation of risk and agents' reactions to uncertainty. The Knightian distinction between risk and uncertainty is a meaningful issue, especially as one considers models of risk management mechanisms. Frank Knight made the distinction that risk, a situation in which the outcome of a given event may be uncertain but the underlying probabilistic framework characterizing the behavior of the events is known, is different from uncertainty–a case where one neither knows the outcome of random processes or the underlying probabilities associated with the random variables of interest. The most prominent example of this distinction comes from gambling markets. In the case of games of chance involving a roulette wheel, dice, or a deck of cards, the probabilistic framework is known with certainty. A standard American roulette wheel has 38 numbers, including 0, 00, and numbers 1-36. The house always wins when a 0 or 00 is hit and thus has a 2/38 = 5.26% advantage in any single number wager. This illustrates a case of risk with no uncertainty. In contrast, parimutuel gambling such as wagers in a horse race, involves payouts that are based upon the composition of wagers in the entire pool. In such a case, the probabilities, as reflected in the parimutuel odds, are unknown until all wagers are made. Gamblers in such a situation are facing both risk and uncertainty.

Much of the risk modeling work in applied agricultural economics involves problems similar to those encountered by the parimutuel bettor. The modeler's task is often to empirically assess the uncertain probabilistic framework underlying risk. Actuarial analysis of insurance contracts is a prime example. The analysis typically seeks to empirically model the probabilistic framework underlying the contingencies being covered by the insurance contract. The range of economic issues and instruments that is modeled is immense, including futures and options contracts, marketing and production contracts, and insurance of all kinds.

Research on insurance has become a central topic in agricultural economics over the last two decades. A highly subsidized federal crop insurance program has existed in the United States since 1938. However, it has recently become the primary mechanism for supporting production agriculture and subsidizing the risks faced by producers. Legislation in 1994, 2000, and 2012 brought about significant changes to the program that boosted participation to about 85% of all crop acreage in the US. The program typically has over $100 billion in total liability and costs US taxpayers about $10 billion annually. Subsidized crop insurance programs have proliferated around the world with programs being introduced throughout the developed and developing world. This prominence has led to significant expansion of crop insurance research, which has become one of the dominant applied research topics in agricultural economics.

In the simplest case, a single random variable is the focus of coverage. A good example is yield insurance, which was the mainstay of crop insurance over most of its history. Another important case is index insurance, where a single index is the focus of coverage. An example is rainfall insurance, where total rainfall at a specific location is the variable that determines the level of coverage and the payout. A simple illustration, that characterizes much of the wide range of coverage offered throughout the world, is that where a single random variable establishes a guarantee and payouts are made if a realization below that guarantee occurs. Consider a random variable Y, which may represent a crop yield or rainfall total. If the expected value of Y is given by μ and the guarantee is set at some proportion λ of this expected value, an actuarially fair contract (a contract priced such that the premium charged is equal to the expected payout) will be determined where Premium $= E(\lambda\mu | Y < \lambda\mu)$. The key factor needed to rate this contract is the probability density function $f(Y)$. The actuarially fair premium will be given by

$$E(\lambda\mu | Y < \lambda\mu) = \int_{-\infty}^{\lambda\mu} f(Y)dY \left(\frac{\lambda\mu - \int_{-\infty}^{\lambda\mu} Yf(Y)dY}{\int_{-\infty}^{\lambda\mu} f(Y)dY} \right) \tag{6.1}$$

The central role played by the proper specification of the density function is obvious from this expression. The typical appeals to normality that are usually invoked through application of the Central Limit Theorem are often inappropriate in these applications. Even though the indexes that are used to establish coverage are typically averages of other random variables, various issues such as dependence and heterogeneity make normality an invalid assumption. Thus, much of applied empirical research is directed toward the correct specification and estimation of the density $f(Y)$. We discuss a wide variety of empirical approaches used to model univariate distributions in the materials that follow.

Other insurance instruments involve multiple, dependent sources of risk. Revenue insurance has become the dominant form of agricultural insurance in recent years. In this case, one is concerned with modeling joint distributions. Many of the same issues relevant to estimating univariate densities arise when modeling joint distributions in that one must characterize the marginal densities. However, the problem is made more interesting by the fact that dependence among jointly distributed random variables must also be modeled.

Copula models have become a significant research issue in agricultural economics in recent years. Copulas allow one to specify a joint distribution in terms of its marginals and a function that "couples" the marginals together to form the joint distribution function. These empirical tools have become the focus of a wide range of research. In the materials that follow, we discuss issues arising in the specification and estimation of copula models for models of risk.

6.2   Frequency and Severity Modeling

For many insurance applications, such as fire and automobile insurance, losses may be modeled by considering the magnitude of loss and frequency of loss. The insurer will sell a number of policies and it is important for the insurer to obtain reliable estimates of the probability of aggregate loss over the entire portfolio of policies. Many insurance companies transfer risk from parts of their portfolios to reinsurers. Pricing these reinsurance agreements depends on accurate measures of portfolio risk, including worst case losses, commonly termed value–at–risk. An insurer that has no idea of the risk of its entire portfolio may be subject to large unexpected portfolio losses, possibly leading to insolvency.

The frequency of loss is a count variable that must be non-negative and integer valued. For instance, we might observe that for a given automobile insurance policy, the policy has two losses in a year. Some of the most popular probability distributions for count variables are the Poisson and negative binomial distributions. The Poisson distribution has mean equal to its variance, an assumption that is often violated in real data. The negative binomial distribution provides an extension to the Poisson as the variance is allowed to exceed the mean. These two distributions may be augmented by placing additional mass at zero. This results in the zero inflated Poisson and zero inflated negative binomial distributions. Zero inflated distributions are useful for modeling real data where losses do not occur in most years.

Severity of loss is also a non-negative variable, but in contrast to frequency, severity is often continuous. Thus the distributions that are best for the modeling of severity will differ from the distributions used to model frequency. There are a fairly large number of distributions that have non-negative support and are continuous. These include Burr, Exponential, Gamma, Generalized Pareto, Inverse Gaussian, Lognormal, Pareto, and Weibull distributions. Given the data, it is up to the analyst to determine the best fitting distribution. In cases where there is little theoretical guidance on the appropriate distribution, the best fitting distribution can be selected according to fit statistics that balance parsimony and flexibility.

6.2.1   Compound Distribution Model

Suppose that an insurer, or other financial firm, is confronted with data on the frequency of losses in a particular time period and the magnitude of each loss. The severity or magnitude of each loss is given by the random variable x. The number of losses is given by the random variable n. Then the aggregate loss can be defined as

$$a = \sum_{i=1}^{n} x_i \tag{6.2}$$

which is simply the sum of the individual losses. The aggregate loss could be, for instance, the total loss over a year for an automobile insurance policy. While most policyholders have no claims or a single claim in a year, some will have multiple claims over the same period of time.

Provided that the frequency and severity of losses over different lines of business are independent, aggregate loss over all business can be computed in a similar way. Consider an insurance company with information on the severity and frequency of losses for two fictional policies: policy 1 and policy 2. Then the aggregate loss over the two policies, provided that the losses are independent, is

$$a = \sum_{i=1}^{n} x_i = \sum_{i=1}^{n_1} x_{i,1} + \sum_{i=1}^{n_2} x_{i,2} \tag{6.3}$$

where n_1 and n_2 are the number of losses under policies 1 and 2 respectively. It is easy to extend this formula to a large number of groups provided that the losses incurred are independent. For this reason, compound distribution models have seen frequent use in the analysis of automobile and fire insurance. Loss events in these lines of insurance are modeled as independent of one another, or the dependence is so weak as to be ignored in the modeling process. Interestingly, recent research has found sizeable accident externalities from driving, suggesting that accident risks in automobile insurance are perhaps not as independent as initially thought (Edlin and Karaca-Mandic 2006).

To describe and calculate the aggregate risk related to the random variables, we would like to have a probability distribution of the aggregate loss. The cumulative distribution function of a can be derived and takes the form

$$F(a) = \sum_{n=0}^{\infty} P(n = \bar{n}) F^*(x) \tag{6.4}$$

where F^* is the n–fold convolution of the cumulative distribution function of x and $Pr(n = \bar{n})$ is the probability of $\bar{n}$ losses from the frequency distribution. You can see from the above equation that to determine the aggregate loss probability, we must have a distribution of the frequency of losses and their severity.

We have seen that when faced with distributions for frequency and magnitude of loss, the probability distribution of aggregate loss can be computed from equation 6.4. While you could derive the distribution analytically, a more efficient method is to estimate the distribution using simulation methods. With the computing power now available to most analysts, simulation methods have become increasingly popular. With a given frequency and severity model, we can simulate data points, compute the aggregate loss from the simulated data, and then let this value form one sample from the compound distribution. By doing this hundreds, thousands, or even millions of times, we arrive at a fairly detailed distribution of aggregate loss.

While the poisson and negative binomial distributions can be fit to count data directly, the counts may be a function of covariates. Similarly, the severity of loss could also be a function of covariates. Including these covariates in the models would lead to more accurate predictions. However, interpretation of the aggregate loss model becomes more complicated. Suppose we know that age affects the frequency of loss. When simulating the cumulative distribution model, we need to know the age of the policyholders and must simulate the loss that different age groups could generate. It turns out that simulation for these types of scenario analyses is again a question of computational power and easily accomplished with modern simulation methods.

Estimation of the compound distribution model occurs in two stages. At the first stage, an appropriate frequency model is proposed, including the effects of any relevant regressors. A severity model is also fit to the data. Frequency and severity models can be compared in terms of model fit and the best-performing model selected. In the second stage, simulations are drawn from the underlying frequency and severity models to generate the compound distribution. The compound distribution is then used to assess the probability of an aggregate loss over the sample, or to generate probabilities of loss for new datapoints.

6.2.2 Empirical Analysis

If we have information of the number of losses and the severity of each loss, then the compound distribution model can be used to determine value-at-risk. This quantity measures the riskiness of a portfolio of investments, assets, or insurance policies. It is often used by financial regulators to determine how much firms need to retain to cover losses. Value-at-risk is defined in terms of the underlying portfolio, a period of time, and a probability. So for an insurance portfolio, the 5% value-at-risk is the loss value that is exceeded 5% of the time over the given time period.

Data on the frequency and severity of losses will be accompanied by additional information about exogenous variables. For instance, we may have data on unemployment insurance claims. This data could include the number of claims and their magnitude for each policyholder. It may also include data on the policyholder's age, salary, job type, education, and other relevant variables. These variables may affect the modeling of counts and severity, so they should be included in the compound distribution model.

In this example, we consider an auto insurance company selling policies to different individuals. The data is shown in Figure 6.1. We have information on the number of claims and the severity of each claim for each policyholder. We also have information on the policyholder's age, gender, vehicle type, vehicle safety rating, vehicle value, and the number of miles that are driven annually. In this data set, gender is a categorical variable with 1 = female and 2 = male, cartype is categorical with 1 = sedan and 2 = SUV, education is categorical with 1 = high school graduate, 2 = college graduate, and 3 = advanced degree. Car safety is measured on a 0 to 1 scale with 1 being the safest possible rating. Both the age of the driver and the income have been normalized. Larger values of both categories represent larger nominal age and income.

```
proc print data = losses(obs = 4);
run;
```

Figure 6.1 Auto Insurance Data

Obs	age	gender	carType	annualMiles	education	carSafety	income	policyholderId	noloss	lossamount
1	0.76	2	1	3.4746	2	0.38192	0.52923	1	1	.
2	1.00	2	1	2.1388	2	0.15068	0.20325	2	0	784.168
3	1.00	2	1	2.1388	2	0.15068	0.20325	2	0	27.639
4	1.00	2	1	2.1388	2	0.15068	0.20325	2	0	69.425

You should first consider the variables that affect the number of losses and the variables that may affect the severity of each loss. These variables will not necessarily be the same. One approach is to consider estimating count and severity models using all regressors and only retaining those variables that are statistically significant. We assume that the number of losses is affected by age, gender, education, and the number of miles driven annually. The severity of each loss is assumed to be affected by the type of car, safety features in the car, and the income of the owner. The categorization of these variables is similar to what one finds in many credit risk analyses. The probability of loss is related to characteristics of the borrower, while severity or loss given default is related to characteristics of the loan itself.

For the frequency component of the compound distribution model (CDM), first fit a negative binomial model to the number of losses. Information on the frequency of loss for each policyholder is in the data set Losscounts. In the PROC COUNTREG procedure, the MODEL statement specifies that the number of losses is modeled as a regression on the covariates mentioned previously. The negative binomial distribution is specified in the DIST option. The parameter estimates from the model are stored in the CountregModel item to be used in simulations from the cumulative distribution model. The second COUNTREG procedure displays the parameters for the model.

```
proc countreg data = losscounts;
   model numloss = age gender carType annualMiles education / dist = negbin;
store work.countregmodel;
run;
```

```
proc countreg restore = work.countregmodel;
   show parameters;
run;
```

Figure 6.2 displays the model fit summary and parameter estimates from the negative binomial model. There are 5,000 observations in the data set and we are also provided with some fit criteria, such as AIC and SBC, that can be used to aid in model selection. The coefficients on the regressors are all statistically significant and should be included in the model. The number of losses decreases with age, miles driven, and the education of the driver. Men and drivers of SUVs are more likely to have losses on the policy.

Figure 6.2 Negative Binomial Model Fit

The COUNTREG Procedure

Model Fit Summary	
Dependent Variable	numloss
Number of Observations	5000
Data Set	WORK.LOSSCOUNTS
Model	NegBin(p=2)
Log Likelihood	-7045
Maximum Absolute Gradient	2.24639E-7
Number of Iterations	6
Optimization Method	Newton-Raphson
AIC	14104
SBC	14150

ITEM STORE CONTENTS: WORK.COUNTREGMODEL

Parameter Estimates					
Parameter	DF	Estimate	Standard Error	t Value	Approx Pr > |t|
Intercept	1	0.910479	0.090515	10.06	<.0001
age	1	-0.626803	0.058547	-10.71	<.0001
gender	1	1.025034	0.032099	31.93	<.0001
carType	1	0.615165	0.031153	19.75	<.0001
annualMiles	1	-1.010276	0.017512	-57.69	<.0001
education	1	-0.280246	0.021677	-12.93	<.0001
_Alpha	1	0.318403	0.020090	15.85	<.0001

Having fit a negative binomial model to the frequency of loss, we must now fit the severity model. PROC SEVERITY allows the scale of the estimated severity distribution to depend on various regressors. In this example, scale depends on car type, car safety, and income. The following code estimates all the predefined distributions in PROC SEVERITY. The PLOTS option is set so that no plots are generated. The data is read in from the data set losses and parameter estimates are placed in the Sevregest item. To obtain estimates of distribution and regression parameters, the SEVERITY procedure uses nonlinear optimization of the likelihood function. In the interest of expediency, we constrain the number of iterations for the optimization routine to 100, although the defaults for the procedure usually perform well.

```
proc severity data = losses plots = none outest = sevregest print = all;
    loss lossamount;
    scalemodel carType carSafety income;
    dist _predef_;
    nloptions maxiter = 100;
run;
```

Figure 6.3 shows the candidate distributions that were estimated by the SEVERITY procedure. All of the estimates converged, and based on the log-likelihood function value, the lognormal model is selected as having the best fit.

Figure 6.3 Severity Model DIstribution Information

The SEVERITY Procedure

Candidate Distributions			
Distribution	Status	Parameters	Description
Burr	Valid	3	Burr Distribution
Exp	Valid	1	Exponential Distribution
Gamma	Valid	2	Gamma Distribution
Igauss	Valid	2	Inverse Gaussian Distribution
Logn	Valid	2	Lognormal Distribution
Pareto	Valid	2	Pareto Distribution
Gpd	Valid	2	Generalized Pareto Distribution
Weibull	Valid	2	Weibull Distribution

Model Selection			
Distribution	Converged	-2 Log Likelihood	Selected
Burr	Yes	127231	No
Exp	Yes	128431	No
Gamma	Yes	128324	No
Igauss	Yes	127434	No
Logn	Yes	127062	Yes
Pareto	Yes	128166	No
Gpd	Yes	128166	No
Weibull	Yes	128429	No

The fit statistics in Figure 6.4 give a more comprehensive look at the different fit criteria for each model. The first four statistics are all based on the likelihood function. The last three are based on the empirical distribution function. In the case of our data, the lognormal distribution is best fitting when using likelihood based fit criteria. The generalized Pareto distribution is best fitting according to the statistics based on the empirical distribution function. Both of the selected distributions are defined by two parameters. We use the lognormal distribution as the severity model in the analysis that follows. Interested readers can extend this exercise by comparing the results from the lognormal to the generalized Pareto.

Figure 6.4 Severity Model Fit Statistics

All Fit Statistics							
Distribution	-2 Log Likelihood	AIC	AICC	BIC	KS	AD	CvM
Burr	127231	127243	127243	127286	7.75407	224.47578	27.41346	
Exp	128431	128439	128439	128467	6.13537	181.83094	12.33919	
Gamma	128324	128334	128334	128370	7.54562	276.13156	24.59515	
Igauss	127434	127444	127444	127480	6.15855	211.51908	17.70942	
Logn	127062	* 127072	* 127072	* 127107	* 6.77687	212.70400	21.47945	
Pareto	128166	128176	128176	128211	5.37453	110.53673	7.07119	
Gpd	128166	128176	128176	128211	5.37453	* 110.53660	* 7.07116	*
Weibull	128429	128439	128439	128475	6.21268	190.81178	13.45425	

Note: The asterisk (*) marks the best model according to each column's criterion.

With frequency and severity models in hand, you can now generate a cumulative distribution model. The simplest approach is to first consider a single policyholder. Because covariates are included in the frequency and severity models, this is a scenario analysis. The policyholder is defined by values for each of the regressors included in the underlying models. Using PROC PRINT to view the data shown in Figure 6.5, you can see that the example policyholder is a male, driving a safe sedan, and holding an advanced degree.

```
proc print data = singlePolicy;
run;
```

Figure 6.5 Data for Single Policyholder

Obs	age	gender	carType	annualMiles	education	carSafety	income
1	1.18	2	1	2.2948	3	0.99532	1.5987

The following code estimates the compound distribution of the aggregate loss that will result for our single policyholder. Several options have been specified in the call to PROC HPCDM. We have asked for 10,000 draws from the cumulative distribution, with the seed for the simulation set so that we can replicate our results. The HPCDM procedure relies on the previously determined frequency and severity models. The estimated frequency model item is specified with the COUNTSTORE= option, while the estimated severity model item is specified with the SEVERITYEST= option. Since we estimated a variety of distributions with the SEVERITY procedure, we can use the SEVERITYMODEL statement to tell SAS which model to use. In this case we specify the lognormal model, as it was best fitting according to the likelihood criteria.

The OUTSUM statement includes several options that specify the types of statistics we are interested in calculating for the simulated compound distribution. These statistics are stored in the OnePolicySum data set. We have asked for the mean, standard deviation, skewness, kurtosis, and median of the distribution. You are also likely interested in the loss that could occur at different percentiles of the distribution. The PCTLPTS option allows you to specify the percentiles you would like to request using list notation. The code requests all percentiles between 97.5 and 99.5 in intervals of 1.

```
proc hpcdm data = singlePolicy nreplicates = 10000 seed = 13579 print = all
        countstore = work.countregmodel severityest = work.sevregest;
    severitymodel logn;
    outsum out = onepolicysum mean stddev skew kurtosis median
        pctlpts = 97.5 to 99.5 by 1;
run;
```

Figure 6.6 displays some of the performance and execution information specific to this high performance procedure. It confirms that the analysis was executed on a single machine and used four threads for computation. It also provides information on where the data was accessed and a summary of the input data set. While these details do not affect this analysis, they can be useful when the high performance procedure is running in a distributed mode. In those cases you will want to confirm that SAS is taking advantage of the available computational resources and also accessing data from correct locations.

Figure 6.6 CDM Performance and Execution Information

The HPCDM Procedure

Performance Information	
Execution Mode	Single-Machine
Number of Threads	4

Data Access Information			
Data	Engine	Role	Path
WORK.SINGLEPOLICY	V9	Input	On Client

Figure 6.6 *continued*

Input Data Summary	
Name	WORK.SINGLEPOLICY
Observations	1
Valid Observations	1

Figure 6.7 shows the results of the HPCDM procedure. We can see that the compound distribution is based on the underlying lognormal model for severity and negative binomial model for frequency. The severity scale depends on three regressors. The mean aggregate loss for the policyholder is just over 214 dollars and the distribution is right skewed. Even up to the 50th percentile, the loss is zero. The losses at high percentiles give a sense of worst case loss. At the 99th percentile, this loss is 1,979.5 dollars. In other words, there is a 1% probability that this policy will realize a loss greater than 1,979.5 dollars.

Figure 6.7 CDM Estimation Results

The HPCDM Procedure
Severity Model: Logn
Count Model: NegBin(p=2)

Compound Distribution Information	
Severity Model	Lognormal Distribution
Scale Model Regressors	carType carSafety income
Count Model	NegBin(p=2) Model in Item Store WORK.COUNTREGMODEL

Sample Summary Statistics			
Mean	217.61476	Median	0
Standard Deviation	429.35923	Interquartile Range	269.28863
Variance	184349.3	Minimum	0
Skewness	3.94508	Maximum	4986.6
Kurtosis	22.88738	Sample Size	10000

Sample Percentiles	
Percentile	Value
0	0
1	0
5	0
25	0
50	0
75	269.28863
95	999.83713
97.5	1417.7
98.5	1774.0
99	2036.5
99.5	2590.1
Percentile Method = 5	

To consider a more advanced scenario, you can extend the analysis to multiple policyholders and then simulate the compound distribution over the entire portfolio. Our data set of five fictional purchasers of auto insurance is shown in Figure 6.8. There are a variety of ages, genders, education levels, and we now also have a few SUVs in the group.

```
proc print data = groupOfPolicies(obs = 5);
run;
```

Figure 6.8 Date for Multiple Policyholders

Obs	policyholderId	age	gender	carType	annualMiles	education	carSafety	income
1	1	1.18	2	1	2.2948	3	0.99532	1.59870
2	2	0.66	2	1	2.6718	2	0.86412	0.84459
3	3	0.64	2	2	1.9528	1	0.86478	0.50177
4	4	0.46	1	2	2.6402	2	0.27062	1.18870
5	5	0.62	1	1	1.7294	1	0.32830	0.37694

The call to PROC HPCDM for the multiple policyholder scenario includes several new options. First, we have asked for a conditional density plot that displays different regions of the compound distribution. The RIGHTQ option instructs SAS to split the distribution at the 95th quantile and then graph conditional distributions on either side of this boundary. The NPERTURBEDSAMPLES option implements parameter perturbation. When we estimated the frequency and severity models, there was uncertainty associated with the parameter estimates for each model. The previous single policy example didn't take this uncertainty into account. It simply took the parameter estimates as given.

The perturbation option creates, in this case, 50 different sets of perturbed parameters. Each set of parameters is then used to generate a full sample from the compound distribution model. Based on these 50 samples, we will then have 50 different estimates of the summary statistics listed in the OUTSUM statement. The sample standard deviations are then used to give some sense of the uncertainty in losses arising from the frequency and severity estimations.

```
proc hpcdm data = groupOfPolicies nreplicates = 10000 seed = 13579 print = all
        countstore = work.countregmodel severityest = work.sevregest
        plots = (conditionaldensity(rightq = 0.95)) nperturbedSamples = 50;
    severitymodel logn;
    outsum out = multipolicysum mean stddev skew kurtosis median
        pctlpts = 97.5 to 99.5 by 1;
run;
```

The results from the perturbed analysis are shown in Figure 6.9. The mean loss over all five policies is about 5,300 dollars with a standard error of 327. The standard deviation of the loss is much larger, at 4,152 dollars. In the worst case scenarios, at the 99th and 99.5th percentiles, the estimated loss is around 20,000 dollars. The relatively small standard errors suggest that our estimate of aggregate loss is not overly sensitive to uncertainty in the parameters of the underlying negative binomial and lognormal models.

Figure 6.9 Perturbed CDM Results

The HPCDM Procedure
Severity Model: Logn
Count Model: NegBin(p=2)

Sample Perturbation Analysis

Statistic	Estimate	Standard Error
Mean	5331.3	559.52182
Standard Deviation	4170.6	346.61321
Variance	17514137	2979306.9
Skewness	2.02770	0.24997
Kurtosis	9.14611	3.75927

Number of Perturbed Samples = 50

Size of Each Sample = 10000

Sample Percentile Perturbation Analysis

Percentile	Estimate	Standard Error
1	216.43966	65.57200
5	765.60278	143.70919
25	2401.0	324.11066
50	4342.7	498.47507
75	7139.4	739.01751
95	13185.9	1217.8
97.5	15858.5	1441.8
98.5	17886.4	1585.0
99	19553.1	1693.9
99.5	22646.0	2001.5

Number of Perturbed Samples = 50

Size of Each Sample = 10000

The conditional density plot is shown in Figure 6.10. The unperturbed sample is used to generate the density plots. By splitting the plot at the 95th percentile, we obtain a visual picture of both the majority of the aggregate loss density and the right tail. The right tail is where the worst case losses occur, so you will probably be especially interested in this region. The conditional densities confirm what was evident in the summary tables of Figure 6.9. The distribution has positive skew with a mean around 5,000 dollars. Once past 20,000 dollars, probabilities of greater losses are especially low.

Figure 6.10 Conditional Density Plots

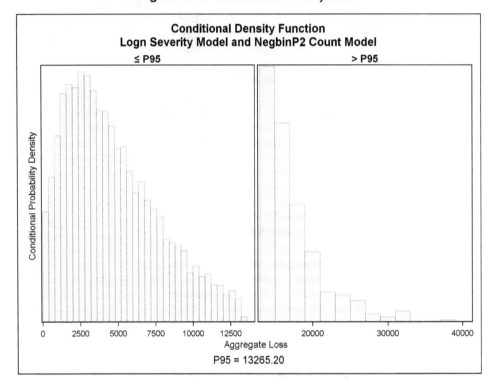

6.3   Agricultural Insurance

This section discusses modeling approaches relevant to the rating of agricultural insurance policies, primarily yield and revenue insurance. The United States operates a large federal crop insurance program where the parameters of policies are determined by the USDA's Risk Management Agency and the policies are then sold and serviced by other insurers. This federal program is now the most expensive instrument of agricultural policy; government outlays on crop insurance exceed those of any other farm program. Private companies (known as approved insurance providers) service the federal policies, which are subsidized at up to 60% of the premium rate. The focus of the U.S. crop insurance program has recently shifted from policies written on crop yields to revenue insurance policies that consider numerous, dependent sources of risk. Research in crop insurance is of interest for the applied economist as it has immediate policy impact. Because of the many sources of risk that affect farmers, statistical modeling associated with crop insurance tends to be of econometric value as well.

The United States is not unique in its provision of agricultural insurance and many developed countries have similar programs. Agricultural insurance has also received attention in developing economics. Much of the developing world derives income from the agricultural sector. Small scale farmers are often particularly exposed to risks from weather, pests, and price movements. Agricultural insurance provides one way of stabilizing farm incomes. One barrier to the implementation of insurance in developing areas is the cost associated with operating such programs. Technological innovation over the last two decades has significantly defrayed this cost. Insurance policies are now written on rainfall and vegetation indices, which can be measured by meteorologists or derived from satellite observation.

For insurance to be actuarially fair, the premium on an insurance policy should be equivalent to the expected loss. A consequence of this type of pricing is that the insurer will not profit from the sale of the policy in expectation. In practice, insurance providers typically calculate the actuarially fair premium and then load the premium to account for operating costs and to generate profits. Underlying pricing of the insurance depends on accurate assessment of probability of loss and expected loss. From the applied economist's perspective, we may not necessarily be interested in the actuarial details of insurance pricing; we are often more concerned with modeling of the random variables that determine the loss. Studying the ways that people respond to variations in these variables is an economic problem.

6.3.1 Yield Insurance

Our empirical analysis is focused on two types of agricultural insurance: yield and revenue insurance. However, these statistical techniques are applicable to many types of insurance outside of the agricultural sector. Yield insurance pays the farmer based on lost yields. Yield insurance policies specify a yield guarantee and a payout price. A loss occurs when

$$\lambda Y_G > Y_H \tag{6.5}$$

where Y_G denotes the yield guarantee specified at the time the insurance policy is purchased and Y_H is the harvest or realized yield. The coverage level $\lambda \in [0, 1]$ is selected by the farmer and higher levels of coverage imply higher premium rates. The payout on a yield insurance policy is given by

$$P(\lambda Y_G - Y_H) \tag{6.6}$$

which is simply the yield shortfall multiplied by a payout price. The payout price is also specified at the time the policy is purchased. It is possible, but not practical, to pay the farmer in–kind, in which case the payout would simply be $\lambda Y_G - Y_H$. The actuarially fair premium on a yield insurance policy is

$$
\begin{aligned}
\text{Premium} &= \text{Expected Loss} \\
&= P(\text{Loss}) E(\text{Loss} \mid \text{Loss Occurs}) \\
&= P(\lambda Y_G > Y_H) E(Y_G - Y_H) \mid \lambda Y_G > Y_H)
\end{aligned}
$$

The only random variable in the equation above is Y_H; the policy may be priced accurately by estimating the probability distribution of crop yields.

There has been a great deal of research in agricultural economics on specifying yield distributions. Botts and Boles (1958), one of the earliest instances of fitting a distribution to yields, suggested that yields followed a normal distribution. Since then, studies have focused on distributions that can accommodate skew and non-normal features. Gallagher (1987) suggested a gamma distribution, while Nelson (1990) suggested a beta distribution. Sherrick et al. (2004) found that a Weibull distribution fit well in small samples. Goodwin and Ker (1998) used nonparametric methods to estimate yield distributions. More recently, Tolhurst and Ker (2015) used parametric mixtures to model yield distributions with components representing catastrophic and normal growing situations. Of course, one can always estimate a number of different distributions and use measures of fit to guide this choice.

6.3.2 Empirical Analysis

This example details the pricing of yield insurance for two counties producing corn and two counties producing soybeans. The data includes measurements of county–level corn yields in Adair County, Iowa and Atchison County, Kansas and soybean yields in Adams County, Illinois and Macon County, Illinois. The time series begins in 1960 and runs through 2014 and is available online from the National Agricultural Statistics Service (NASS) at http://www.nass.usda.gov. In the case of both corn and soybeans, crop yield is measured in bushels per acre. First read in the data, set labels for the yield variables, and then print the data to confirm that it has been read correctly.

```
data yields;
set yields;
    label adair_corn = "Adair, IO Corn (Bu/Ac)"
          atchison_corn = "Atchison, KS Corn (Bu/Ac)"
          adams_soybeans = "Adams, IL Soybeans (Bu/Ac)"
          macon_soybeans = "Macon, IL Soybeans (Bu/Ac)";
run;
```

```
proc print data = yields(obs = 10);
run;
```

The printout of the first ten observations of yield data in Figure 6.11 suggests that there may be a trend in the data. We can plot the entire series of yields over time to obtain a more accurate picture of the trend in yields and their variability.

Figure 6.11 Yield Data

Obs	year	adair_corn	atchison_corn	adams_soybeans	macon_soybeans
1	2014	169.3	183.8	50.7	67.4
2	2013	137.8	129.1	43.6	56.5
3	2012	104.4	58.5	40.7	44.8
4	2011	152.8	128.2	41.4	46.7
5	2010	139.1	108.9	48.7	60.4
6	2009	179.3	152.0	47.0	55.0
7	2008	169.0	132.0	41.0	51.0
8	2007	160.7	124.0	37.0	53.0
9	2006	164.9	111.0	43.0	56.0
10	2005	159.0	121.0	43.0	54.0

```
proc sgplot data = yields;
    scatter x = year y = adair_corn;
    title 'Adair, IO Corn';
    xaxis label = 'Year';
    yaxis label = 'Bushels/Acre';
run;

proc sgplot data = yields;
    scatter x = year y = atchison_corn;
    title 'Atchison, KS Corn';
    xaxis label = 'Year';
    yaxis label = 'Bushels/Acre';
run;

proc sgplot data = yields;
    scatter x = year y = adams_soybeans;
    title 'Adams, IL Soybeans';
    xaxis label = 'Year';
    yaxis label = 'Bushels/Acre';
run;

proc sgplot data = yields;
    scatter x = year y = macon_soybeans;
    title 'Macon, IL Soybeans';
    xaxis label = 'Year';
    yaxis label = 'Bushels/Acre';
run;
```

Figure 6.12 Agricultural Output

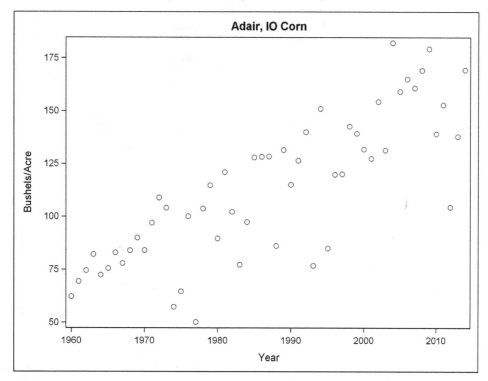

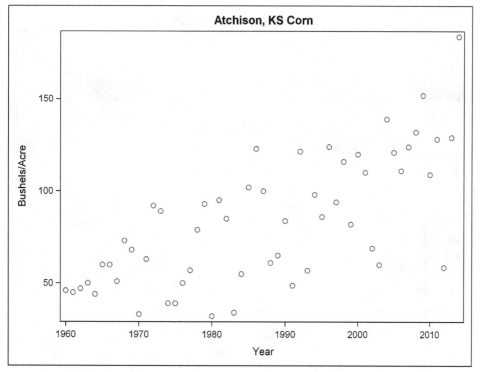

Figure 6.12 *continued*

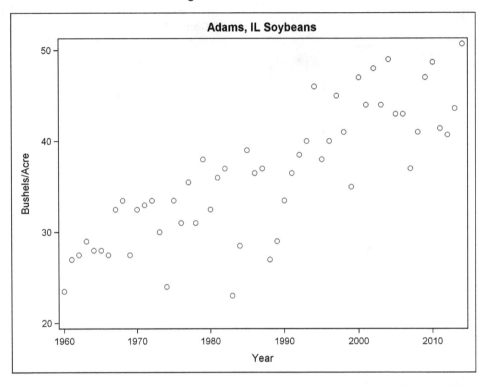

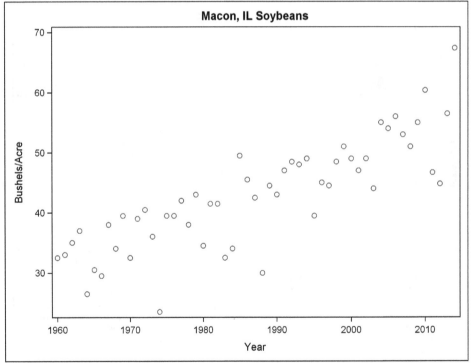

The time series plots of yields show both an upward trend and evidence of heteroskedasticity. Yield distributions change over time as new technologies are introduced, innovative farm management methods are applied, or changes in long run climate phenomena occur. These changes are not limited in impact to any particular moment of the yield distribution. For instance, applications of biotechnology and genetically modified seeds might raise the mean of the distribution and simultaneously lower the variance. The practical consequence is that the farmer will receive a higher yield on average, with less risk of extreme loss. Because of the obvious increases in yields over time, it is necessary to detrend observed yields. As a practical concern, most density estimation methods require that variables are independently and identically distributed. Nonstationary yields violate this assumption.

There are a number of ways that we can account for time trends in random variables. SAS contains several procedures that might be used depending on the detrending method selected. PROC REG can be used to fit a trend line using ordinary least squares or a quadratic trend via polynomial regression. You can also use PROC LOESS to implement a nonparametric procedure known as local regression. Both of these methods are detailed below. The basic idea is that the observed yield Y_t in any given year follows some unknown trend function so that

$$Y_t = f(t) + \epsilon_t \tag{6.7}$$

The trend function can be generated in a number of ways. Perhaps the most basic approach is to allow $f(t) = \beta t$, where β is a constant, in which case the function could be captured by an ordinary least squares regression of yields on time. We might also want to consider a quadratic function in time, which could be accommodated by considering additional powers. In that case, $f(t) = \beta_1 t + \beta_2 t^2$.

The following code uses PROC REG to fit a linear trend to the observed yields. The MODEL statement regresses corn yields in Adair, Iowa on year. Because the yield plots in Figure 6.12 showed possible evidence of heteroskedasticity, the SPEC option is included in the MODEL statement. This option performs a model specification test with the maintained hypothesis that the error terms in the regression are homoskedastic and independent of the regressor. If the model is correctly specified, then rejection of the null hypothesis is evidence of heteroskedasticity.

```
proc reg data = yields;
   model adair_corn = year / spec;
   output out = pred_adair_reg predicted = predicted_adair_reg;
run;
```

The PROC REG output in Figure 6.13 shows that the linear model has fairly good fit with an R-square value of 0.6588. The estimate of the coefficient on Year indicates that the county yield grows by roughly 1.7 bushels per acre in each year. The test for heteroskedasticity is rejected at the 10% level, providing further evidence that we may want to correct for heteroskedasticity before estimating the conditional yield distribution.

Figure 6.13 PROC REG Output

The REG Procedure
Model: MODEL1
Dependent Variable: adair_corn Adair, IO Corn (Bu/Ac)

Root MSE	20.06385	R-Square	0.6588
Dependent Mean	113.18182	Adj R-Sq	0.6524
Coeff Var	17.72709		

Parameter Estimates

Variable	Label	DF	Parameter Estimate	Standard Error	t Value	Pr > |t|
Intercept	Intercept	1	-3312.71584	338.64475	-9.78	<.0001
year		1	1.72416	0.17042	10.12	<.0001

Figure 6.13 *continued*

The REG Procedure
Model: MODEL1
Dependent Variable: adair_corn Adair, IO Corn (Bu/Ac)

Test of First and Second
Moment Specification

DF	Chi-Square	Pr > ChiSq
2	5.78	0.0555

Fit and diagnostic plots in Figure 6.14 show decent fit in the middle of the distribution, but worse fit at both high and low quantiles. The residual plot provides some visual evidence of heteroskedasticity, with residuals for years in the middle and end of the sample having greater variation. The plot of the fitted regression also includes 95% confidence and prediction limits. From 1960 to 1970, almost all of the observations fall within the 95% confidence limits, while very few observations past 1970 meet this criteria. There were four years with low realized yields relative to the trend, and all four of these observations fall outside of the 95% prediction limits.

Figure 6.14 PROC REG Fit Plots

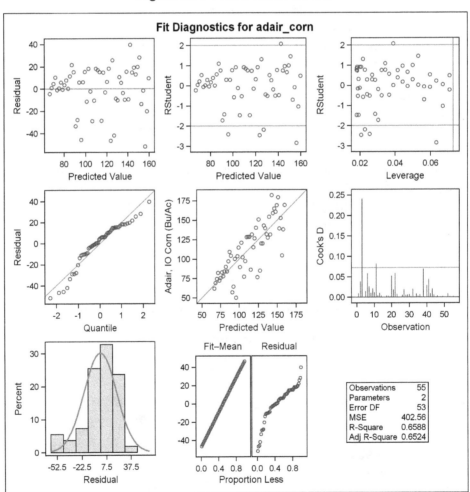

Figure 6.14 *continued*

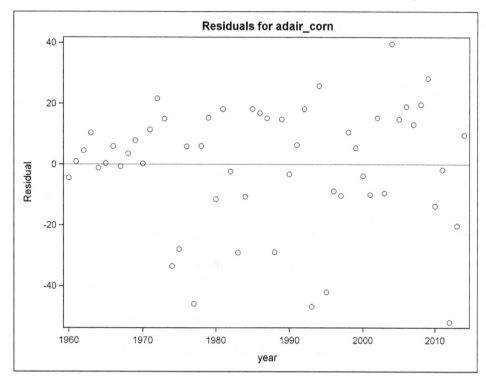

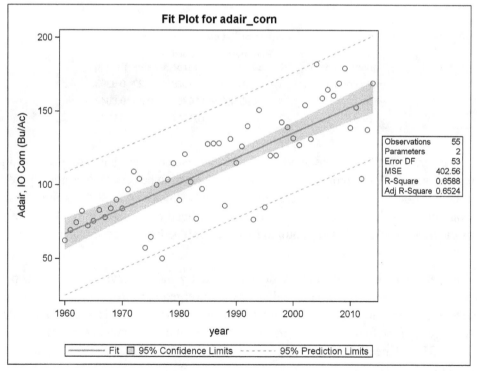

Fitting a quadratic function of time is one way to incorporate nonlinear behavior in the trend model. By including time and the square of time as regressors, the model allows for yields to increase at an increasing rate, increase at a decreasing rate, and other types of behavior. The following code adds a year squared variable to the data and then uses PROC REG to fit the quadratic function.

```
data yields;
set yields;
   yearsq = year * year;
run;

proc reg data = yields;
   model adair_corn = year yearsq;
   output out = pred_adair_quad predicted = predicted_adair_quad;
run;
```

The output from the regression in Figure 6.15 provides some insight into the perils of strict parametric models. In this case, the fit of the model as measured by R-square is almost identical to the linear regression model. However, the coefficient values are entirely nonsensical. The general trend of yields is decreasing over time. In fact, the highest expected yield is in the first year of the sample. Given the only slight increase in R-square of this model with one additional parameter, and the odd coefficient estimates, we prefer the simple linear regression to the quadratic.

Figure 6.15 PROC REG Output

The REG Procedure
Model: MODEL1
Dependent Variable: adair_corn Adair, IO Corn (Bu/Ac)

Root MSE	20.24008	R-Square	0.6594
Dependent Mean	113.18182	Adj R-Sq	0.6463
Coeff Var	17.88280		

			Parameter Estimates			
			Parameter	Standard		
Variable	Label	DF	Estimate	Error	t Value	Pr > |t|
Intercept	Intercept	1	10304	47828	0.22	0.8303
year		1	-11.98224	48.14282	-0.25	0.8044
yearsq		1	0.00345	0.01211	0.28	0.7770

Instead of fitting parametric functions for the yield trend, you can also consider generating $f(t)$ using nonparametric methods. Local regression (LOESS) is more flexible than linear regression because it does not require any assumptions about the form of the functional relationship. In the previous trend estimations, we first assumed that the relationship between the two variables was linear, and then also considered a quadratic relationship. This brings up an obvious question. Perhaps the trend would be better captured by a cubic? The list of possible parametric models is clearly quite long.

One advantage of nonparametric methods is that we do not have to try and estimate all conceivable parametric models. With enough data, the nonparametric estimates will always converge to the true model. The advantage is that the nonparametric model grows with the data set, allowing the data to speak for itself. The following code implements the LOESS procedure for each of the four counties in the data set. The MODEL statement specifies yield as a function of time, just as in PROC REG. Three output data sets are generated for each county, including a data set of predicted values and a data set of residuals.

```
proc loess data = yields;
   model adair_corn = year;
   output out = pred_adair predicted = predicted_adair_corn
         residual = residual_adair_corn;
run;

proc loess data = yields;
```

```
    model atchison_corn =year;
    output out = pred_atchison predicted = predicted_atchison_corn
            residual = residual_atchison_corn;
run;

proc loess data = yields;
    model adams_soybeans = year;
    output out = pred_adams predicted = predicted_adams_soybeans
            residual = residual_adams_soybeans;
run;

proc loess data = yields;
    model macon_soybeans = year;
    output out = pred_macon predicted = predicted_macon_soybeans
            residual = residual_macon_soybeans;
run;
```

Figure 6.16 shows the fit summary for the LOESS procedure for Adair, IA corn. The fit method is a kd tree which divides the initial cell containing the 55 data points into rectangular cells. This division continues until no child cell has more than the bucket size of the kd tree, which we can see from the procedure output is four. PROC LOESS locally fits at the vertices of all of the cells of the kd tree. For our analysis, there were 17 fitted points. The LOESS procedure automatically selects a value for the smoothing parameter that controls model fit and model complexity. The default value is based on a corrected Akaike information criterion obtained by Hurvich, Simonoff, and Tsai (1998). The larger the value of the smoothing parameter, the smoother the resulting function and the less flexible the function is in capturing local fluctuations in the data. If the value of the smoothing parameter is too small, the regression function can be greatly influenced by random error.

Figure 6.16 PROC LOESS Output

The LOESS Procedure
Selected Smoothing Parameter: 0.409
Dependent Variable: adair_corn

Fit Summary	
Fit Method	kd Tree
Blending	Linear
Number of Observations	55
Number of Fitting Points	17
kd Tree Bucket Size	4
Degree of Local Polynomials	1
Smoothing Parameter	0.40909
Points in Local Neighborhood	22
Residual Sum of Squares	19583
Trace[L]	5.08900
GCV	7.86097
AICC	7.12924

Fit plots and diagnostic plots in Figure 6.17 suggest that the LOESS procedure is a better choice for detrending our data. Interestingly, growth in yields seems to be slower after 2000, but this result is largely driven by low yields due to drought in 2012. One advantage of LOESS methods is that as the sample size grows and we obtain more data, the estimate will converge to the true model. There is also very little reason to believe that yields should grow at a constant rate over time. Flexible nonparametric methods can account for other more complex types of trends.

Figure 6.17 Fit Plot

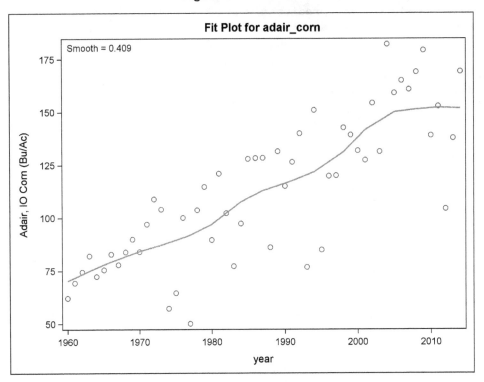

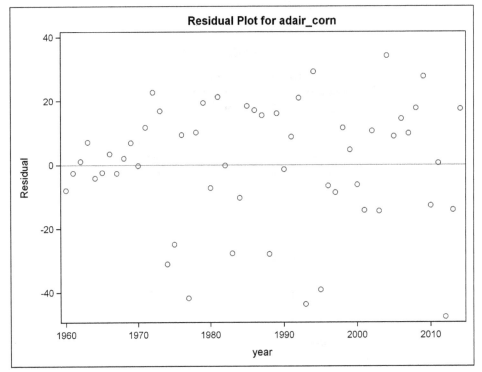

Figure 6.17 *continued*

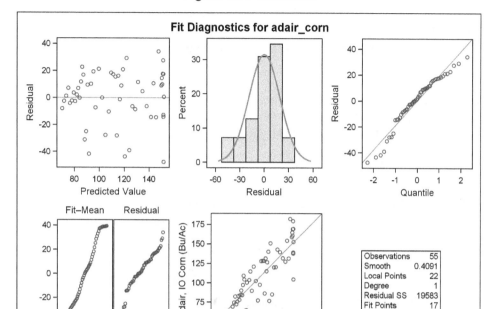

Given evidence of heteroskedasticity in yields, a correction can be made to the yield series. The normalized yields are constructed as

$$Y_t^N = \hat{Y}_{2014} + \epsilon_t \tag{6.8}$$

where Y_t^N is the normalized yield in year t, $\hat{Y}_{2014}$ is the predicted yield in the last year of the sample, and ϵ_t is the residual from the trend in any given year. You can use DATA steps to combine the data from the four counties and then construct the normalized yields.

```
data predictedyields;
    merge pred_adair pred_atchison pred_adams pred_macon;
run;

data predicted2014(keep = yhat_adair yhat_atchison yhat_adams yhat_macon);
set predictedyields;
    if year ne 2014 then delete;
    rename predicted_adair_corn = yhat_adair predicted_atchison_corn = yhat_atchison
        predicted_adams_soybeans = yhat_adams predicted_macon_soybeans = yhat_macon;
run;

data normalizedyields;
    if _N_ = 1 then set predicted2014;
set predictedyields;
    norm_adair_corn      = yhat_adair    + residual_adair_corn;
    norm_atchison_corn   = yhat_atchison + residual_atchison_corn;
    norm_adams_soybeans  = yhat_adams    + residual_adams_soybeans;
    norm_macon_soybeans  = yhat_macon    + residual_macon_soybeans;
run;
```

Once we have normalized yields, standard methods of density estimation can be used to obtain the yield distribution. We consider parametric and nonparametric methods of estimating the yield distributions. Because yields cannot be negative, the SEVERITY procedure is the easiest method for estimating a variety of possible distributions using SAS. The following code obtains estimates of Gamma, Inverse Gaussian, Lognormal, Burr, and Weibull distributions. The CRIT option specifies BIC as our fit criteria of choice, but we also ask for all fit statistics to be printed. In the interest of space, we only consider corn yields from Adair, IA and leave the estimation of other yield distributions to the reader.

```
proc severity data = normalizedyields crit = bic
              print = allfitstats outest = yieldests
              outmodelinfo = sevmodels;
   loss norm_adair_corn;
   dist Gamma Igauss Logn Burr Weibull;
run;
```

The fit statistics in Figure 6.18 show that the Weibull distribution has the best fit under BIC and the majority of the other criteria. The Burr distribution is selected according to Kolmogorov-Smirnov and Cramer-von Mises statistics.

Figure 6.18 Fit Statistics

The SEVERITY Procedure

		All Fit Statistics				
Distribution	-2 Log Likelihood	AIC	AICC	BIC	KS	AD
Gamma	483.14967	487.14967	487.38044	491.16434	0.84972	1.27202
Igauss	485.60325	489.60325	489.83402	493.61792	0.73889	1.30611
Logn	485.53021	489.53021	489.76098	493.54488	0.91825	1.49195
Burr	472.85010	478.85010	479.32069	484.87210	0.49635	* 0.27942
Weibull	472.83378	* 476.83378	* 477.06455	* 480.84845	* 0.49870	0.27942 *

Note: The asterisk (*) marks the best model according to each column's criterion.

All Fit Statistics	
Distribution	CvM
Gamma	0.19126
Igauss	0.15474
Logn	0.22801
Burr	0.03256 *
Weibull	0.03283

Note: The asterisk (*) marks the best model according to each column's criterion.

It is often instructive to examine plots of the cumulative distribution functions of the estimated distributions with the empirical distribution function. The last three fit statistics in Figure 6.18 are calculated by comparing the EDF with the estimated CDF. While all of the distributions perform poorly at low yield levels, the Weibull distribution closely approximates the empirical distribution function at cumulative probabilities above 0.2. It is particularly effective at capturing the distribution at high yields over 170 bushels per acre.

Figure 6.19 Fit Plot

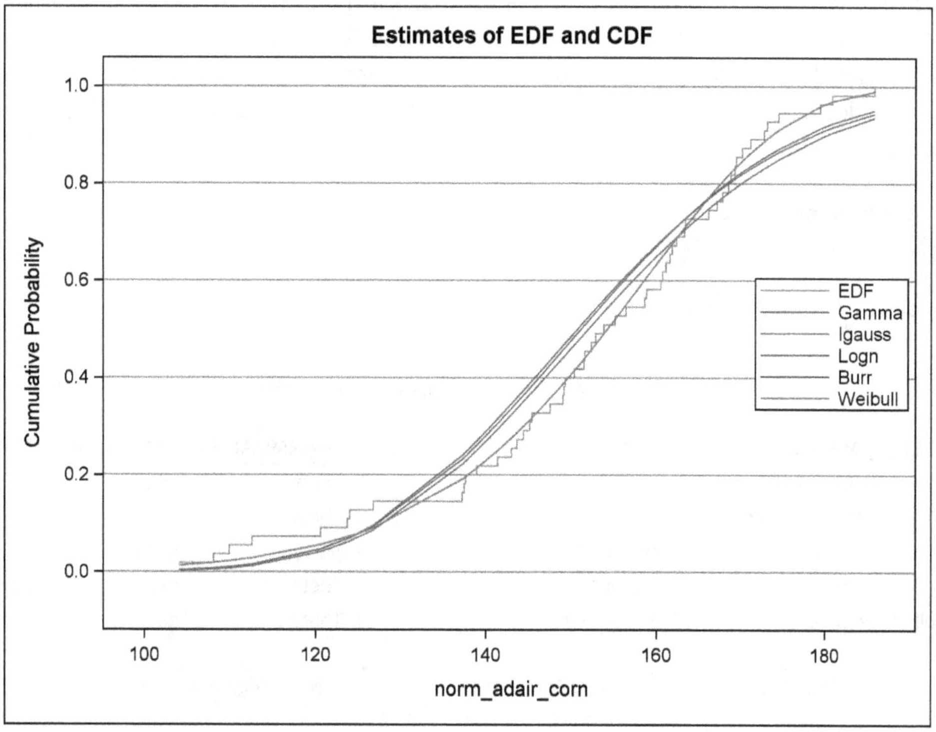

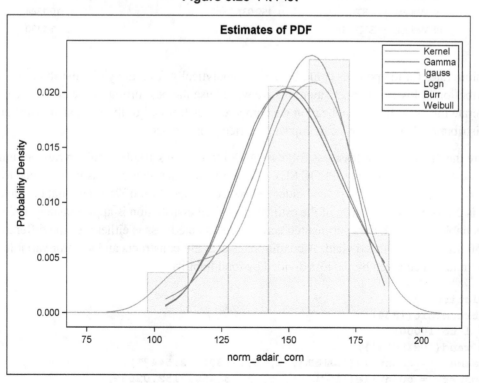

The PDF plot in Figure 6.20 overlays the probability density functions of the estimated distributions, and a kernel density, with a histogram. There is evidence from the histogram and kernel density of negative skew in the yield distribution. Of the parametric distributions, the Weibull distribution captures this feature of yields, aligning with the results obtained from the table of fit statistics.

Figure 6.20 Fit Plot

The SEVERITY procedure stored model information and parameter estimates in the data sets SevModels and YieldEsts. While PROC SEVERITY reports parameter estimates as part of its standard output, the following PROC PRINT statements display model information and parameter values for each estimated distribution. On advantage of the Weibull over the Burr distribution is that it is defined by two parameters instead of three. This parsimony comes at no cost in terms of adequately describing the distribution of yields, as evidenced by the fit criteria considered and plots of estimated density functions.

```
proc print data = sevmodels;
run;

proc print data = yieldests;
run;
```

Figure 6.21 Severity Model Information

Obs	_MODEL_	_DEPVAR_	_DESCRIPTION_	_VALID_	_PARMNAME1	_PARMNAME2	_PARMNAME3
1	Gamma	norm_adair_corn	Gamma Distribution	1	Theta	Alpha	
2	Igauss	norm_adair_corn	Inverse Gaussian Distribution	1	Theta	Alpha	
3	Logn	norm_adair_corn	Lognormal Distribution	1	Mu	Sigma	
4	Burr	norm_adair_corn	Burr Distribution	1	Theta	Alpha	Gamma
5	Weibull	norm_adair_corn	Weibull Distribution	1	Theta	Tau	

Obs	_MODEL_	_TYPE_	_STATUS_	Theta	Alpha	Mu	Sigma	Gamma	Tau
1	Gamma	EST	0	2.544	59.75	.	.	.	.
2	Gamma	STDERR	0	0.495	11.58	.	.	.	.
3	Igauss	EST	0	152.026	56.35	.	.	.	.
4	Igauss	STDERR	0	2.782	11.00	.	.	.	.
5	Logn	EST	0	.	.	5.01566	0.13256	.	.
6	Logn	STDERR	0	.	.	0.01821	0.01288	.	.
7	Burr	EST	302	288.490	397.83	.	.	10.1466	.
8	Burr	STDERR	0	105.266	1426.44	.	.	1.1367	.
9	Weibull	EST	0	159.931	.	.	.	.	10.1344
10	Weibull	STDERR	0	2.277	.	.	.	.	1.1130

While the premium rates for the policies could be derived analytically from the yield distributions, it is far easier to simulate a distribution of losses. In most situations we would use the best fitting of the candidate distributions, the Weibull, to generate the rates. In this application we compare rates from all of the estimated distributions to obtain a sense of how distributional assumptions can impact the price of insurance.

You can simulate the distribution of losses as follows. A DO loop draws 10,000 uniform random numbers z. Based on the parameter estimates computed by PROC SEVERITY for each distribution, z is transformed to the scale of the original yield data. We assume that the policyholder selects a coverage level of 75% and that the payout price for the yield insurance is 2.50 dollars. The mean of the estimated Weibull distribution is approximately 152 bushels per acre, so the insurer is liable for 285 dollars per insured acre. The simulated loss is either 0 or the difference between this liability and 2.50 times the simulated yield. A conditional statement constructs an indicator variable for whether the loss occurs. The rate is then given by the loss divided by total liability.

```
data simulation;
   call streaminit(1234);
   do i = 1 to 10000;
      z = rand('UNIFORM');
      y_gamma  = quantile('GAMMA', z, 59.75391, 2.54421);
      y_igauss = quantile('IGAUSS', z, 56.35450, 152.02639);
```

Figure 6.24 Kernel Density Estimate Output

The KDE Procedure

Inputs	
Data Set	WORK.NORMALIZEDYIELDS
Number of Observations Used	55
Variable	norm_adair_corn
Bandwidth Method	Sheather-Jones Plug In

Controls	
	norm_adair_corn
Grid Points	1000
Lower Grid Limit	0
Upper Grid Limit	185.93
Bandwidth Multiplier	1

Univariate Statistics	
	norm_adair_corn
Mean	152
Variance	363
Standard Deviation	19.04
Range	81.83
Interquartile Range	24.16
Bandwidth	7.96

The following code numerically integrates under the kernel density using the grid of evaluation points. Dividing the total grid width by the number of points, each cell has width 0.18593. The probability associated with each cell is the cell width multiplied by the density. The mean of the KDE density is 152, and assuming a coverage level of 75%, if the yield value is greater than 152 times the coverage level, set the probability variable to zero. To price the insurance we need an estimate of the probability of loss and the expected loss given that a loss occurs. PROC MEANS is used to sum the probabilities below the yield guarantee providing an estimate of the probability of loss.

```
data kernel;
set kernel;
    width = 0.18593;
    prob = density * width;
    y_guarantee = 152;
    if value > (.75 * y_guarantee) then prob = .;
    uno = 1;
run;

proc means sum noprint;
    by uno;
    var prob;
    output out = probsum sum = prob_sum;
run;

data kernel;
merge kernel probsum;
by uno;
    e_y_75 = value * prob / prob_sum;
    if value > (.75 * y_guarantee) then e_y_75 = .;
run;
```

```
proc means sum noprint;
   by uno;
   var e_y_75;
   output out = exsum sum = e_y_75_sum;
run;
```

If we assume the same payout price of 2.50 dollars, then total liability per acre is again 285 dollars. The expected loss is the product of the probability of loss and expected loss conditional on a loss occurring. The premium rate is expected loss divided by liability.

```
data kderates;
   merge probsum exsum;
   by uno;
   liab = 2.50 * .75 * 152;
   e_loss = prob_sum * (liab - 2.50 * e_y_75_sum);
   rate_kernel = e_loss / liab;
run;
```

Printing the premium rates, Figure 6.25 shows that the probability of loss is about 5% using the kernel density estimate. The premium rate is about 4/10 to 5/10 of a cent per dollar of liability. The rates obtained from the kernel density are closest to those obtained from the Weibull distribution. Note that because we numerically integrated under the candidate density, we didn't have to use PROC MEANS to obtain a rate from the simulated data.

```
proc print data = kderates;
run;
```

Figure 6.25 KDE Rates

Obs	uno	_TYPE_	_FREQ_	prob_sum	e_y_75_sum	liab	e_loss	rate_kernel
1	1	0	1000	0.061850	105.567	285	1.30394	.004575230

The preceding analysis of the distribution of yields has revealed the sensitivity of crop insurance prices to modeling assumptions. Because the program is subsidized, these assumptions inevitably affect government expenditures. In attempting to identify a best modeling procedure, we saw that the analyst must consider time trends in crop yields, parametric and nonparametric approaches to distribution estimation, and heteroskedasticity. We did not deal with the effects of weather or soil quality, although these variables influence crop yields and their effects have been quantified empirically. While characterizations of the yield distribution remain important for crop insurance pricing, farmers in the United States are increasingly purchasing revenue insurance; revenue insurance introduces additional actuarial complications and problems of economic interest.

6.3.3   Revenue Insurance

Revenue insurance policies pay the farmer on lost revenue, which is a function of both yields and prices. Unlike yield insurance where there is a single source of risk (yields), rating revenue insurance requires the modeler to deal with multiple dependent sources of risk. Under the most basic revenue insurance policy sold through the federal crop insurance program, a loss occurs when

$$\lambda Y_G P_P > Y_H P_H \tag{6.9}$$

where Y_G again denotes the yield guarantee and Y_H the harvest or realized yield. The price P_P is a planting time futures price, while P_H is the harvest price. The prices are obtained from futures contracts traded on the Chicago Mercantile Exchange. For instance, the planting time price for corn is the average February price for a corn contract expiring in December. The harvest price for corn is the average October price for the same contract expiring in December. The payout on a revenue insurance policy is given by

$$\lambda Y_G P_P - Y_H P_H \qquad (6.10)$$

which is simply the revenue shortfall created when realized revenue falls below projected revenue scaled by the coverage level. The actuarially fair premium on a revenue insurance policy is

Premium $=$ Expected Loss

$$P(\text{Loss}) E(\text{Loss} \mid \text{Loss Occurs})$$

$$P(\lambda Y_G P_P > Y_H P_H) E(\lambda Y_G P_P - Y_H P_H \mid \lambda Y_G > Y_H)$$

The obvious difference is that we are now dealing with two random variables: Y_H and P_H. The probability distribution underlying actuarial calculations will be bivariate, and in more general frameworks, could be multivariate.

To generate the joint distribution of prices and yields, actuarial procedures in the federal crop insurance program first assume that linear correlation between prices and yields is fixed within states. A joint distribution across a county level yield and price at the Chicago Mercantile Exchange is then formed using the technique of Iman and Conover (1982). This technique imposes several assumptions on dependence relationships between prices and yields; it is equivalent to the use of a Gaussian copula. Goodwin and Hungerford (2015) showed that resulting revenue insurance rates were sensitive to these assumptions. As with yield insurance, if modeling methods are flexible, such assumptions do not need to be imposed. The best model can be selected according to empirical fit criteria.

6.3.4 Dependence and Copulas

A well-known result from introductory statistics is that if two variables are uncorrelated they are not necessarily independent. On the other hand, if two variables are independent, they are uncorrelated. Indeed two variables are independent only if $F_{xy}(x, y) = F_x(x) F_y(y)$ for all x and y. Much of statistics and econometrics is concerned with dependence between variables and associations between variables. A number of methods have accordingly been developed to measure association between variables, or dependence in general. Confronted with two or more variables, these measures provide a good first look at how the variables might be related and how dependence between the variables might be modeled.

You are likely already familiar with Pearson correlation which measures the strength and direction of a linear relationship between two variables. When two variables are exactly related by a linear function and a positive relationship exits, the Pearson correlation takes the value 1. If the exact linear relationship is negative, then the correlation coefficient is -1. The Pearson correlation is

$$\psi_{xy} = \frac{\text{Cov}(x, y)}{\text{Var}(x)^{1/2} \text{Var}(y)^{1/2}} \qquad (6.11)$$

where x and y are the variables whose correlation we wish to measure. The covariance and variance of these variables are usually computed using the sample covariance and sample variance.

One problem with using Pearson correlation to measure dependence is that it is only a measure of linear dependence. In many cases, a better measure of dependence can be obtained by using nonparametric and nonlinear measures that are based on sample ranks. Let R_i^x be the rank of x_i and R_i^y the rank of y_i. The respective means of the ranks are given by $\bar{R}^x$ and $\bar{R}^y$. Then the Spearman correlation is given by

$$\theta = \frac{\sum_i (R_i^x - \bar{R}^x)(R_i^y - \bar{R}^y))}{\sqrt{\sum_i (R_i^x - \bar{R}^x)^2 \sum_i (R_i^y - \bar{R}^y)^2}} \qquad (6.12)$$

It is clear from the formula that Spearman correlation is a rank–based generalization of Pearson correlation. For this reason it is often called rank-order correlation.

We can also use Kendall's tau (Kendall 1938) to investigate dependence between two variables. This measure of dependence is based on the number of concordances and discordances in a pair of observations. Concordance is when two observations vary together, and discordance is when two observations vary differently. Kendall's tau is given by

$$\tau = \frac{\sum_{i<j}(\text{sgn}(x_i - x_j))(\text{sgn}(y_i - y_j))}{\sqrt{(T_0 - T_1)(T_0 - T_2)}} \tag{6.13}$$

where $T_0 = n(n-1)/2$, $T_1 = \sum_k t_k(t_k - 1)/2$, and $T_2 = \sum_l u_l(u_l - 1)/2$. The t_k is the number of tied x values in the kth group of tied x values while u_l is the number of tied y values in the lth group of tied y values. The sign function $\text{sgn}(x)$ is 1 if $z > 0$, 0 if $z = 0$ and -1 if $z < 0$.

Lastly, we can compare values of Hoeffding's D (Hoeffding 1948). This is a more general measure of association.

$$D = 30\frac{(n-2)(n-3)D_1 + D_2 - 2(n-2)D_3}{n(n-1)(n-2)(n-3)(n-4)} \tag{6.14}$$

where $D_1 = \sum_i(Q_i - 1)(Q_i - 2)$, $D_2 = \sum_i(R_1^x - 1)(R_i^x - 2)(R_i^y - 1)(R_i^y - 2)$ and $D_3 = \sum_i(R_i^x - 2)(R_i^y - 2)(Q_i - 1)$. For each point in the data, R_i^x is the rank of x_i, R_i^y is the rank of y_i, and Q_i is the bivariate rank of (x_i, y_i). Spearman rank correlation and Kendall's tau can capture monotonic dependence, while Hoeffding's D captures dependence that can be nonmonotonic.

While these measures of association can provide some insight into the nature of dependence between two variables, they don't necessarily provide an effective modeling approach. Many standard "named" multivariate distributions are restrictive in one way or another. The univariate margins of the multivariate normal distribution, for instance, must be normal themselves. Such an assumption is unrealistic when modeling crop yields and prices. We have already seen that yield distributions are often skewed and may be multimodal. The basic problem is that multivariate distributions contain information about both the dependence structure between variables and the marginal distributions. If it was possible to separate these two elements of the model, then their estimation could proceed independent of one another.

Sklar (1959) showed that this separation was theoretically possible by introducing the copula function. His existence theorem is as follows. Let F be a distribution function in d dimensions with marginal distribution functions F_i for $i = 1, \ldots, d$. Then there exists a copula function $C : [0, 1]^d \rightarrow [0, 1]$ such that $F(x_1, \ldots, x_d) = C(F_1(x_1), \ldots, F_d(x_d))$ for all $x \in [-\infty, \infty]$. C is unique if the margins are continuous, as is the case in most practical applications. The copula is itself a multivariate distribution function on Uniform(0,1) margins.

The are two major classes of copula functions: elliptical and Archimedean. Elliptical copulas are derived from corresponding elliptical multivariate distributions such as the multivariate normal and multivariate Student's t. If the densities of these distributions are plotted in the bivariate case, the contour plot will show their elliptical shapes. The Gaussian copula in k dimensions takes the form

$$C_N(u_1, ..., u_k) = \Phi\left(\phi^{-1}(u_1), ..., \phi^{-1}(u_k)\right) \tag{6.15}$$

where Φ is the multivariate standard normal distribution with mean $\mathbf{0}$ and a given covariance matrix. ϕ is the distribution function of a standard normal random variable. The copula is then defined by $k(k-1)/2$ parameters.

The t copula takes the form

$$C_t(u_1, ..., u_k) = \mathbf{t}\left(t_v^{-1}(u_1), ..., t_v^{-1}(u_k)\right) \tag{6.16}$$

where t_v is the univariate t distribution with v degrees of freedom and $\mathbf{t}$ is the multivariate Student's t distribution with a given correlation matrix and v degrees of freedom. The t copula has $1 + k(k-1)/2$ parameters. Both the Gaussian and t copulas have symmetric dependence structures.

The second class of copula functions are the Archimedean copulas. Archimedean copulas have the general form $C(u_1, \ldots, u_d) = \rho^{-1}(\rho(u_1), \ldots, \rho(u_d))$ where $\rho(\cdot)$ is a function known as the generator function of the copula. To be a valid generator function $\rho : [0, 1] \rightarrow [0, \infty)$ with $\rho(0) = \infty$ and $\rho(1) = 0$. It must also be differentiable and monotone increasing. If these conditions are satisfied then the generator function will form a valid copula according to the equation above. A large number of functions meet the requirements to form a valid generator function and there are many Archimedean copulas. The most widely used Archimedean copulas are the Gumbel, Clayton, and Frank copulas. Each of these is indexed by a single parameter.

The Clayton copula is defined as

$$C_C(u_1, ..., u_k) = \left(\sum_{i=1}^{k} u_i^{-\theta} - k + 1 \right)^{-1/\theta} \tag{6.17}$$

with $\theta > 0$.

The Gumbel copula is

$$C_G(u_1, ..., u_k) = \exp\left(-\left(\sum_{i=1}^{k} -(\log u_i)^{\theta} \right)^{1/\theta} \right) \tag{6.18}$$

where $\theta > 1$.

The Frank copula is

$$C_F(u_1, ..., u_k) = \frac{1}{\theta} \log \left(1 + \frac{\sum_{i=1}^{k}(\exp(-\theta u_i) - 1)}{(\exp(-\theta) - 1)^{k-1}} \right) \tag{6.19}$$

where $\theta \in (-\infty, \infty)/0$ in two dimensions and $\theta > 0$ in three or more dimensions. The Frank copula has a symmetric dependence structure, while the Clayton and Gumbel copulas have asymmetric dependence.

One dependence feature of interest is tail dependence. Tail dependence is an asymptotic measure that describes dependence between two variables that both take extreme values. Upper tail dependence is defined as

$$\lambda_U = \lim_{u \to \infty} P(X > F_X^{-1}(u)|Y > F_Y^{-1}(u)) \tag{6.20}$$

and lower tail dependence is defined as

$$\lambda_L = \lim_{u \to -\infty} P(X > F_X^{-1}(u)|Y > F_Y^{-1}(u)) \tag{6.21}$$

The degree of tail dependence is restricted by the choice of copula. The Gaussian copula cannot have any tail dependence, whereas the t copula can have tail dependence. Since the t copula is symmetric, tail dependence will be the same in the upper and lower tails. The degree of dependence is controlled by the degrees of freedom parameter. The Gumbel copula has tail dependence in the upper tail, but not the lower. This is in contrast to the Clayton copula which has tail dependence in the lower tail, but not the upper. The Frank copula has no dependence in either tail. With two elliptical copulas and three Archimedean copulas, it is then possible to cover a range of different symmetry and tail dependence scenarios. Selection of the optimal copula can be driven by the data.

Schweizer and Wolff (1981) showed that the study of copulas and the study of rank statistics are one in the same. Spearman rank correlation and Kendall's tau can both be expressed as functions of the copula with

$$\begin{aligned} \theta &= 12 \int_0^1 \int_0^1 (C(u, v) - uv)\, du\, dv \\ \tau &= 4 \int_0^1 \int_0^1 C(u, v) dC(u, v) - 1 \end{aligned} \tag{6.22}$$

Moving from an approach to dependence based on Pearson correlation to the use of copulas, we drop any assumption of linearity. This also implies a direct correspondence between the copula parameters and values of the rank statistics. Copulas can be fit to data using calibration methods. For instance, an estimate of Kendall's tau is computed and then plugged in to determine the parameter of the copula. One exception is the t copula because the degrees of freedom parameter is independent of the theoretical value of the rank statistics.

6.3.5 Empirical Analysis

This empirical application uses the same yield data as our yield insurance example. For simplicity we only consider a revenue insurance policy for Adair, IA corn. The interested reader can extend the analysis to the other three counties using the data provided. The average monthly closing prices in February and October for the December corn futures contract are obtained from the Chicago Board of Trade. Like the yield data, these prices run from 1960 to 2014 and we provide data for both corn and soybeans. The following code merges the data sets containing the corn and soybean prices.

```
data prices;
   merge corn_prices soy_prices;
run;

proc print data = prices(obs = 10);
run;
```

Figure 6.26 Price Data

Obs	year	c_price_feb	c_price_oct	s_price_feb	s_price_oct
1	1960	110.194	108.393	207.619	214.875
2	1961	122.197	109.926	238.105	240.057
3	1962	116.026	106.853	239.375	240.277
4	1963	114.375	118.294	249.388	276.880
5	1964	119.132	121.085	255.961	271.580
6	1965	120.704	114.738	254.868	246.816
7	1966	120.954	135.399	268.531	292.992
8	1967	133.401	113.926	276.999	263.635
9	1968	128.355	106.196	271.485	250.748
10	1969	115.743	118.612	240.360	242.314

We will refer to the the logarithm of the ratio of the October and February prices as a relative price, or return over the growing season. It contains information about the change in prices between the two months; this is the relevant information for rating the revenue insurance policies. Because the February price is known at the time the policy is sold we will be able to simulate rates for the parameters of a given contract. Additionally, monthly average prices are not stationary across years. Commodity price levels have increased since 1960 and particularly over the past decade. Even if the level of monthly average prices follows a trend, the log price difference may not.

Our expectation is that the relative price is negatively related to the county yield. Without storage, and with consistent demand for an agricultural commodity, downward sloping market demand curves imply that prices rise when yields are low. Conversely, high yields imply low prices. This theoretical relationship is known as the natural hedge. Because revenue is a function of prices and yields, a strong natural hedge causes consistent farm revenues over time. Our estimate of dependence between yields and prices is therefore an estimate of the strength of the natural hedge. A DATA step is first used to create the log price ratios or relative prices.

```
data prices;
set prices;
   c_log_price = log(c_price_oct/c_price_feb);
   s_log_price = log(s_price_oct/s_price_feb);
run;
```

The code below plots both of the relative price series. Based on the plots in Figure 6.27, the relative price series appear to be stationary.

```
proc sgplot data = prices;
   scatter x = year y = c_log_price;
   title 'Relative Futures Price, Corn';
   yaxis label = 'Relative Price';
run;

proc sgplot data = prices;
   scatter x = year y = s_log_price;
   title 'Relative Futures Price, Soybeans';
   yaxis label = 'Relative Price';
run;
```

Figure 6.27 Relative Futures Prices

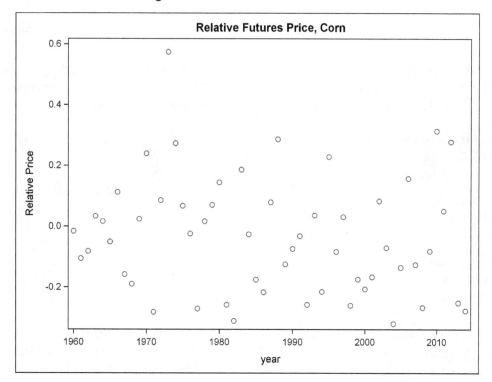

Figure 6.27 *continued*

In the yield insurance example, code was provided to account for trends and heteroskedasticity. The last step before fitting the copulas is to merge the normalized yield data with the data set of relative prices. The copula is fitted to the normalized prices from the Chicago Mercantile Exchange and the yield data in each county.

```
proc sort data = normalizedyields;
   by year;
run;

proc sort data = prices;
   by year;
run;

data prices_yields;
   merge prices normalizedyields;
   by year;
run;
```

Before fitting the copulas, PROC CORR can be used to analyze dependence between the normalized Adair County, Iowa yields and the relative prices obtained from the Chicago Mercantile Exchange. The options for the CORR procedure specify estimates of the Pearson correlation, Spearman's rho, Kendall's tau, and Hoeffding's D. The VAR statement specifies the two variables from the input data set to be used in the estimation. With these four measures of association, we are able to capture both nonlinear and nonmonotonic dependence. In applications with massive amounts of data, the HPCORR procedure can be used, but it only calculates Pearson product moment correlation.

```
proc corr data = prices_yields
   pearson spearman kendall hoeffding
   plots = matrix(histogram);
   var norm_adair_corn c_log_price;
run;
```

The results of the CORR procedure are shown in Figure 6.28. There were 55 observations in the input data set. For each dependence measure, the procedure gives a dependence matrix that shows the estimated dependence or correlation coefficient and probabilities associated with tests of statistical significance. The null hypotheses for the tests are explained in the output headers. Both the Pearson correlation coefficient and the Spearman rank-order correlation indicate a negative relationship between prices and yields with significant p-values less than 0.01. Kendall's tau, based on the number of concordances and discordances, gives similar results. The Hoeffding D statistic indicates weak dependence between the two variables, but it is not significantly different from 0 at the 1% level. Overall, these results are suggestive of weak but significant negative association between price and yield. Determining the direction of this relationship is particularly important as it informs our choice of copula models.

Figure 6.28 Correlation Matrices

The CORR Procedure

Pearson Correlation Coefficients, N = 55 Prob > |r| under H0: Rho=0		
	norm_adair_corn	c_log_price
norm_adair_corn	1.00000	-0.36468
		0.0062
c_log_price	-0.36468	1.00000
	0.0062	

Spearman Correlation Coefficients, N = 55 Prob > |r| under H0: Rho=0		
	norm_adair_corn	c_log_price
norm_adair_corn	1.00000	-0.36595
		0.0060
c_log_price	-0.36595	1.00000
	0.0060	

Kendall Tau b Correlation Coefficients, N = 55 Prob > |tau| under H0: Tau=0		
	norm_adair_corn	c_log_price
norm_adair_corn	1.00000	-0.25522
		0.0059
c_log_price	-0.25522	1.00000
	0.0059	

Hoeffding Dependence Coefficients, N = 55 Prob > D under H0: D=0		
	norm_adair_corn	c_log_price
norm_adair_corn	1.00000	0.02873
		0.0150
c_log_price	0.02873	1.00000
	0.0150	

The following code estimates a Gaussian copula on the corn yield and price. The VAR statement again specifies the variables to be used in the estimation. The FIT statement instructs SAS to fit a normal copula to the data. The marginal distributions of the data are not specified and the empirical marginal distributions are used to transform the input variables to the Uniform(0,1) scale. The METHOD option specifies estimation of the copula parameters via maximum likelihood, while the PLOTS option calls for scatterplot matrices of both the raw and uniform data. Simulated data from the copula will be used to construct a distribution of losses, so the SIMULATE statement produces 10,000 uniform draws from the estimated Gaussian copula. These draws are stored in the data set NormalSim. We also output the uniform pseudovariables used in the copula estimation to the data set Pseudos.

PROC COPULA provides several methods for estimating the copula: maximum likelihood and calibration. For calibration, Kendall's tau is estimated on the data and then mapped to the copula parameter of interest. For maximum likelihood, the variables are first transformed to the uniform scale and the copula likelihood is then maximized. To make the transformation, one can use parametric representations of the marginals or nonparametric estimates. Parametric marginals were suggested by Joe and Xu (1996) in a technique that has become known as Inference Functions for Margins (IFM). The use of nonparametric marginals is discussed in Genest, Ghoudi, and Rivest (1995). As with IFM and maximum likelihood approaches, the semiparametric estimator of the copula parameters is consistent and asymptotically normal. Two step approaches, where marginal distributions are obtained first and then taken as given, have proven to be exceptionally useful in the copula paradigm. Their popularity arises because they allow for the problems of the estimation of the dependence structure and the marginal distributions to be separated.

```
proc copula data = prices_yields;
   var norm_adair_corn c_log_price;
   fit NORMAL / marginals = empirical
       method = MLE
       plots = (datatype = both)
       outpseudo = pseudos;
   simulate /
         ndraws = 10000
         seed    = 1234
         outuniform  = normalsim;
run;
```

The matrix plots in Figure 6.29 confirm the results of PROC CORR. There appears to be a negative relationship between price and yield. We also have observations in the tails of the distribution, possibly indicating tail dependence. The matrix of transformed data contains scatterplots of ranks. The transformed data is more useful for visualizing dependence between the variables because the raw data plots are affected by the scaling of the marginal distributions.

Figure 6.29 Matrix Plot

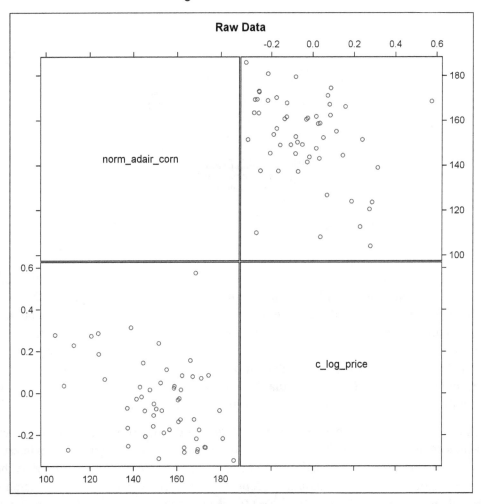

Figure 6.29 *continued*

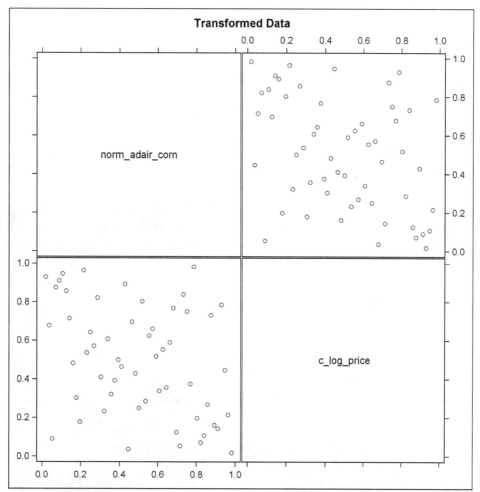

The correlation matrix for the Gaussian copula in Figure 6.30 indicates negative dependence between the two variables with a correlation parameter of -0.3935.

Figure 6.30 Fit Summary

The COPULA Procedure

Model Fit Summary	
Number of Observations	55
Data Set	WORK.PRICES_YIELDS
Copula Type	Normal

Correlation Matrix		
	norm_adair_corn	c_log_price
norm_adair_corn	1.0000	-0.3935
c_log_price	-0.3935	1.0000

In making use of the Gaussian copula, we implicitly assumed that there is no tail dependence between prices and yields. Extreme prices and yields, whether characterized by a positive or negative relationship, never occur together. A more flexible approach is to use the *t* copula, which is able to capture possible tail dependence. The *t* copula can be fit to the data with a similar call to PROC COPULA. The only change to the code comes from the FIT statement, where NORMAL has been changed to T. Note that calibration methods of estimation cannot be used with the t copula because the degrees of freedom parameter is independent of the copula's theoretical value for Kendall's tau.

```
proc copula data = prices_yields ;
   var norm_adair_corn c_log_price;
   fit T / marginals = empirical
       method = MLE
       plots = (datatype = both);
   simulate /
         ndraws = 10000
         seed   = 1234
         outuniform = tsim;
run;
```

The results of the t copula estimation are shown in Figure 6.31. The correlation parameter is -0.4019, similar to the correlation parameter of the normal copula. However, the degrees of freedom parameter, which measures tail dependence, is 2.03. As the degrees of freedom parameter goes to infinity, the t copula converges to the normal copula. The small degrees of freedom parameter that we observe indicates strong dependence in the tails of the distribution.

Figure 6.31 Fit Summary

The COPULA Procedure

Model Fit Summary	
Number of Observations	55
Data Set	WORK.PRICES_YIELDS
Copula Type	T
Log Likelihood	7.21199
Maximum Absolute Gradient	7.24032E-6
Number of Iterations	2
Optimization Method	Newton-Raphson
AIC	-10.42397
SBC	-6.40931

Parameter Estimates				
Parameter	Estimate	Standard Error	t Value	Approx Pr > |t|
DF	2.034393	1.004467	2.03	0.0428

Correlation Matrix		
	norm_adair_corn	c_log_price
norm_adair_corn	1.0000	-0.4019
c_log_price	-0.4019	1.0000

Thus far, we have only considered copulas with symmetric tail dependence. This assumption may not be reasonable if the response of prices to exceptionally low yields is different from the response to exceptionally high yields. Archimedean Gumble and Clayton copulas have asymmetric tail dependence. However, these basic Archimedean copulas can only capture positive dependence between the variables. If we believe that the natural hedge holds, then we would expect a negative relationship. By way of rotation, Archimedean copulas can be fit to data that exhibits negative dependence. In the two dimensional case, the transformations

$$u_{1,t} = u_1 \qquad u_{2,t} = 1 - u_2$$
$$u_{1,t} = 1 - u_1 \qquad u_{2,t} = u_2$$
$$u_{1,t} = 1 - u_1 \qquad u_{2,t} = 1 - u_2$$

have the effect of rotating the copula 90, 270, and 180 degrees respectively. In d dimensions, there are 2^d possible orientations. If we did not have any economic theory to guide us in choosing a suitable rotation, all four rotations could be estimated and the best fitting rotation could be selected according to fit statistics. Before we fit the Gumbel and Clayton copulas to the data, first rotate the copulas 90 degrees by constructing a rotated version of the price variable. Instead of starting from the raw data, we can use the pseudovariables that were output from our previous estimation of the Gaussian copula.

```
data arch_prices_yields;
set pseudos;
   c_log_price_rot = 1 - c_log_price;
run;
```

The Gumbel copula is fit to the rotated data using PROC COPULA. Because the input data are already on the uniform scale, the MARGINALS option is specified as uniform.

```
proc copula data = arch_prices_yields ;
   var norm_adair_corn c_log_price_rot;
   fit gumbel / marginals = uniform
       method = MLE
       plots = (datatype = both);
   simulate /
           ndraws = 10000
           seed   = 1234
           outuniform = gumbelsim;
run;
```

A quick look at the matrix plot in Figure 6.32 confirms that we correctly rotated the data.

Figure 6.32 Matrix Plot

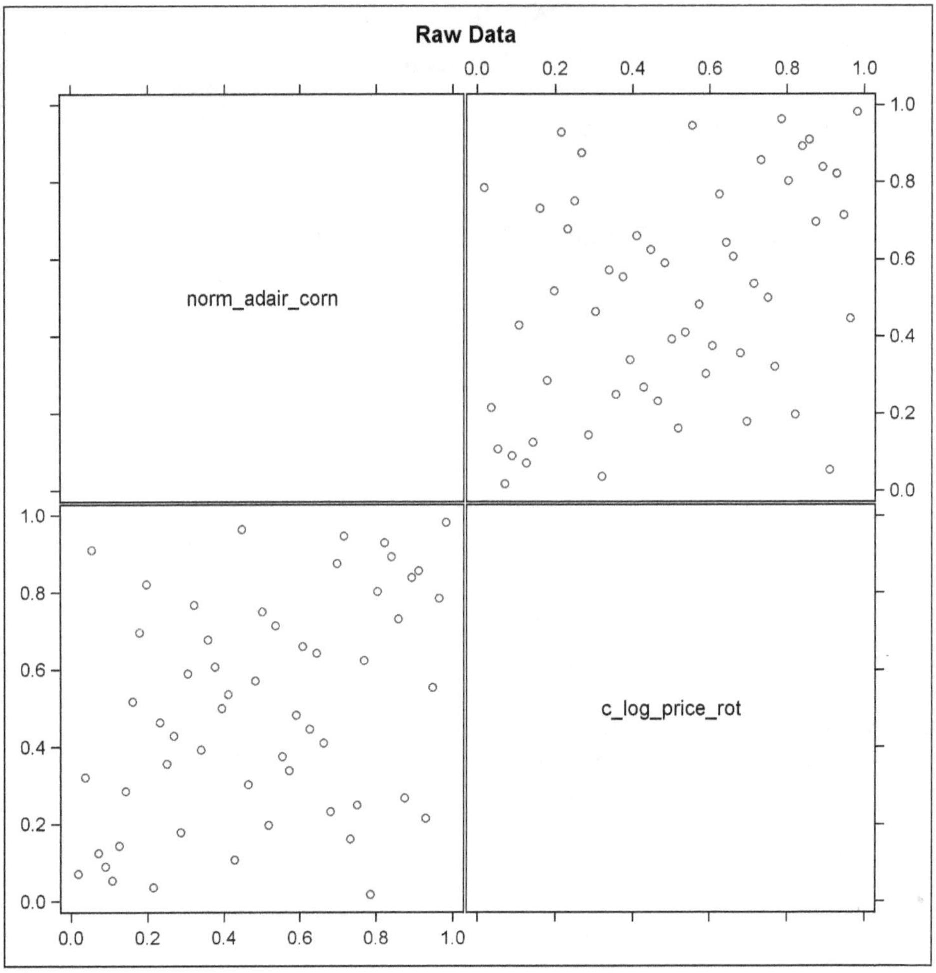

Results from the Gumbel copula are shown in Figure 6.33. There is weak dependence given the small value of the copula's single parameter θ. Notice also that when the copulas are estimated using maximum likelihoods, the SAS output contains standard errors and t values for the estimated parameters. This is in contrast to the calibration approach where only the parameter estimate is provided.

Figure 6.33 Parameter Estimates

The COPULA Procedure

Model Fit Summary	
Number of Observations	55
Data Set	WORK.ARCH_PRICES_YIELDS
Copula Type	Gumbel
Log Likelihood	5.83833
Maximum Absolute Gradient	4.34857E-8
Number of Iterations	3
Optimization Method	Newton-Raphson
AIC	-9.67665
SBC	-7.66932

Figure 6.33 *continued*

		Standard		Approx
Parameter	Estimate	Error	t Value	Pr > |t|
theta	1.423891	0.158315	8.99	<.0001

Parameter Estimates

The Clayton copula is estimated in a similar manner from the rotated data. Instead of estimating the copula using maximum likelihood estimation, the copula is calibrated from Kendall's tau by specifying METHOD = CAL.

```
proc copula data = arch_prices_yields ;
   var norm_adair_corn c_log_price_rot;
   fit clayton / marginals = uniform
       method = CAL
       plots = (datatype = both);
   simulate /
         ndraws = 10000
         seed   = 1234
         outuniform = claytonsim;
run;
```

Figure 6.34 Parameter Estimates

The COPULA Procedure

Model Fit Summary

Number of Observations	55
Data Set	WORK.ARCH_PRICES_YIELDS
Copula Type	Clayton

Parameter Estimates

		Standard		Approx
Parameter	Estimate	Error	t Value	Pr > |t|
theta	0.685353	.	.	.

We can estimate the same Clayton copula using maximum likelihood. Notice that output from the procedure, when using maximum likelihood estimation, also includes various fit statistics. In particular, we are provided with Akaike information criterion and the Schwarz Bayesian criterion. The fit of different copulas can be compared based on the values of the fit statistics. The best fitting copula, for instance, is that with minimum AIC. It is important to remember that the marginal distributions must be held constant when comparing the fit of the copula. Using AIC as a measure of fit, the *t* copula has minimum AIC compared to the rotated Gumbel and rotated Clayton.

Figure 6.35 Parameter Estimates

The COPULA Procedure

Model Fit Summary	
Number of Observations	55
Data Set	WORK.ARCH_PRICES_YIELDS
Copula Type	Clayton
Log Likelihood	4.08568
Maximum Absolute Gradient	3.56818E-7
Number of Iterations	2
Optimization Method	Newton-Raphson
AIC	-6.17136
SBC	-4.16403

		Parameter Estimates		
Parameter	Estimate	Standard Error	t Value	Approx Pr > |t|
theta	0.652664	0.251184	2.60	0.0094

We may be interested in how the choice of a copula for modeling dependence affects the price of insurance. The following DATA steps use the uniform draws from the copulas to create a simulated distribution of losses. Remember that the February average price is known at the time the policy is sold, so you must assume a synthetic price for the purposes of the loss simulation. A February average price of 400 cents per bushel of corn is assumed in the simulations that follow. Based on the results of the SEVERITY procedure estimates, we use the Weibull distribution as the marginal distribution of yields. The normalized yield is constructed using the QUANTILE function of the Weibull distribution. The log ratio of the October and February prices is assumed to follow a normal distribution with conditional volatility of 20. Inverting this expression you can solve for the October average price.

```
data ncoprates;
set normalsim;
   y_n_copula = quantile('WEIBULL', norm_adair_corn, 10.1344, 159.931);
   p_feb = 4;
   p_n_oct = p_feb * exp(-.2**2/2 + .2 * quantile('NORMAL', c_log_price, 0, 1));
run;

data tcoprates;
set tsim;
   y_t_copula = quantile('WEIBULL', norm_adair_corn, 10.1344, 159.931);
   p_feb = 4;
   p_t_oct = p_feb * exp(-.2**2/2 + .2 * quantile('NORMAL', c_log_price, 0, 1));
run;

data gcoprates;
set gumbelsim;
   c_log_price = 1 - c_log_price_rot;
   y_g_copula = quantile('WEIBULL', norm_adair_corn, 10.1344, 159.931);
   p_feb = 4;
   p_g_oct = p_feb * exp(-.2**2/2 + .2 * quantile('NORMAL', c_log_price, 0, 1));
run;

data ccoprates;
set claytonsim;
   c_log_price = 1 - c_log_price_rot;
   y_c_copula = quantile('WEIBULL', norm_adair_corn, 10.1344, 159.931);
```

```
   p_feb = 4;
   p_c_oct = p_feb * exp(-.2**2/2 + .2 * quantile('NORMAL', c_log_price, 0, 1));
run;
```

Armed with simulated prices and yields, we can generate a distribution of losses. As calculated in the following code, guaranteed revenue is the February average price multiplied by the average yield and the coverage level. We earlier found the average yield to be 152 bushels per year and we can assume a coverage level of 90%. The loss under the policy is then either zero or the difference between the guaranteed revenue and realized revenue. Realized revenue is simply the product of the October average price and the simulated yield.

```
data ncoprates;
set ncoprates;
   g = p_feb * .90 * 152;
   loss_normal = max(0, g - p_n_oct * y_n_copula);
   ld_normal = (g > p_n_oct * y_n_copula);
   rate_normal = loss_normal / g;
run;

data tcoprates;
set tcoprates;
   g = p_feb * .90 * 152;
   loss_t   = max(0, g - p_t_oct * y_t_copula);
   ld_t     = (g > p_t_oct * y_t_copula);
   rate_t = loss_t / g;
run;

data gcoprates;
set gcoprates;
   g = p_feb * .90 * 152;
   loss_g   = max(0, g - p_g_oct * y_g_copula);
   ld_g     = (g > p_g_oct * y_g_copula);
   rate_g = loss_g / g;
run;

data ccoprates;
set ccoprates;
   g = p_feb * .90 * 152;
   loss_c   = max(0, g - p_c_oct * y_c_copula);
   ld_c     = (g > p_c_oct * y_c_copula);
   rate_c = loss_c / g;
run;

data rates;
merge ncoprates tcoprates gcoprates ccoprates;
run;
```

After merging the data from the different copulas, PROC MEANS can be used to summarize the simulated distribution of losses. Remember that, according to AIC, the t copula fit best among the copulas considered. In this case, we do not see much difference in the rates obtained from the different copulas. The simulated policy has a price of about 3.5 cents per dollar of liability under the t copula. Because the Gaussian copula is similar to the t, except for tail independence, the Gaussian rate should be higher than the t when the relationship between prices and yields is negative. This appears to be the case based on output from the MEANS procedure.

```
proc means data = rates;
run;
```

Figure 6.36 Revenue Insurance Rates

The MEANS Procedure

Variable	N	Mean	Std Dev	Minimum	Maximum
norm_adair_corn	10000	0.4963087	0.2887150	1.7957715E-6	0.9998816
c_log_price	10000	0.5014690	0.2902143	0.000214505	0.9999715
y_n_copula	10000	152.1018135	18.1870286	62.7111826	201.6312804
p_feb	10000	4.0000000	0	4.0000000	4.0000000
p_n_oct	10000	3.9972076	0.8063806	1.6287516	9.4866699
g	10000	547.2000000	0	547.2000000	547.2000000
loss_normal	10000	21.4523518	40.8991358	0	285.5961266
ld_normal	10000	0.3357000	0.4722582	0	1.0000000
rate_normal	10000	0.0392039	0.0747426	0	0.5219227
y_t_copula	10000	151.8890493	18.2712027	63.7344638	204.1731199
p_t_oct	10000	4.0129866	0.8142238	1.5197466	8.1250415
loss_t	10000	19.2574697	42.5625593	0	394.7376718
ld_t	10000	0.3087000	0.4619801	0	1.0000000
rate_t	10000	0.0351927	0.0777825	0	0.7213773
c_log_price_rot	10000	0.4985310	0.2902143	0.000028497	0.9997855
y_g_copula	10000	151.9657424	17.9238221	55.1134217	198.8257196
p_g_oct	10000	4.0124224	0.8146818	1.8168199	8.2757160
loss_g	10000	20.0379902	39.1508356	0	289.4954792
ld_g	10000	0.3318000	0.4708831	0	1.0000000
rate_g	10000	0.0366191	0.0715476	0	0.5290488
y_c_copula	10000	151.9681595	18.1189867	43.3488593	198.7415430
p_c_oct	10000	4.0062341	0.8120428	1.9386303	8.7694911
loss_c	10000	20.7177429	41.1905035	0	315.5520113
ld_c	10000	0.3220000	0.4672663	0	1.0000000
rate_c	10000	0.0378614	0.0752750	0	0.5766667

This chapter has detailed several basic models for measuring risk. Because the measurement of risk involves probability distributions, the different models essentially involved creative ways of obtaining a probability distribution for a random variable. The earlier compound distribution model relies on independence between the units of interest. This assumption is relaxed in the copula models which allow for models of multiple dependent variables. In both cases, we also dealt with fitting univariate marginal distributions, whether the underlying variables were counts, continuous, etc.

While the examples may seem specific, the general principles and tools underlying the examples are common to many risk modeling applications. The goal is to measure the probability that a loss occurs and an expected loss. Through the SEVERITY, HPCDM, and COPULA procedures, SAS provides powerful tools for obtaining these measurements. Our hope is that applied practicioners, even if they are working outside of automotive or agricultural insurance, can take the general principles and techniques of this chapter and apply them in their own areas of interest. Start from the basics and then modify the model and code as needed.

References

Aigner, D. J., Lovell, C. A. K., and Schmidt, P. (1977). "Formulation and Estimation of Stochastic Frontier Production Function Models." *Journal of Econometrics* 6:21–37.

Allen, R. G. D. (1938). *Mathematical Analysis for Economists*. London: Macmillan.

Alson, J. M., and Chalfant, J. A. (1993). "The Silence of the Lambdas: A Test of the Almost Ideal and Rotterdam Models." *American Journal of Agricultural Economics* 75:304–313.

Alston, J. M., Chalfant, J. A., and Piggott, N. E. (2002). "Estimating and testing the compensated double–log demand model." *Applied Economics* 34:1177–1186.

Asche, F., and Wessels, C. R. (1997). "On Price Indices in the Almost Ideal Demand System." *American Journal of Agricultural Economics* 79:1182–1185.

Atkinson, S. E., and Dorfman, J. H. (2005). "Bayesian measurement of productivity and efficiency in the presence of undesirable outputs: crediting electric utilities for reducing air pollution." *Journal of Econometrics* 126:445–468.

Banks, J., Blundell, R. W., and Lewbel, A. (1997). "Quadratic Engel curves and consumer demand." *Review of Economics and Statistics* 79:527–539.

Barnett, W. A. (1979). "Theoretical Foundations for the Rotterdam Model." *Review of Economic Studies* 46:109–130.

Barnett, W. A., and Seck, O. (2008). "Rotterdam model versus almost ideal demand system: will the best specification please stand up?" *Journal of Applied Econometrics* 23:795–824.

Barnett, W. A., and Serletis, A. (2009). "The Differential Approach to Demand Analysis and the Rotterdam Model." In *Quantifying Consumer Preferences*, edited by D. Slottje, 61–81. Bingley, UK: Emerald Group.

Barten, A. P. (1964). "Consumer Demand Equations under Conditions of Almost Additive Preferences." *Econometrica* 32:1–38.

Battese, G. E. (1992). "Frontier Production Functions and Technical Efficiency: A Survey of Empirical Applications in Agricultural Economics." *Agricultural Economics* 7:185–208.

Battese, G. E., and Coelli, T. J. (1995). "A Model for Technical Efficiency Effects in a Stochastic Frontier Production Function for Panel Data." *Empirical Economics* 20:325–332.

Battese, G. E., Harter, R. M., and Fuller, W. A. (1988). "An Error-Components Model for Prediction of County Crop Areas Using Survey and Satellite Data." *Journal of the American Statistical Association* 83:28–36.

Becker, G. S. (1973). "A Theory of Marriage: Part I." *Journal of Political Economy* 81:813–846.

Becker, G. S. (1983). "A theory of Competition Among Pressure groups For political Influence." *The Quarterly Journal of Economics* 97:371–400.

Berry, S., Levinsohn, J., and Pakes, A. (1995). "Automobile Prices in Market Equilibrium." *Econometrica* 63:841–890.

Blackorby, C., Primont, D., and Russell, R. R. (2007). "The Morishima gross elasticity of substitution." *Journal of Productivity Analysis* 28:203–208.

Blackorby, C., and Russell, R. R. (1989). "Will the Real Elasticity of Substitution Please Stand Up? (A Comparison of the Allen/Uzawa and Morishima Elasticities)." *American Economic Review* 79:882–888.

Botts, R. R., and Boles, J. N. (1958). "Use of Normal-Curve Theory in Crop INsurance Ratemaking." *Journal of Farm Economics* 40:733–740.

Chambers, R. G. (1988). *Applied Production Analysis: A Dual Approach.* New York: Cambridge University Press.

Chavas, J., and Segerson, K. (1987). "Stochastic specification and estimation of share systems." *Journal of Econometrics* 35:337–358.

Christensen, L. R., Jorgenson, D. W., and Lau, L. J. (1975). "Transcendental Logarithmic Utility Functions." *American Economic Review* 65:367–383.

Christensen, L. R., and Manser, M. E. (1977). "Estimating U.S. Consumer Preferences for Meat with a Flexible Utility Function." *Journal of Econometrics* 5:37–53.

Clements, K. W., and Gao, G. (2015). "The Rotterdam demand model half a century on." *Economic Modelling* 49:91–103.

Coelli, T. J., Rao, D. S. P., O'Donnell, C. J., and Battese, G. E. (2005). *An Introduction to Efficiency and Productivity Analysis.* New York: Springer.

Cornes, R. (1992). *Duality and modern economics.* New York: Cambridge University Press.

Davis, G. C., and Gauger, J. (1996). "Measuring Substitution in Monetary-Asset Demand Systems." *Journal of Business and Economic Statistics* 14:203–208.

Deaton, A., and Muellbauer, J. (1980a). "An Almost Ideal Demand System." *American Economic Review* 70:312–326.

Deaton, A., and Muellbauer, J. (1980b). *Economics and consumer behavior.* New York: Cambridge University Press.

Diewert, W. E. (1971). *Choice on Labour Markets and the Theory of The Allocation of Time.* Tech. rep., Research Branch, Department of Manpower and Immigration Canada, Ottawa.

Diewert, W. E. (1976). "Exact and Superlative Index Numbers." *Journal of Econometrics* 4:115–145.

Diewert, W. E., and Nakamura, A. O. (2003). "Index number concepts, measures and decompositions of productivity growth." *Journal of Productivity Analysis* 19:127–159.

Diewert, W. E., and Wales, T. J. (1987). "Flexible Functional Forms and Global Curvature Conditions." *Econometrica* 55:43–68.

Douglas, P. H. (1976). "The Cobb-Douglas Production Function Once Again: Its History, Its Testing, and Some New Empirical Evidence." *Journal of Political Economy* 84:903–915.

Duffy, M. (1987). "Advertising and the inter-product distribution of demand: A Rotterdam model approach." *European Economic Review* 31:1051–1070.

Eales, J., and Unnevehr, L. (1988). "Demand for Beef and Chicken Products: Separability and Structural Change." *American Journal of Agricultural Economics* 70:521–532.

Edgerton, D. (1997). "Weak Separability and the Estimation of Elasticities in Multistage Demand Systems." *American Journal of Agricultural Economics* 79:62–79.

Edlin, A. S., and Karaca-Mandic, P. (2006). "The Accident Externality from Driving." *Journal of Political Economy* 114:931–955.

Evans, G. H. (1967). "The Law of Demand–The Roles of Gregory King and Charles Davenant." *The Quarterly Journal of Economics* 81:483–492.

Farrell, M. J. (1957). "The measurement of productive efficiency." *Journal of the Royal Statistical Society: Series A* 120:253–290.

Fisher, D., Fleissig, A. R., and Serletis, A. (2001). "An empirical comparison of flexible demand system functional forms." *Journal of Applied Economics* 16:59–80.

Fleissig, A., and Swofford, J. (1996). "A dynamic asymptotically ideal model of money demand." *Journal of Monetary Economics* 37:371–380.

Gallagher, P. (1987). "U.S. SOybean Yields: Estimation and Forecasting with Nonsymmetric Disturbances." *American Journal of Agricultural Economics* 69:796–803.

Genest, C., Ghoudi, K., and Rivest, L. P. (1995). "A Semiparametric Estimation Procedure of Dependence Parameters in Multivariate Families of Distributions." *Biometrika* 82:543–552.

George, P. S., and King, G. A. (1971). *COnsumer Demand for Food Commodities in the United States With Projections for 1980*. Berkeley: California Agricultural Experiment Station.

Goodwin, B. K., and Hungerford, A. (2015). "Copula-Based Models of Systemic Risk in U.S. Agriculture: Implications for Crop Insurance and Reinsurance Contracts." *American Journal of Agricultural Economics* 97:879–896.

Goodwin, B. K., and Ker, A. P. (1998). "Nonparametric Estimation of Crop Yield DIstributions: Implications for Rating Group-Risk Crop Insurance Contracts." *American Journal of Agricultural Economics* 80:139–153.

Green, H. (1964). *Aggregation in Economic Analysis: An Introductory Survey*. Princeton, NJ: Princeton University Press.

Green, R., and Alston, J. (1990). "Elasticities in AIDS Models." *American Journal of Agricultural Economics* 72:442–445.

Greene, W. H. (2018). *Econometric Analysis*. New York: Pearson.

Griliches, Z. (1957). "Hybrid Corn: An Exploration in the Economics of Technological Change." *Econometrica* 25:501–522.

Hayami, Y., and Ruttan, V. W. (1970). "Factor Prices and Technological Change in Agricultural Development: The United States and Japan, 1880-1960." *Journal of Political Economy* 78:1115–1141.

Hayashi, F. (2000). *Econometrics*. Princeton, NJ: Princeton University Press.

Hoeffding, W. (1948). "A Non-parametric Test of Independence." *Annals of Mathematical Statistics* 19:546–557.

Hurvich, C. M., Simonoff, J. S., and Tsai, C.-L. (1998). "Smoothing Parameter Selection in Nonparametric Regression Using an Improved Akaike Information Criterion." *Journal of the Royal Statistical Society, Series B* 60:271–293.

Hurwicz, L., and Uzawa, H. (1971). "On the integrability of demand functions." In *Preferences, Utility, and Demand*, edited by M. R. J. Chipman, L. Hurwicz, and H. Sonnenschein, 114–148. Jovanovich, NY: Harcourt Brace.

Iman, R. L., and Conover, W. J. (1982). "A Distribution-Free Approach to Inducing Rank Correlation among Input Variables." *Communications in Statistics—Simulation and Computation* 11:311–334.

Joe, H., and Xu, J. (1996). *The Estimation Method of Inference Functions for Margins for Multivariate Models*. Technical Report 166, University of British Columbia.

Jondrow, J., Lovell, C. A. K., Materov, I. S., and Schmidt, P. (1982). "On the Estimation of Technical Efficiency in the Stochastic Frontier Production Function Model." *Journal of Econometrics* 19:233–238.

Jorgenson, D. (1986). "Econometric Methods for Modeling Producer Behavior." In *Handbook of Econometrics*, edited by Z. Griliches and M. D. Intriligator, 1841–1915. Amsterdam: North-Holland.

Kastens, T. L., and Brester, G. W. (1996). "Model Selection and Forecasting Ability of Theory-Constrained Food Demand Systems." *American Journal of Agricultural Economics* 78:301–312.

Kendall, M. G. (1938). "A New Measure of Rank Correlation." *Biometrika* 30:81–93.

Kinnucan, H. W., Xiao, H., Hsia, C., and Jackson, J. D. (1997). "Effects of Health Information and Generic Advertising on U.S. Meat Demand." *American Journal of Agricultural Economics* 79:13–23.

Kirwan, B. E., Uchida, S., and White, T. K. (2012). "Aggregate and Farm-Level Productivity Growth in Tobacco: Before and After the Quota Buyout." *American Journal of Agricultural Economics* 94(4):838–853.

Kumbhakar, S. C., and Lovell, C. A. K. (2000). *Stochastic Frontier Analysis*. New York: Cambridge University Press.

Kumbhakar, S. C., and Tsionas, E. G. (2011). "Stochastic Error Specification in Primal and Dual Production Systems." *Journal of Applied Econometrics* 26:270–297.

LaFrance, J. T. (2004). "Integrability of the Linear Approximate Almost Ideal Demand System." *Economics Letters* 84:297–303.

Lehfeldt, R. A. (1914). "The ELasticity of Demand for Wheat." *The Economic Journal* 24:212–217.

Leontief, W. (1993). "Can Economics be Reconstructed as an Empirical Science?" *American Journal of Agricultural Economics* 75:2–5.

Marsh, T. L., Schroeder, T. C., and Mintert, J. (2004). "Impacts of meat product recalls on consumer demand in the USA." *Applied Economics* 36:897–909.

Matsuda, T. (2006). "Linear approximations to the quadratic almost ideal demand system." *Empirical Economics* 31:663–675.

McElroy, M. B. (1987). "Additive General Error Models for Production, Cost, and Derived Demand or Share Systems." *Journal of Political Economy* 95:737–757.

McFadden, D. L. (1964). *Existence Conditions for Theil-Type Preferences*. Tech. rep., University of California, Berkeley, California.

Morishima, M. (1967). "A Few Suggestions on the Theory of Elasticity (in Japanese)." *Keizai Hyoron (Economic Review)* 16:144–150.

Moro, D., and Sckokai, P. (2000). "Heterogeneous preferences in household food consumption in Italy." *European Review of Agricultural Economics* 27:305–323.

Morrison, C. (1988). "Quasi-fixed Inputs in U.S. and Japanese Manufacturing: A Generalized Leontief Restricted Cost Function Approach." *Review of Economics and Statistics* 70:275–287.

Moschini, G. (1995). "Units of Measurement and the Stone Index in Demand System Estimation." *American Journal of Agricultural Economics* 77:63–68.

Moschini, G., Moro, D., and Green, R. (1994). "Maintaining and Testing Separability in Demand Systems." *American Journal of Agricultural Economics* 76:61–73.

Mountain, D. C. (1988). "The Rotterdam Model: An Approximation in Variable Space." *Econometrica* 56:477–484.

Mundlak, Y. (1968). "Elasticities of substitution and the theory of derived demand." *Review of Economic Studies* 35:225–236.

Mundlak, Y., Butzer, R., and Larson, D. F. (2012). "Heterogeneous technology and panel data: The case of the agricultural production function." *Journal of Development Economics* 99:139–149.

Nelson, C. H. (1990). "The Influence of Distributional Assumptions on the Calculation of Crop Insurance Premia." *North Central Journal of Agricultural Economics* 12:71–78.

Nerlove, M. (1963). "Returns to Scale in Electricity Supply." In *Measurement in Economics: Studies in Mathematical Economics and Econometrics in Memory of Yehuda Grunfeld*, edited by C. Christ, 167–198. Stanford, CA: Stanford University Press.

Nevo, A. (2001). "Measuring Market Power in the Ready-To-Eat Cereal Industry." *Econometrica* 69:307–342.

Petrin, A., and Levinsohn, J. (2012). "Measuring aggregate productivity growth using plant-level data." *RAND Journal of Economics* 43:705–725.

Pollak, R. A., and Walkes, T. J. (1987). "Specification and Estimation of Nonseparable Two-Stage Technologies: The Leontief CES and the Cobb-Douglas CES." *Journal of Political Economy* 95:311–333.

Roy, R. (1947). "La distribution du revenu entre les divers biens." *Econometrica* 15:205–225.

Samuelson, P. A. (1950). "The Problem of Integrability in Utility Theory." *Economica* 68:355–385.

Schultz, H. (1925). "Appendix I: Comments on Professor Lehfeldt's Method of Deriving the Elasticity of Demand for Wheat." *Journal of Political Economy* 33:632–633.

Schweizer, B., and Wolff, E. F. (1981). "On Nonparametric Measures of Dependence for Random Variables." *Annals of Statistics* 9(4):879–885.

Selvanathan, E. (1991). "Cross-country alcohol consumption comparison: an application of the Rotterdam demand system." *Applied Economics* 23:1613–1622.

Shephard, R. W. (1953). *Cost and Production Functions*. Princeton: Princeton University Press.

Sherrick, B. J., Zanani, F. C., Schnitkey, G. D., and Irwin, S. H. (2004). "Crop insurance valuation under alternative yield distributions." *American Journal of Agricultural Economics* 86:406–419.

Shumway, C. R., and Davis, G. C. (2001). "Does consistent aggregation really matter?" *Australian Journal of Agricultural and Resource Economics* 45:161–194.

Sklar, A. (1959). "Fonctions de répartition à n dimensions et leurs marges." *Publications de l'Institut de Statistique de L'Université de Paris* 8:229–231.

Small, K. A., and Rosen, H. S. (1981). "Applied Welfare Economics with Discrete Choice Models." *Econometrica* 49:105–130.

Stern, D. I. (2010). "Elasticities of substitution and complementarity." *Journal of Productivity Analysis* 36:79–89.

Stone, R. (1954). "Linear Expenditure Systems and Demand Analysis: An Application to the Pattern of British Demand." *The Economic Journal* 64:511–527.

Theil, H. (1965). "The Information Approach to Demand Analysis." *Econometrica* 33:67–87.

Tolhurst, T. N., and Ker, A. P. (2015). "On Technological Change in Crop Yields." *American Journal of Agricultural Economics* 97:137–158.

Uzawa, H. (1962). "Production Functions with Constant Elasticities of Substitution." *Review of Economic Studies* 29:291–299.

Uzawa, H., and Goldman, S. M. (1964). "A Note on Separability in Demand Analysis." *Econometrica* 32(3):387–398.

Villas-Boas, S. (2009). "An Empirical Investigation of the Welfare Effects of Banning Wholesale Price Discrimination." *Rand Journal of Economics* 40:20–46.

Index

A

Absolute Price model 30–33
adding-up
    elasticities and 19
    as a property of Hicksian demands 15
    as a property of Marshallian demand function 8–9
aggregate level data 66–68
aggregation 20–22, 81–82
agricultural insurance 124–158
AIDS (almost ideal demand system) 3, 44–54
Aigner, D.J. 106
Akaike Information Criterion 111
Allen, R.G.D. 19
Allen-Uzawa Elasticity 19, 20, 80
almost ideal demand system (AIDS) 3, 44–54
Alson, J.M. 44
Alston, J.M. 25, 45
Archimedean copulas 144–145, 152–153
Asche, F. 45
Atkinson, S.E. 106

B

Banks, J. 46
Barnett, W.A. 30, 32, 36, 44, 46
Barten, A.P. 29, 36
Battese, G.E. 104, 108, 109, 111
Becker, G.S. 75
Berry, S. 3
Blackorby, C. 19, 20
Blundell, R.W. 46
Boles, J.N. 125
Botts, R.R. 125
Brester, G.W. 24
Burr distribution 136, 138
BY statement 64

C

CDM (compound distribution model) 115–116
Central Limit Theorem 114
Chalfant, J.A. 25, 44
Chambers, R.G. 76
"characteristics space" 54
Chavas, J. 78
Chow Test 101–102
Christensen, L.R. 2–3, 44, 46
CLASS statement 64, 69
Clayton copula 145, 152–153, 155
Clements, K.W. 30

Cobb-Douglas utility function 9–13, 84–91, 112
Coelli, T.J. 107, 111
COLLIN option 90
compensated price elasticities of demand 18
completeness, as a preference axiom 6
compound distribution model (CDM) 115–116
concavity
    as a property of cost function 77
    as a property of expenditure function 16
    as a property of production function 77
Conover, W.J. 143
consumer welfare 59–60
CONTENTS procedure 61
continuity, as a preference axiom 7
continuous, as a property of expenditure function 16
convexity
    as a preference axiom 7
    as a property of profit function 79
copula models 114, 143–146
COPULA procedure 4, 149, 151, 153, 158
Cornes, R. 5, 8, 76
CORR procedure 148–149, 150
cost function 77–78
COUNTREG procedure 4, 117
COUNTSTORE= option 120
Cramer-von Mises statistic 136
cross price elasticity 58

D

DATA option 27, 97
Davenant, Charles 23
Davis, G.C. 20, 22
Deaton, A. 3, 5, 8, 25, 44
demand theory
    about 5–6
    aggregation 20–22
    elasticities 18–20
    Hicksian demands and expenditures 15–17
    indirect utility 14–15
    preference axioms 6–7
    separability 20–22
    utility and Marshallian demands 8–13
    utility function 6–7
dependence, copulas and 143–146
derived factor demands 77–78
Diewert, W.E. 2–3, 92
differentiated products, demand for 54–74
discrete choice models 55–57
DIST option 117
DO loop 138
Dorfman, J.H. 106

double logarithmic demand functions 24–29
Duffy, M. 43

E

Eales, J. 45
economic analysis, applications of 2–3
Edgerton, D. 22
elasticities 18–20, 28, 58–59, 80–81
elliptical copulas 144
empirical demand analysis
    about 23–24
    almost ideal demand system (AIDS) 44–54
    demand for differentiated products 54–74
    double logarithmic demand functions 24–29
    Rotterdam model 29–43
empirical supply analysis
    about 83–84
    Cobb-Douglas utility function 84–91
    frontier production functions 104–112
    translog cost function 91–104
ENDOGENOUS statement 27, 70, 71, 97, 108
essentiality, as property of production function 76
ETS procedures 2
exactly aggregable translog model 44
exhaustive, as a property of discrete choice models 55
EXOGENOUS statement 27, 71, 97
expenditures, Hicksian demands and 15–17

F

Farrell, M.J. 104
finite, as a property of discrete choice models 55
Fisher D. 46
FIT statement 27, 71, 97, 101, 149, 151–152
Fleissig, A.R. 15, 46
Frank copula 145
FREQ procedure 62
frequency, severity modeling and 114–124
frontier production functions 104–112
full approximate AIDS models 44–46
Fuller, W.A. 108, 109

G

Gallagher, P. 125
Gao, G. 30
Gauger, J. 20
Gaussian copula 145, 151
GCHART procedure 62–63
generalized composite commodity theorem 22
generalized Leontief 2–3
Genest, C. 149
George, P.S. 22
Ghoudi, K. 149
Giffen goods 17, 19
Goldman, S.M. 22

Goodwin, B.K. 125, 143
Green, H. 22
Green, R. 21, 45
Greene, W.H. 57
Griliches, Z. 83
Gumbel copula 145, 152–153, 155
Gumbel distribution 57–58

H

hands-on practice 4
Harter, R.M. 108, 109
Hayashi, F. 85
Hessian matrix 32
Hicks, John 15–17
Hicks composite commodity theorem 22
Hicks-Allen elasticity 20, 92–93, 103
Hicksian demands 15–17, 18
Hoeffding D statistic 149
homogeneity
    elasticities and 19
    as a property of cost function 77
    as a property of expenditure function 16
    as a property of Hicksian demands 15
    as a property of indirect utility function 14
    as a property of Marshallian demand function 9
    as a property of profit function 79
homogenous separability 21
homothetically separable production 22
Hotelling's lemma 80
HPCDM procedure 120–122, 158
HPCORR procedure 148
Hungerford, A. 143
Hurvich, C.M. 133
Hurwicz., L. 9

I

IFM (Inference Functions for Margins) 149
IIA (Independence of Irrelevant Alternatives) property 66
Iman, R.L. 143
IML (interactive matrix language) 4
IML procedure 2, 4, 28, 39, 50, 81, 102
implicit separability 21
IMPORT procedure 61, 68–69, 107
income elasticity of demand 18
Independence of Irrelevant Alternatives (IIA) property 66
index number approach 83
indirect utility 14–15
Inference Functions for Margins (IFM) 149
An Inquiry into the Nature and Causes of the Wealth of
    Nations (Smith) 23
INSTRUMENT statement 70, 71
Integrability Theorem 9
interactive matrix language (IML) 4
ITSUR option, FIT statement 97–98

J

Joe, H. 149
Jondrow, J. 108
Jorgenson, D.W. 2–3, 44, 92

K

Kastens, T.L. 24
KDE procedure 140
Kendall, M.G. 144
Kendall's tau 144–146, 149, 152, 155
Ker, A.P. 125, 140
kernel density estimate 142
King, G.A. 22
King, Gregory 23
Kinnucan, H.W. 43
Kirwan, B.E. 83
Knight, Frank 113
Kolmogorov-Smirnov statistic 136
Kronecker delta 45
Kumbhakar, S.C. 3, 78

L

LaFrance, J.T. 46
Lau, L.J. 2–3, 44
Law of Demand 13, 23
Lehfeldt, R.A. 2
Leontief, W. 24
Leontief composite commodity theorem 22
Levinsohn, J. 3, 112
Lewbel, A. 46
linear approximate AIDS models 44–46
local regression 129, 132–133
LOESS procedure 129, 132–133
LOGISTIC procedure 64
logit models 57–58
Lovell, C.A.K. 3, 106
LR option 98

M

Manser, M.E. 46
MARGINALS option 153
MARKERS option 94
Marsh, T.L. 43
Marshall, Alfred 8
Marshallian demands, utility and 8–13
matrix of price elasticities 28
Matsuda, T. 46
McElroy, M.B. 78
McFadden, D.L. 30
MEANS procedure 33–34, 39, 47, 64, 102, 107, 139, 141–142, 157
METHOD option 149
Mintert, J. 43

MODEL procedure 4, 25–26, 36–38, 47–49, 52, 71–73, 81, 96–100
MODEL statement 64–65, 110, 117, 129, 132
monotonicity
  as a property of expenditure function 16
  as a property of indirect utility function 14
  as a property of production function 77
  as a property of profit function 79
Morishima, M. 19
Morishima Elasticity 19–20, 81, 93, 103
Moro, D. 21, 46
Morrison, C. 3, 81
Moschini, G. 21, 45
Mountain, D.C. 30
Muellbauer, J. 3, 5, 8, 25, 44
Mundlak, Y. 20
Mundlak elasticity 20
mutual exclusivity, as a property of discrete choice models 55

N

NCOL function 102
negativity
  elasticities and 19
  as a property of Hicksian demands 16
  as a property of Marshallian demand function 9
Nelson, C.H. 125
Nerlove, M. 85, 87
Nevo, A. 3
NHINT option 11
nondecreasing, as a property of cost function 77
nonsatiation, as a preference axiom 7
NPERTURBEDSAMPLES option 122

O

options
  See specific options
OUTSUM statement 120, 122

P

Pakes, A. 3
PARAMETERS statement 27, 71, 97
PCTLPTS option 120
Pearson correlation 143, 149
Petrin, A. 112
Piggott, N.E. 25
PIGLOG preferences 44
PLOTS option 118, 149
Poisson distribution 115
Pollak, R.A. 112
positivity
  as a property of Hicksian demands 15
  as a property of indirect utility function 14
  as a property of Marshallian demand function 8

practice, hands-on 4
preference axioms 6–7
PRINT procedure 93, 120, 138
procedures
    See specific procedures
production, time in 81
production function 76–77
profit function 79–81
profit-derived factor demands 80

Q

QLIM procedure 4, 106, 108, 109, 110
quadratic almost ideal demand system (QUAIDS) 46
QUANTILE function 156

R

R software package 2
reflexivity, as a preference axiom 6
REG procedure 4, 26, 69, 85–87, 90, 109, 129, 131–132
Relative Price model 30–33
RESTRICT statement 37–38, 100
revenue insurance 142–143
RIGHTQ option 122
risk
    about 113–114
    agricultural insurance 124–158
    frequency and severity modeling 114–124
Rivest, L.P. 149
Rosen, H.S. 59
Rotterdam model 29–43
Roy's identity 14–15, 16
Russell, R.R. 19, 20

S

Samuelson, P.A. 9
SAS OnDemand for Academics (website) 4
Schmidt, P. 106
Schroeder, T.C. 43
Schultz, H. 2
Schwarz Criterion 111
Schweizer, B. 145
Sckokai, P. 46
Seck, O. 36, 44, 46
Segerson, K. 78
Selvanathan, E. 43
separability 20–22, 81–82
SERIES statement 94–95
Serletis, A. 30, 32, 46
severity modeling, frequency and 114–124
SEVERITY procedure 4, 118–119, 136, 138– 140, 156, 158
SEVERITYEST= option 120
SEVERITYMODEL statement 120
SGPLOT procedure 34–35, 94, 95

SGRENDER procedure 10, 11
Sheather-Jones Plug In method 140
Shephard's lemma 16, 78, 80, 92
Sherrick, B.J. 125
SHOW option, FIT statement 101
Shumway, C.R. 22
Simonoff, J.S. 133
SIMULATE statement 149
Sklar, A. 144
Slutsky Equation 17, 18–19
Small, K.A. 59
Smith, Adam
    An Inquiry into the Nature and Causes of the Wealth of Nations 23
Spearman rank-order correlation 149
SPEC option 90, 129
statements
    See specific statements
Stern, D.I. 20
Stone, R. 30
Stone's index 45–46, 47
strict quasi-convexity, as a property of indirect utility function 14
strong separability 21, 82
SUM function 94
SUMMARY procedure 69
superscripts 18
supply theory
    about 75–76
    aggregation 81–82
    concepts of time in production 81
    cost function 77–78
    derived factor demands 77–78
    production function 76–77
    profit function 79–81
    separability 81–82
SURFACETYPE option 10
Swofford, J. 15
symmetry
    elasticities and 19
    as a property of Hicksian demands 16
    as a property of Marshallian demand function 9
SYSLIN procedure 70, 71, 72–73

T

technical efficiency, estimates of 106–107
TEMPLATE procedure 10
TEST statement 36, 86, 97–98, 101
Theil, H. 29
theory of demand
    See demand theory
theory of supply
    See supply theory
time, in production 81
TITLE statement 95
Tolhurst, T.N. 125, 140
transcendental logarithmic 2–3
transivity, as a preference axiom 7

translog cost function 91–104
trend function 129
TRUNCATED option 110
Tsai, C.-L. 133
Tsionas, E.G. 78
TYPE option 108

U

Uchida, S. 83
Unnevehr, L. 45
utility
    indirect 14–15
    Marshallian demands and 8–13
utility function 6–7
Uzawa, H. 9, 19, 22

V

VALUESFORMAT option, SGPLOT procedure 34–35
VAR statement 149
Villas-Boas, S. 3

W

Wales, T.J. 92
Walkes, T.J. 112
weak separability 21, 82
Weibull distribution 125, 136, 138, 140, 142, 156
Wessels, C.R. 45
White, T.K. 83
Wolff, E.F. 145

X

Xu, J. 149

Y

yield insurance 125–142
Young's Theorem 1, 92

Ready to take your SAS® and JMP® skills up a notch?

Be among the first to know about new books, special events, and exclusive discounts.
support.sas.com/newbooks

Share your expertise. Write a book with SAS.
support.sas.com/publish

sas.com/books
for additional books and resources.

§.sas.
THE POWER TO KNOW.